ROMANTICISM IN PERSPECTIVE:
TEXTS, CULTURES, HISTORIES

General Editors:
Marilyn Gaull, *Professor of English,*
Temple University/New York University
Stephen Prickett, *Regius Professor of English Language and Literature,*
University of Glasgow

This series aims to offer a fresh assessment of Romanticism by looking at it from a wide variety of perspectives. Both comparative and interdisciplinary, it will bring together cognate themes from architecture, art history, landscape gardening, linguistics, literature, philosophy, politics, science, social and political history and theology to deal with original, contentious or as yet unexplored aspects of Romanticism as a Europe-wide phenomenon.

Titles include

Richard Cronin (*editor*)
1798: THE YEAR OF THE *LYRICAL BALLADS*

Péter Dávidházi
THE ROMANTIC CULT OF SHAKESPEARE: Literary
Reception in Anthropological Perspective

David Jasper
THE SACRED AND SECULAR CANON IN ROMANTICISM
Preserving the Sacred Truths

Malcolm Kelsall
JEFFERSON AND THE ICONOGRAPHY OF ROMANTICISM
Folk, Land, Culture and the Romantic Nation

Andrew McCann
CULTURAL POLITICS IN THE 1790s: Literature, Radicalism
and the Public Sphere

Ashton Nichols
THE REVOLUTIONARY 'I': Wordsworth and the Politics of
Self-Presentation

Jeffrey C. Robinson
RECEPTION AND POETICS IN KEATS: 'My Ended Poet'

Anya Taylor
BACCHUS IN ROMANTIC ENGLAND: Writers and Drink,
1780–1830

Michael Wiley
ROMANTIC GEOGRAPHY: Wordsworth and
Anglo-European Spaces

Eric Wilson
EMERSON'S SUBLIME SCIENCE

Romanticism in Perspective
Series Standing Order ISBN 0–333–71490–3
(*outside North America only*)

You can receive future titles in this series as they are published by placing a
standing order. Please contact your bookseller or, in case of difficulty, write to us at
the address below with your name and address, the title of the series and the ISBN
quoted above.

Customer Services Department, Macmillan Distribution Ltd
Houndmills, Basingstoke, Hampshire RG21 6XS, England

First published in Great Britain 1999 by
MACMILLAN PRESS LTD
Houndmills, Basingstoke, Hampshire RG21 6XS and London
Companies and representatives throughout the world

A catalogue record for this book is available from the British Library.

ISBN 0–333–72521–2

First published in the United States of America 1999 by
ST. MARTIN'S PRESS, INC.,
Scholarly and Reference Division,
175 Fifth Avenue, New York, N.Y. 10010

ISBN 0–312–21499–5

Library of Congress Cataloging-in-Publication Data
Taylor, Anya.
Bacchus in romantic England : writers and drink, 1780–1830 / Anya
Taylor.
p.   cm. — (Romanticism in perspective)
Includes bibliographical references (p.   ) and index.
ISBN 0–312–21499–5 (cloth)
1. English literature—19th century—History and criticism.
2. English literature—18th century—History and criticism.
3. Drinking customs—England—History—19th century.   4. Drinking
customs—England—History—18th century.   5. Drinking of alcoholic
beverages in literature.   6. Authors, English—19th century–
–Biography.   7. Authors, English—18th century—Biography.
8. Romanticism—England.   I. Title.   II. Series.
PR457.T39   1998
820.9'355—dc21   98–3237
                                                                                              CIP

This book is printed on paper suitable for recycling and made from fully managed and
sustained forest sources.

10   9   8   7   6   5   4   3   2   1
08   07   06   05   04   03   02   01   00   99

Printed and bound in Great Britain by
Antony Rowe Ltd, Chippenham, Wiltshire

Bacchus in Romantic England

Writers and Drink, 1780–1830

Anya Taylor
Professor of English
John Jay College of Criminal Justice
The City University of New York

For Mark

Contents

List of Plates

Acknowledgements

Many people have helped to gather, structure, and find meaning in the unusual materials that form the substratum of this book. The staffs of The Senate House Library of London University, The British Library and The Wellcome Institute Library in London brought up musty temperance tracts and songs without complaint. Librarians at Manhattan College, especially Catherine Shanley, and at Columbia University kindly found and shared their holdings. Librarians in the Rare Book Collection of the Hunter College Library permitted me to roam amid women's novels published between 1780 and 1830; the New York Public Library annex shared its Temperance Collection. The PSC–CUNY Research Foundation supported my work in London for four summers. Early versions of some ideas in Chapters 4, 5 and 6, appeared in very different forms in my '"A Father's Tale": Coleridge Foretells the Life of Hartley', *Studies in Romanticism* (Spring 1991), in my 'Coleridge and Alcohol', *Texas Studies in Literature and Language* (Fall 1991), and in my 'Coleridge, Keats, Lamb, and Seventeenth-Century Drinking Songs,' in *Milton, the Metaphysicals, and Romanticism*, edited by Lisa Low and Anthony John Harding (1994).

A number of friends have struggled with my interpretations and sharpened them, though I fear I have not always done justice to their insights. Willard Spiegelman and Nicholas Roe commented incisively on Chapter 2; Judith Ryan brought a keen psychological perspective to Chapter 5, along with suggestions for bibliography about father-and-son relations; Jeffrey Robinson studied Chapter 6 with Keatsian gusto; and Andrew Taylor reassured me of the current relevance of my description of male groups in Chapter 7. Marilyn Gaull, who has fostered my work since she published my first article in 1972, grappled with many recalcitrant sentences. I am grateful to J. Robert Barth, S. J., John Beer, James Engell, Roger Forseth, Norman Fruman, Debbie Lee, Larry Lockridge, Allen Mandelbaum, Millicent Pinckert, Robert Pinckert, Judith Plotz, and Donald Reiman for advice and encouragement. I thank Anthony Harding for finding Plate 5, Karl Kroeber for suggesting the pertinence to my study of Wordsworth's 'Letter to a Friend of Burns', and John Nagle for the title of Chapter 7.

My colleagues in the English department at John Jay College of Criminal Justice have continued to provide a stimulating community. Elisabeth Gitter in particular has spurred me to persistence and clarity; over many years she has discovered and brought to the surface submerged meanings in the book as a whole and in a number of chapters that yearned for definition. Benjamin Hellinger broke down and rebuilt the styles of Chapter 1; Jane Bowers and Patricia Licklider worked to improve, respectively, Chapters 2 and 7. My chairman Robert Crozier has created a gracious and good-humoured oasis in a beleaguered university. In the John Jay College Library Janice Dunham has plied me with important facts, and Anthony Simpson introduced me, years ago, to the work of Roy Porter. For helping me over nine years to think about the 'real' connections between alcohol and literature I thank the lively students in my alcohol and literature seminars, given as part of the Alcohol and Substance Abuse programme at the college.

I feel as always my debt to the presences of my two sets of parents, Virgil and Jean Bozeman, and the late Adda Bozeman Barkhuus and the late Arne Barkhuus. I thank my growing family – Andrew, Kristin and Jack; Nicholas, Jenny, Dustin and Courtney – for the life of pleasure they share with me. Most of all I am grateful for Mark Taylor's work in criticizing these chapters in their metamorphoses, for propping up my spirits, for giving me the daily gift of his hilarity and wisdom, and for inspiring me to *carpe diem*. To his buoyant health I raise a glass, and dedicate to him this long-fermenting vintage, *Bacchus in Romantic England*.

Abbreviations

Introduction

Although many books have studied writers and drink in modern American literature, not even an article has noted the rich culture of drinking and the many poems and narratives about it in the Romantic period in England. *Bacchus in Romantic England: Writers and Drink 1780–1830* is the first study to describe the bulk and variety of writings about drink; to set these poems, novels, essays, letters and journals in a historical, sociological and medical context; to demonstrate the importance of drunkenness in the works of a number of major and minor writers of the period; and to suggest that during these years, for a short time, the pleasures and pains of drinking are held in a vivacious balance. The book argues that the figure of the drinker tests the margins of the human being, either as a beast, savage or thing, or, on the other edge of the human range, as a free, inspired spirit.

Chapter 1 establishes the double context – mythical and historical – of drunkenness in the period. After reviewing the dual role of Dionysus in classical and Renaissance literature, it unearths previously unexamined writings by doctors and philanthropists who voice alarm at a newly dangerous intensity of drinking. Analyses by Drs Trotter, Fothergill, Lettsom, Darwin, Beddoes, Carlisle and MacNish, and by philanthropic observers such as Colquoun, Dunlop, Place and Montagu indicate a shift in attitudes toward drinking, especially of distilled spirits, and toward drunkards, whom they see as patients suffering from a new disease of the will.

Having established the historical realities of drinking, the book turns to focus on the fatal drunkenness of Robert Burns, as seen through the admiring but worried eyes of the abstemious William Wordsworth. Burns's passionate celebration of drunkenness in poems such as 'Tam O'Shanter' and the revelations of his drunkenness in Dr Currie's 1800 biography shocked temperate bards and inspired intemperate ones. Wordsworth struggles with the risk-taking genius Burns in a series of writings about his drunkenness: three elegies at his grave; *Benjamin the Waggoner*; and 'Letter to the Friends of Burns'. The figure of Burns provokes Wordsworth to examine the image of the wild, self-destructive poet, to measure himself and his friends against it, and to learn a guarded tolerance for excess. While expressing his sorrow for Burns's 'irregularities',

1

Wordsworth finally affirms his own temperate power as a ground of success and thus he angers the emulators of Burns.

Chapter 3 sets the legendary drunkard Charles Lamb in the context of a new awareness of personal fragmentation initiated by eighteenth-century sceptical philosophers. Hume's witty pulverization of the coherence of the person, fragmented into moments, moods, forgetfulness and feelings, gave additional resonance to drunken self-loss, especially to the extent that it was self-willed or permitted. How stable was the human being if a litre of liquid could transform him or her into an animal or a thing, and if that human being 'decided' out of some unfathomable depth of self-destructiveness to be so transformed? Hume's insights into dissolving subjectivities had a real effect on how people lived lives of new anxiety, already painfully true for an earlier figure like Boswell (who has been dubbed 'the first alcoholic of historical record'[1]), who learned his inner fragmentation in part from his fellow Scot's writings on personal identity.[2] It is no coincidence that Lamb and Coleridge, also heavy drinkers, also take Hume's theory personally. When David Hartley and Immanuel Kant describe the destabilizing influence of wine and spirits on already fragile personal identities, they enhance an atmosphere of uncertainty that riddles Lamb's *John Woodvil: A Tragedy* and 'Confessions of a Drunkard'. Lamb's many references to the joys and pains of drinking punctuate his essays, letters and poems. Lamb's drunkenness is far more central to his art and the multifariousness of his presentation of self than has previously been thought; the divided self of alcoholism and the divided self of late-eighteenth-century psychology overlap in his person and writing. He himself observes his dividedness, and so do his friends and detractors.

One of Lamb's favourite drinking partners, the man whom Wordsworth called 'the most wonderful man I know' and also 'a rotten drunkard' – Samuel Taylor Coleridge – occupies the centre of the book. An antic Coleridge, a man of pleasure, steps onto the stage. His drinking amused his cronies, inspired joyful drinking songs, accelerated his metre, wit and imagination, and led him to celebrate Dionysus. In different moods, however, it worried him more than his opium eating; it was the subject of several of his essays about the social milieu and the dilemma of workers; it prompted him to analyse the bestiality and thingness of the drunkard as a human being at the margins of humanity; it led him to imagine a cure for the affliction; it brought him to the dark abyss of the human will in himself and in others.

Drinking was one of his legacies to his son David Hartley Coleridge, whose drunkenness is an extension of his own. Chapter 5, informed by recent work on father-and-son relations and on adult children of alcoholics, looks at the interplay of poems, letters and memoirs by Coleridge and by Hartley to see how Coleridge influences his son's alcoholism through inheritance, example, and a complex form of the prophecy that was thought to be one of Bacchus's powers. The alcoholic boy-man becomes for Coleridge a figure of failure: he is a partial self, a gnome, a beast, even a thing, in his father's self-projecting eyes.

Keats's interest in Bacchus, derived from some of the same sources as Coleridge's, evolves in his argument with Milton on temperance, and finds expression in lyrics, narratives and odes on the pleasures of the senses and on sorrow. Keats's hedonism comes to the surface in his observations of the effects of claret on his sensations and imagination, and with his moments of release from pain. But, more important, for him as for Coleridge, drink energizes art and verse; it marks the point of evaporation of the senses into the spirit; it is a spur to music and an antidote to loss.

Chapter 7 explores the divergence between Romantic men and women in their attitudes toward drinking. This divergence widens during this period, as gender roles freeze, husbands roam, and wives wait. Drinking defines manliness then as now, in upper and well as lower classes: Byron and his cronies, as well as John Clare and his, boasted about their binges in poems and memoirs. Meanwhile, women become outspoken in their newly genteel disgust. While the Restoration poet Anne Finch had flirtatiously twitted drinking males, Romantic women writers frankly describe their outrage at being dependent on such animals. Hannah More, Charlotte Smith, Mary Wollstonecraft, and Maria Edgeworth anticipate by fifty years Anne Brontë's *Tenant of Wildfell Hall* (1848) in detailing the sufferings of the wives and daughters of drunkards. Contemporary studies of wives of alcoholics clarify in retrospect these family dynamics, showing a continuity in 'why women don't like Romanticism'.[3]

The book connects writers as various as Burns, Clare, Hannah More, Blake, Tom Moore, Crabbe, Byron, Coleridge, Maria Edgeworth, Lamb, Wordsworth, Hartley Coleridge, Francis Place,

William Hazlitt, Basil Montagu, Dr Thomas Beddoes, Dr Thomas Trotter, Charlotte Smith, and Keats, showing these writers in dialogue about the dangers of drink among the lower classes and the joys of drinking among themselves.

1

Dionysian Myths and Alcoholic Realities

Drinking permeates writing in England during the period 1780–1830, in songs of celebration, narrative poems, elegies for those who drank too much, studies of drinking patterns among the lower classes, analyses of the intoxicated self, and confessions of inebriation. The abundance of these writings about drink, the complexity of their analyses, the urgency of their tone, and the elaborateness of their themes and variations indicate that men and women worried about drinking fifty years earlier than the familiar temperance writings of the mid-nineteenth century and a hundred and fifty years before the often-studied alcoholic fictions of twentieth-century America. In public and in private, in high culture and in low, in formal and in casual exchanges, Romantic writers describe the pleasures and pains of drinking.

The existence of these many alcohol-intensive texts raises questions: Why does the drinker become noticeable at this time? Is there a difference in the way the drinker is viewed during the Romantic period as opposed to earlier and later periods? Does the drinker, or the drunkard, carry slightly different values at this time, in the wake of altered theories of mind, of personal integrity, or of artistic representation? Does a new religious scepticism isolate the drinker in his guilt? Does it make him more self-conscious about his pleasures?

The drinker tests the boundaries of the human person at a time when scepticism, secularism and psychology were calling into doubt assumptions about personal integrity; the drinker becomes either a less than human figure or a more than human one. Seen as less than human, the drinker verges on the savage or the animal; seen as more, the drinker seems like a god, inspired and boundless. The drinker is under observation as a test case: does his consciousness expand or does it contract? Is he free or bound? Does he choose intoxication or can he not help himself?

Judgements about drunkards as more or less than human, as divine or bestial, occur in the earliest literature when non-drunken observers describe a being who seems oblivious to their gaze. In the inscriptions of the Greek anthology a drunkard is already an emblem, as he lies insouciant by the side of the road, his empty jar his only remaining possession. The icon of the bottle, full or empty, the tankard foaming or upset, tells well-known stories. The drunkard – enclosed in the transformations going on within and sometimes unaware of how on-lookers will interpret the actions that result from these transformations – makes a spectacle of himself. On-lookers may feel wonder at the witty, dazzling drunkard, or may feel pity, or even disgust, at the wilful loss of control or decorum. As an object of observation, he is already a thing.

Looking from inside, the drinker sees a multiplied and trans-formed being, released from previous roles, free to explore alternative selves. Drinkers since antiquity have expressed such a goal: to be an other, to be a different self, to get out of the boundaries of self, to allow the self to be unpredictable. Samuel Johnson knew why he drank: 'to throw myself away, to get rid of myself.' He told Anna Williams that 'he who makes a beast of himself gets rid of the pain of being a man.' He knew that people drink to suspend consciousness and to fill the 'vacuity of life'.[1] Anthropologists studying diverse cultures have shown that transformation and oblivion are often the goals of drinkers. Alcohol introduces festivity and dissolves hierarchy. It allows the drinker to say 'I was not myself.'[2] In permitting or excusing lapses in behaviour, alcohol produces pleasure and self-forgetfulness; it dissolves predictable roles of social position or gender; it threatens to release the 'wild man', or woman, hidden within.[3] However brief the escape, or harsh the consequences, often clearly anticipated, the metamorphosis seems worth it, for the time being.

Although the drunkard sees himself as a vitally fluid person making choices from a still infinite set of possibilities, from the outside the drunkard has become a figure of freedom or a figure of bondage. He has either dared to transgress the boundaries of humanness, or he cannot help slipping out of them. His quest to be free of expected patterns of behaviour sometimes turns around: he becomes 'the drunkard' driven to drink and forfeiting free agency. Sometimes he makes himself, or lets himself become, a beast. Why would a person choose this dangerous route: out of fulness or out of emptiness? Out of courage or out of terror? Out of sufficiency or out of self-dissatisfaction? Such questions from such multiple perspectives complicate the literature of drinking.

1.

The ambiguity of the drinker already unsettles classical and Renaissance literary representations of drunkenness. The mythic tradition centring on Dionysus as a composite idea of abandon, fertility and drunkenness provides one of several contexts in which to place Romantic investigations of the drinker's meaning.

In Euripides's *The Bacchae*, the meanings of Dionysus bifurcate into the divinely metamorphic and the ragingly bestial. Dionysus names powers of fertility, joy and riot, powers outside or deep within the human being. Dionysus dispenses food, drink and comfort, and inspires communal energy, song and dance; he is rapture and rage, illumination and blindness. Wine is only one aspect of his realm, and is never actually drunk in the play, though Pentheus imagines that it is. Instead, wine as a transformative substance functions as a metonymy for the holy drunkenness that pervades the play, spurs the women's mountain dancing, and, obliterating or intensifying their senses, rouses them to see the lion in the boy and to commit horrific human sacrifice. Dionysus is '"the Liberator" – the god who by very simple means, or by other means not so simple, enables you for a short time to *stop being yourself*, and thereby sets you free.'[4]

Simultaneously, and darkly, Dionysus stirs these blind communal energies to destroy rationality, will and restraint.[5] Euripides's play enacts this double-edged power by showing the god possessing the women of Thebes. He sends them up to the mountains away from their chores at looms and cradles to consort with animals, gives them superhuman strength to kill with bare hands, and obliterates their understanding of what they do. The play shows this transformation as the god possesses Pentheus, mesmerizes him into passivity, makes him dress as a woman to explore this female self hidden beneath his male postures.[6] Under the god's power (which does not require intoxicating drinks, only the god's magical force) Pentheus is led to discard his role as king, his image of maleness, his faith in his own ability to make decisions and keep order. He is ripped to shreds even as he tries to identify himself to his mother – 'It is I, your son' – but this fragile voice is lost in the uproar of the bestial females under the god's power.[7] The ambiguity of the god's power matches the ambiguity of the human response: if Pentheus refuses to yield he is torn apart; if he yields he is also torn apart. Dionysus as a force destroys him as it destroys his mother who joined the dancers. For the god sets out to punish mortals who refuse and those who accept his oblivion.

Wine's power to change, release, debase or exalt circulates through classical figures of speech. Images in Greek and Latin identify wine with life, blood, semen, the liquid in plants, the life-fluid and vitality, and even the genius in human beings.[8] It can be imagined as divine, to be worshipped for its power to unify, inspire and magnify. The god of dancing, singing and prophecy 'rises out of the earth in the form of an elixir which intoxicates. This is the vine.' Wine has 'the intrinsic power to enchant, to inspire, to raise up the spirit', even as it drives the human mind to a terrible wildness.[9]

Virgil and Ovid turn to Dionysian figures but choose his followers, Silenus and Dypsas, making them literally drunk as they speak. The substance itself, rather than the god's spirit, inspires them. In the sixth eclogue Virgil's Silenus, old and wise, sings of creation and excess. He tells myths about family relations distorted by inappropriate desire. Drunk when he sings, awakened from a stupor, Silenus dwells on Pasiphae's desire for her bull and on Philomela's cruel fate, violated and punished by her imbruted brother-in-law. Drink reveals human brutishness in lust and violence, while it inspires the song itself: 'The music struck the valleys and the valleys tossed it to the stars.'[10]

Ovid's drunken Dypsas is a prophetess, however disreputable. In the *Amores* I, viii, she knows 'the ways of magic, and Aeaean incantations, and by her art turns back the liquid waters upon their source; she knows well what the herb can do, what the thread set in motion by the whirling magic wheel, what the poison of the mare in heat.' She has supernatural powers: 'Whenever she has willed, the clouds are rolled together over all the sky.' Like Dionysus, she, too, is a shape-shifter; 'she changes form and flits about in the shadows of night, her aged body covered with plumage.' She sees into the past and future, inspires poetry, and love. Her wisdom is released in drunkenness.[11]

Edgar Wind, describing the Renaissance revival of the Bacchic mysteries, shows that 'the torture of the mortal by the god who inspires him was a central theme' among Florentine Neoplatonists such as Pico della Mirandola, for whom 'the mysteries of Bacchus are both destructive and consoling'.[12] The figure of Bacchus, with his joyful, naked and sensuous companions Silenus and the satyrs, parades through Florence's sculpture and painting. Sometimes gross and gluttonous, sometimes satirical, always playful, Bacchic figures enliven works by Piero, Mantegna, Michelangelo, Bellini and Titian, and recall the secret of living well.[13] In the Renaissance revival of paganism, Bacchus liberates: he encourages an explosive nature, a multiplying personal being, and an intense quest (because secular) for artistic expansion.[14]

But even then, Dionysus posed dangers for the human being seeking freedom. Although Dionysus himself is sinuous and slippery, creative and destructive by turns, the human being who takes on his drunkenness can become fixed as a caricature. In the *Phaedrus* Plato describes such a process of narrowed ways of being:

When judgment guides us rationally toward what is best, and has the mastery, that mastery is called temperance, but when desire drags us irrationally toward pleasure, and has come to rule within us, the name given to that rule is wantonness. But in truth wantonness itself has many names, as it has many branches or forms, and when one of these forms is conspicuously present in a man it makes that man bear its name, a name that it is no credit or distinction to possess.... . if desire has achieved domination in the matter of drink, it is plain what term we shall apply to its subject who is led down that path.[15]

Plato points to the difficulty of preserving a balance between expansiveness and fixity: the wanton drinker can become a figure of ridicule or menace, reduced to a type: 'the sot'. The freedom that Dionysus brings turns into its opposite: a fixity in addiction.

Although Falstaff demonstrates this narrowed inflexibility at the end of his festive reign, Rabelais' Pantagruel expands to include joy and energy; he celebrates wine as the quintessence of all our vital fluids. Inspiration is the 'joyful, spontaneous, free-flowing cascade of words; its symbol is Bacchus' wine'. Beyond artistic creation, wine represents also a larger principle: it is 'a symbol of the primal energy in all its forms, be it inspiration or action. It is the blind force in all men that makes them live and act and create despite the counsels of reason which tell them that their endeavors are in vain.'[16] Rabelais' bottle is a symbol of artistic creativity and of large

and happy life: 'intoxication is not escape but integration, acceptance. "Drinking" is a collective, free, enthusiastic acceptance of life',
generative of laughter, words and joy.[17] Even the temperate
Montaigne declares 'Let us get back to our bottles.'[18]

Renaissance literary Dionysianism lives ebulliently in England in
Falstaff's carnival,[19] in Ben Jonson's drinking-songs and masques,
in cavalier drinking-songs by Herrick, Cowley and Rochester, and
in John Gay's 'A Ballad. On Ale'. Gay's mock-epic 'Wine, A Poem'
invokes the tradition that wine inspires great poetry:

> Of Happiness Terrestrial, and the Source
> Whence human pleasures flow, sing *Heavenly* Muse,
> Of sparkling juices, of th'enliv'ning Grape,
> Whose *quickning* tast adds vigour to the Soul,
> [...]
> BACCHUS Divine, aid my *adventrous* Song,
> That with no middle flight intends to soar.[20]

Gay parodies the opening of Milton's *Paradise Lost* on a topic ironically subversive of Milton's temperance; praising the terrestrial
world as an unfallen paradise where drink flows, he satirizes
Milton for transforming the creative Bacchus into a demon.[21] Gay
anticipates A. E. Housman's quip in 'Terence, This is stupid stuff' –

> And malt does more than Milton can
> To justify God's ways to man –[22]

and urges his readers to savour 'human pleasures', the heaven
that earth makes by its own natural processes of fermentation, the
divinity within human reach.

In these classical and Renaissance literary and artistic representations Dionysus rides leopards, swims with dolphins, waves the
thrysus; on friezes and in garden nooks, he and his laughing companions encourage indulgence and oblivion, pleasure and idleness.
The mythical context continues to offer its multiple meanings into
the Romantic period, as the statue of Dionysus in Plate 1 attests.
This sculpture, a Roman copy of a Greek original, presided over
Thomas Hope's Duchess Street galleries from 1796 to 1841, and lent
its twice-removed classical lustre to carousings of the Georgian and
Regency eras. But Romantic drinkers tinge this classical joy with
melancholy; while shouting '*carpe diem*', they look anxiously ahead
at the void.

2.

Subtle changes beginning around 1780 shift the quality of drinking and the attitude toward drunkards. The transformed selves of classical and Renaissance drinkers emerge from the realm of myth and enter the seemingly more real realm of psychology and auto-biography. Doubt and uncertainty destabilize the human being,[23] who, precariously differentiated from the animal under the best of circumstances, now teeters into drunkenness. While scepticism contributes to the shift, economic, social and technological changes such as the decline of raucous seasonal festivity,[24] the regulation of labour patterns and the disparagement of play,[25] the crowded lone-liness of industrial towns,[26] and, most important, the increased flow of distilled liquor mark a decisive turn toward a perception of drinking as illness.

Historians and literary critics alike have ignored the shift occurring at this time in the reality and perception of drunkenness. They view the fifty years between 1780 and 1830 as a transition between two well-known eras of heavy drinking: the mid-eighteenth century gin mania and the mid-nineteenth century drunkenness of industrial labourers assailed by the temperance movement. M. Dorothy George and John Frederick Logan believe that drinking during this period was winding down;[27] Brian Harrison and M. M. Glatt see these fifty years as gearing up for the next binge. In his study of mid- to late nineteenth-century drunkenness, Harrison begins his bibliography at 1815 'because only the ending of the Napoleonic Wars could give full rein to the latent contemporary concern with problems of public order, social reform and poverty.'[28] Harrison implies that material on alcohol use in the period before 1815 is either inaccessible or non-existent, when in fact it is abundant. So, too, M. M. Glatt imagines a fifty-year-long pause in British drinking: '[t]here was a definite improvement of conditions in the second half of the 18th century. ... Having lost its hold on the masses in the second half of the 18th century, gin drink-ing, however, once more became universal in the 19th century and in particular in its third decade.'[29] Instead, during these fifty years drinking reached an alarming pitch.

Among historians Roy Porter is almost alone in showing that whatever the actual amount of drinking, the quality of drinking became more dangerous in the mid-eighteenth century. He traces the arrival of 'stronger liquors' such as port, brandy, gin, rum and whisky, the strengthening of beer into 'porter', and the addition of 'noxious additives' for preservation; 'potent, dangerous, and often extremely cheap, the spread of ardent spirits raised the problem of drunkenness onto a new plane.'[30] William Hogarth, Henry Fielding, and other mid-eighteenth-century opponents of distilled spirits worked to force legislation against 'a new Kind of Drunkenness, unknown to our Ancestors ... that acquired by the strongest intoxicating Liquors, and particularly by that Poison called *Gin*.'[31] Although the legislation that they fostered saved many lives, the new 'poison' continued to transform drunkenness into sickness and addiction.

New technology for distilling caused what Fernand Braudel calls a 'revolution' in drinking: 'The great innovation, the revolution in Europe, was the appearance of brandy and spirits made from grain – in a word, alcohol. The sixteenth century created it; the seventeenth consolidated it; the eighteenth popularized it.'[32] In his view, the use of spirits follows a clear rise to 1800. Spirits 'increased by leaps and bounds', particularly in northern Europe, where transportation, storage and manufacture of the more fragile fermented drinks proved difficult. Even with the increase, 'production remained on the scale of a craft-type organization' until the early Romantic era, when stills invented by Weigert in 1773 and by Magellano in 1780 'made continuous cooling by a double current possible. The crucial changes that made it possible to distill wine in one operation came even later. They were the work of a little-known inventor, born in 1778, Edouard Ardant. They lowered manufacturing costs and contributed to the enormous spread of alcohol in the nineteenth century' (172–8). W. J. Rorabaugh shows that an increase in the use of distilled liquors took place concurrently in the United States in the early Federal period, in response to difficulties with transportation, isolation, and a raw and alienated culture, where 'the cult of individuality gave rise to acute drinking' of corn liquor.[33] In 1784 Dr Benjamin Rush, surgeon-general of the continental army of the new United States, urged all rational men to drink 'moderate quantities' of wine, beer and cider, which cause 'cheerfulness, strength, and nourishment' and to reject grog, gin, brandy and whisky, which lead to vice, murder, disease, apoplexy, death and punishment, including 'the Hulks, Botany Bay, and Gallows'.[34] Late eighteenth century men and women imbibed distilled spirits in huge quantities because they were cheap, plentiful, easily transported and quick in effect. These spirits turned celebrants into alcoholics.

Even though historians neglect the drunkenness of the decades from 1780 to 1830, doctors and observers of the period tell their own stories and thus fill a gap in the history of drinking. While the classical and Renaissance context of Dionysus and his Bacchante is familiar, this medical context is not, because many of these writings are being published only now, or lie still unpublished in The Wellcome Institute Library, in the Temperance Library of London University, or in the British Library. In their writings doctors and social observers deplore the excesses of drink and bear witness to a new kind of drinking; they confirm Samuel Taylor Coleridge's declaration in a 1799 letter from Germany that 'no Country in God's Earth labours under the tremendous curse of Drunkenness equally with England'.[35]

These Romantic doctors and philanthropists share with the better known poets and essayists of their day a concern with the poor; a passion for sensation and psychology; an interest in the workings of pleasure and pain, consciousness and unconsciousness, and rationality and dreams; and a faith in the healing power of imagination. Though earlier doctors discuss the drunkenness of their contemporaries in their diaries,[36] and mention the many notorious eighteenth-century drunks – Lord Bolingbroke, Queen Anne herself, Joseph Addison, Pitt the Younger, Richard Sheridan, Richard Savage, Nathaniel Lee, William Collins, Christopher Smart, Samuel Johnson's wife Tetty, Erasmus Darwin's wife, Samuel Johnson, and James Boswell – who, as Roy Porter expresses it, 'had their careers blighted and lives truncated by the sequelae of alcohol',[37] Romantic doctors develop at this time a new professional approach and a new ethical standard in medicine.[38] Perceiving people as 'patients', subjects to be studied and healed, these doctors see addiction generally, and drunkenness specifically, as a physical ailment rather than a moral failing.[39] While noting the pleasurable highs of drink, they watch sickness and ruin; they look into shadowy doorways of slums and hospitals, and voice their outrage at the debasement of human life.[40] Their testimonies embed in reality Romantic 'literary' writings about drink, a realism grossly depicted in Plate 2.

Dr Thomas Trotter initiates the public study of the conditions and effects of drunkenness. His doctoral thesis, submitted to the University of Edinburgh in 1788 and published in 1804 as *An Essay,*

*Medical, Philosophical, and Chemical, on Drunkenness, and its Effects on
the Human Body*, ranges widely over this newly dangerous condition.[41] Trotter shares with Dr Benjamin Rush the honour of
inventing the 'disease concept of alcoholism', although their
definitions of 'disease' include mental and spiritual aspects that
many modern theorists reject.[42] Trotter believes that the disease can
only be cured by treating the complex interplay of soul and body:
'It is to be remembered that a bodily infirmity is not the only thing
to be corrected. *The habit of drunkenness is a disease of the mind.* The
soul itself has received impressions that are incompatible with its
reasoning powers' (p. 179).

In describing the troubled souls and bodies of drunkards,
Dr Trotter includes the special cases of women drunkards and of
their impaired children suffering from what we now call 'foetal
alcohol syndrome'. He enriches his method with references to
Tacitus, Shakespeare's Cassio, Robert Burton, Dr Johnson and
James Thomson. Having no 'precursor in my labours', he must
invent his method on his own, for he sees that drunkenness has
been ignored because it is unseemly:

> Most instances of casual or sudden death, and suspended anima-
> tion, have obtained rules for recovery; while the drunkard,
> exposed in the street and highway, or stretched in the kennel, has
> been allowed to perish, without pity and without assistance; as if
> his crime were inexpiable, and his body infectious to the touch.
> Our newspapers give us too frequent accounts of this kind. The
> habit of inebriation, so common in society, to be observed in all
> ranks and stations of life, and the source of inexpressible
> affliction to friends and relatives, has seldom been the object of
> medical admonition and practice. (p. 3)

Noting the prevalence of drunkenness in his society, and not just
among the lower ranks or labouring poor, Trotter seeks the often
contradictory causes of this self-destructive illness:

> A due acquaintance with the human character will afford much
> assistance; for the objects of our care are as diversified as the vari-
> eties of corporeal structure. Pleasure, on the one hand, presents
> the poisonous bowl: low spirits, on the other, call for the cheering
> draught. There business and the duties of office have plunged
> one man into frequent hard drinking; while cares and misfor-

tunes have goaded on another. The soldier and the sailor get drunk while narrating the dangers of the battle and the storm: the huntsman and the jockey, by describing the joys of the chace and the course. Here genius and talent are levelled with the dust, in trying to forget, in wine, the outrages of fortune, and the ingratitude of the world; while more ponderous and stupid mortals, in attempting to seek in the bottle the feelings and sentiments of exalted beings, gravitate to their original clay, or sink deeper into their parent mud. (p. 4)

In addition to these paradoxical inner motivations for drinking, Trotter believes that the inhabitants of Great Britain and Ireland are more than usually convivial because more than usually democratic.

There is no business of moment transacted in these islands without a libation to Bacchus. It prevails among the Peers of the realm down to the parish committee. These convivial parties are a luxuriant scyon of a free country; where all ranks and degrees of society meet to enjoy friendly intercourse, without the dread of interruption from a jealous Inquisition, or the domiciliary visits of a tyrant's spies. But they have often the bad effect of mixing the profligate with the good, and debauching the sober citizen.

Twenty years after Trotter's praise of Britain's democratic drinking customs, his fellow Scot John Dunlop called these bibulous customs 'Artificial and Compulsory Drinking', convivial transactions that lure the light-headed to ruin.[43] Dunlop finds these rules themselves autocratic, and their enforcers thugs who insult, beat, and steal the tools of reluctant drinkers. In his compendium of tradesmen's drinking practices throughout Great Britain, Dunlop argues that this system of festive compulsion is unknown on the continent and alien to the United States, where solitary drinking is common:

The system of rule and regulation, as to times and occasions of drinking, pervades all branches of society in Great Britain – at meals, markets, fairs, baptism, and funerals; and almost every trade and profession has its own code of strict and well-observed laws on this subject. There are numerous occasions when general custom makes the offer and reception of liquor as imperative as the laws of the land. Most other countries have, on the whole,

only *one general motive* to use liquor – viz. natural thirst, or desire
for it; but in Great Britain there exists a large plurality of motives,
derived from etiquette and rule. (p. 3)

An example was the poet Burns, who could not walk past tradesmen
without feeling compelled to take a drink, lest he offend their sense
of honour. Dunlop mourns the consequent destruction of Burns's
genius, career, and life (pp. 90–102), as Dr Currie, another Scottish
doctor worried about alcohol abuse, will blame the seductions of the
rich.

Thomas Trotter saw drunkenness on all levels of his society
when he first composed his study in 1780 and when he revised it
for publication in 1804 and 1805. He is less class-specific than
Patrick Colquhoun and Dr Fothergill in the 1790s or than Dunlop
or Francis Place in the 1820s.

The eventual founder of the metropolitan police force began his
career by recording his youthful disgust at the epidemic of drunkenness that he saw about him. Patrick Colquhoun set down
*Observations and Facts relative to licenced Ale-Houses, in the City of
London and its Environs* in 1794, when he served as a young magis-
trate in the counties of Surrey, Kent and Essex. Aiming to restrict
the licences available for new ale-houses, Colquhoun numbers the
ale-houses at 6,000 in the county of Middlesex, and foresees that
the addition of new ale-houses will render the publicans desperate
for business. When needy, they will be tempted to serve children,
to adulterate liquors, to water the spirits, and to indulge in other
subterfuges. 'When they see nothing but impending ruin staring
themselves in the face, such occupiers are glad to encourage the
most profligate part of the community, men, women, children,
vagrants, and thieves, to frequent their houses' (p. 12). Colquhoun's
imagination enables him to see through the eyes of the needy publicans, and also through the eyes of the families that crowd into
their impoverished establishments:

it certainly never was the intention of the legislature, that such
public conveniences should be prostituted to the purpose of har-
bouring thieves, pick pockets, or lewd and profligate people of
either sex, neither was it intended that they should become re-
ceptacles for whole families (men, women and children) of many
of the labouring poor, who unhappily for themselves and for
society, have gradually got into the habit of resorting to the

public-houses, where all their little earnings are spent in eating expensively, and drinking ale and spirits; which earnings, with proper management, and by remaining at home in their own dwellings, might have procured a sufficiency of vituals and drink. (pp. 15–16)

Colquhoun paints a picture of lewdness and inebriation, robbery and mischief; he holds out a melancholy prospect to the rising generation in the poor education of those children. Extrapolating from poverty to drink to crime, he anticipates the insights of Francis Place and Charles Dickens.

His signature in the end-leaf reveals that Colquhoun possessed a copy of a powerful tract published the year after his own, 1795: Dr A. Fothergill's *Essay on the Abuse of Spirituous Liquors, being an attempt to exhibit, in its genuine colours, its pernicious effects upon the property, health, and morals, of the People, with Rules and Admonitions respecting the prevention and cure of this GREAT NATIONAL EVIL.* Fothergill's study is 'chiefly designed for the benefit of the inferior ranks, among whom this vice is most predominant; would we could add, and to them wholly confined! for then would it soon become as unfashionable as it is contemptible.' Where Colquhoun lamented the corruption of the labouring poor and the inevitable degradation of their children, Fothergill wishes vainly that the higher ranks would set a better example. Fothergill sees that 'the appetite among the common people for strong liquors is their darling passion.' He believes that drinking is learned in infancy and steadily indulged and increased, despite the poisonous taste of 'base English malt spirit, distilled from coarse turpentine'. As a doctor, Fothergill has seen the effects first hand:

Yet so unaccountable is the rage for this disgusting composition that thousands of poor half-famished creatures daily swallow it with insatiable avidity. Though supported, together with their helpless families, at the expense of the public, yet some of them have been known to pledge their allowance of bread, their clothes, nay, the very beds they lie on, to procure their accustomed dose of this detestable potion! When we descend into their comfortless abodes, what an affecting scene do we behold! Disease, poverty, and wretchedness, pourtrayed in their darkest and most gloomy colours! None but those who have witnessed such scenes can conceive the unspeakable misery into which this vice has plunged innumerable poor families. (p. 10)

Thirty years before Charles Dickens was moved to write about drunken families in 'The Drunkard's Death',[44] Fothergill is descending the steps into basement rooms where families sprawl in ruin because of distilled spirits.

Dr Fothergill sees not only the individual suffering but the broad sociological picture. 'Drunkenness is the secret bane of society, it ruins the peace of families, destroys conjugal endearments, and strikes at the very root of population' (p. 10). His analysis could apply to twentieth century urban problems:

> In the year 1794 the produce of ten capital distilleries in London only ... amounted to the enormous quantity of 237, 233, 960 gallons! What then must be the amount through the whole kingdom, and how immense the annual consumption from the year 1755 to the year 1795! If to this we should add all the foreign spirits that have been consumed in Great Britain during the above period, the sum total would almost baffle calculation! Can we longer wonder why our parishes are overburthened with poor? Why our prisons overflow with debtors and desperate felons, or why our poor's rates, amounting to a sum little short of three millions a year, should be rapidly increasing? (p. 12)

In view of Fothergill's combination of precise individual observation and far-ranging and prophetic extrapolation from specific instances, it is not surprising that the young Coleridge chose to quote long sections of this tract in his tenth issue of *The Watchman* for 13 May 1796. In doing so he issued warnings to his countrymen and hinted at his own fascination with addictions. The mutual respect among Colquhoun, Fothergill and Coleridge gleams through the signatures, quotations and references to each other's works, for each seeks corroboration for his alarm.

Unexpectedly early, Dr John Coakley Lettsom also sees the difficulty of curing habitual drunkenness. In *Bonner Middleton's Bristol Journal*, 13 May 1797, the surgeon understands the dangers of abrupt withdrawal: 'But in some cases where the habit of [drinking] has been long continued the total and sudden omission of them has sunk the person into irretrievable debility. Here the pernicious custom must be left off gradually. ... Painful indeed is this truth, that where the indulgence in spirituous liquors is rendered habitual it is extremely difficult to overcome.'[45] Lettsom realizes that ceasing to drink is not a matter of will, for spirits create a physiological compulsion.

Where Trotter, Fothergill, Lettsom and MacNish had specialized medical reputations, Dr Erasmus Darwin and Dr Thomas Beddoes participated in many aspects of the Romantic intellectual and social community and through their broader engagement helped turn attention to the dangers of spirit-drinking. Darwin, in *Zoonomia* (1801), sets drunkenness in the context of pleasures as general as the rocking of infants, where the sensations of glow and heat lead the 'voluntary power to become feebly exerted'. Using a sensation-alist approach similar to David Hartley's, he examines the experience of drunkenness, so like dreams and delirium, and notes the doubling of objects of sight, the irritated susceptibility to smells and light, the frequency of certain diseases, especially gout, which he believes to be an inherited disposition. Darwin worries that where people are alarmed if someone ingests a poisonous mushroom, they are 'so familiarised ... to the intoxication from vinous spirit, that it occasions laughter rather than alarm.'[46] Darwin reads the Prometheus myth as a temperance allegory, with Prometheus's tortured liver a symptom of cirrhosis: Prometheus's stealing fire from heaven, might 'well represent the inflammable spirit produced by fermentation; which may be said to animate or enliven the man of clay; whence the conquests of Bacchus, as well as the temporary mirth and noise of his devotees. But the after punishment of those who steal this accursed fire, is a vulture gnawing the liver; and well allegorizes the poor inebriate, lingering for years under painful hepatic diseases.'[47]

Author of *Hygeia: or Essays Moral and Medical, on the Causes Affecting the Personal State of our Middling and Affluent Classes* (1802), Dr Thomas Beddoes maintained close connections with major Romantic writers of the period, learning from Mary Wollstonecraft and influencing S. T. Coleridge, who refers often to Dr Beddoes in his early lectures, when Beddoes worked at his Pneumatic Institute at Clifton, very near Coleridge's Bristol and Nether Stowey lodgings. Two long essays in his three volumes explore the sources of alcohol abuse in the late eighteenth century. The first, 'Essay on the Means of Avoiding Habitual Sickliness and Premature Mortality', exposes the evils of schools for girls and boys, where cold, hunger, boredom, lack of exercise, and 'early sexual intemperance' stunt the growth and vitality of children. Among boys, boredom leads to

drinking: 'little boys, if I am not grossly misinformed, guzzle
at their meals so strong a fermented liquor as porter. The bigger
frequently super-add wine; and not in very sparing quantities.'
Dr Beddoes sees this early training as the source of later illness: 'It
is impossible that three or four glasses of port wine – a quantity,
which usage miscalculates as small – should be regularly swal-
lowed by under-graduates of our universities without curtailing
life, or making it miserable; and indeed, without doing both in a
tremendous number of instances.'[48] Dr Beddoes admires Dr Pilger's
experiments on drunken horses in Bavaria, including poisoning
and dissecting them to demonstrate from the condition of the
stomach lining the ravages of alcohol.[49]

Dr Beddoes's eighth essay, 'On The Preservation of the Physical
Power of Enjoyment, with remarks on Food and Digestion', begins,
like Erasmus Darwin's work, with a study of pleasure and the
difficulty of moderating it in a luxurious age:

> Our danger arises from untutored appetite. To indulge in such a
> way, that desire may constantly spring up anew to administer
> the occasion of fresh indulgence, constitutes the *virtue of temper-
> ance*, which, according to my apprehension, can be no otherwise
> considered than as synonymous with the *art of enjoyment*.[50]

How, indeed, can a doctor (especially one whose girth made him a
by-word for self-indulgence) propose 'self-denying measures,
when [he has] no authority to enforce them'? Beddoes believes that
the stomach suffers much more from the intake of brandy and
spirits than from ale and wine. Though he watches the heavy
drinker's growing dissatisfaction and hypochondria, he nevertheless praises the glow of near intoxication as it gives pleasure to
young people of genius:

> But what shall we say to our young men, and men of genius,
> who derive such exquisite delight from the glow of imagination,
> and who are therefore apt to embrace with so much avidity every
> means of kindling this glow? According to the general feelings of
> mankind ... that effervescence of the animal spirits which takes
> place just this side of intoxication, ranks among the highest of
> human pleasures. It has the advantage of being enhanced by par-
> ticipation; and if the human frame were otherwise constituted,
> the free use of wine would not only be an allowable indulgence

but might properly be inculcated as a duty. For there are none of the ingenious arts, of which the cultivation have a more healthy effect on the mind, and a more humanising, than the frequent excitement of the chearful spirits.[51]

Dr Beddoes's acknowledgement of the pleasures of intoxication – which we will see again in Francis Place, in the drinking-songs of Coleridge and Keats, and in the delicious reminiscences of Charles Lamb – is shadowed by the realities of the fragile 'human frame', which cannot endure such excess.

In addition to setting alcohol use in the context of pleasure and inspiration, Beddoes pioneers the study of women's drinking as it leads to hysteria and depression. Women's drinking can be ascribed to 'their wretched education, and the life they afterwards lead; to the neglect of that exercise, which the human animal was formed for taking; to close confinement in unwholesome apartments; to books that have too great a power to melt; and to other habits and privations, already described at large.'[52] Such analyses suggest that he has absorbed Mary Wollstonecraft's *Vindication of the Rights of Women* (1792), especially her chapters on women's shallow education and sedentary lives.

Revealing a similar interest in the pleasure of drink, especially for geniuses, Dr Anthony Carlisle, a fashionable but indiscreet London physician who briefly treated Coleridge, is quoted at length in Basil Montagu's 1814 *Enquiries*. Dr Carlisle examines the causes and processes of drunkenness as they transform the drunkard's psychology. At first, the 'moral influence of fermented liquors' has a heightening effect:

At the beginning of intoxication the ideas flow with a more than natural rapidity; self-love soars above our prudence and shews itself openly; we lay aside the scales of deliberation, the slow pondering, measuring and comparing instruments of the judgement. In this condition every man is a hero to himself, he feels as he wishes, and the state of his mind is betrayed by boastings and falsehoods, by pretensions to abilities beyond his possession, and by a delusive contempt for the evils that beset him.[53]

Too soon this ecstasy tips over into assorted derangements – 'the destruction of continuity in the memory', 'the dissolution of moral integrity', a 'disorderly imagination', 'an acquired habit of slovenly and heedless inductions', ending often in insanity.

The witty Scottish doctor Robert MacNish, much admired in America, presented *Anatomy of Drunkenness* (1825) as his inaugural essay for the faculty of physicians and surgeons. One of his several studies of the irrational, including sleep, dreams, metempsychosis and *diablerie, Anatomy of Drunkenness* seeks in literature and myth, including the drunkenness of Noah, Lot and Alexander, and the drunken songs of Scandinavian skalds, for help in understanding this complex new illness. MacNish believes that drunkenness is decreasing among the upper classes but increasing among the lower:

> If we turn to our own times, we shall find little cause to congratu-late ourselves upon any improvement. The vice has certainly di-minished among the higher orders of society, but there is every reason to fear that, of late, it has made fearful strides among the lower. Thirty or forty years ago, a landlord did not conceive he had done justice to his guests unless he sent them from his table in a state of intoxication. (pp. 23–4)

Covering the whole subject of drunkenness, its physiology, its causes (which will enhance the study of Lamb in a later chapter), its symptoms, and its cures, MacNish classifies drunks, a topos famil-iar from the Renaissance,[54] describing sanguinaceous drunks like Roderick Random as ruddy, animalistic, combative and obstreper-ous; melancholy drunks like Robert Burns; surly drunks, gloomy, discontented and suspicious; and phlegmatic drunks, 'heavy-rolling machines', whose 'energies are as stagnant as the dead sea'. From such 'animated clods' 'the words come forth as if they were drawn from his mouth with a pair of pincers and the ideas are as frozen as if compacted in the bowels of Lapland. Such persons are very apt to be played upon by their companions. There are few men who, in their younger days, have not assisted in shaving the heads and painting the faces of these lethargic drunkards' (pp. 64–5). Before his death of typhoid at 34, MacNish worked to cure these varied drunkards.

While most Romantic doctors and observers preserve their ob-jectivity in treating and describing individual and family cases, two contemporaries complicate their observations with personal involvement. Though from very different backgrounds, Francis

Place and Basil Montagu both write at length about alcohol use as a serious problem in the London of the Romantic era. Both men overcame early alcoholism, though Place was far more frank about his than Montagu, and both wrote to help others escape the same sufferings. Both were also philanthropists in a variety of causes, central figures in different milieus, and social friends of Romantic writers. To compare them is to see two different characters, two different attitudes to past drunkenness and indulgence, and two different relations to telling the truth.

Francis Place had a remarkable ability to see the drunkenness of poor workers as the middle classes saw them, but also to feel from the inside what an individual drinker craves. Although his work on labour and class has been studied, his work on alcoholism has so far been ignored. The son of a brutal drunkard, a tailor by trade, and an influential political figure among London tradesmen in the 1790s and early 1800s, Place defended the behaviour of working-class drunks against the snobbish attacks of gentry like J. Silk Buckingham in hearings before a select committee of the House of Commons in 1834. His *On Drunkenness,* a pamphlet from 1829, is a wide-ranging analysis of the social and psychological phenomena of drinking. In his own lifetime, from 1771 to 1854, Place observes the improvement in the education of working men and consequently the decrease in heavy drinking. But he is moved to explain that working men need moments of leisure just like upper-class men, and that working men are criticized for their behaviour whereas upper-class men are coddled and forgiven. He looks back to the situations of working men in his own early decades and tries to convey the emptiness, hopelessness and brutality of their lives, and thus the inevitability of their drunkenness.

Although many working men have employment only half the time, and therefore enforced idleness the other half, the working man who works all the time works long hours, 'excluded from all rational enjoyment, shut out from reasonable conversation, doing the same thing, generally in the same place, always against his will and on compulsion, without hope of bettering his condition and with a conviction that it will become worse and worse as he grows older and his family increase. ... His thoughts are necessarily of a gloomy cast; his home is seldom comfortable.'[55] Place describes the wearying process by which a poor man and his wife gradually degenerate, spirits breaking, love forgotten, children neglected, until the only enjoyments left are sexual intercourse and drinking,

the latter 'by far the most desired' (p. 10). Speaking to the middle
and upper classes, Place points out that working men feel as
intensely as anyone the hopelessness of their lives: 'the most
unthinking, the least intelligent ... feel acutely at times: they never
reflect on their condition without a perfect consciousness, amount-
ing to absolute certainty, that their mortal career will terminate in
the most abject poverty and misery, and this has a marked effect on
them: few, indeed, are they who can at all times escape from
depressing thoughts, and still fewer who can at all times bear up
against them' (p. 11). Aware of their own spiritual emptiness, lack
of education, and consequent lack of hope, these men turn to drink:
'no one then need be surprised that they should occasionally get
drunk, the only matter for surprise is that it should be only occasional. Drinking is the sole means such men have of getting away
from themselves, the only resource against the most depressing
thoughts' (p. 12).

The warmth, power, and pleasure of alcohol Place remembers
intensely from his own labouring days.

> It is not easy for any one who has not himself been a working
> man, accurately to estimate the agreeable sensations produced by
> the stimulus of strong liquor in the stomach of the working man,
> or the intimate connexion between these sensations and the
> pleasurable ideas they excite in uncultivated men; yet so constant
> are these effects, that he who has scarcely any other means of
> excitement producing enjoyment, will in almost all cases, and to
> some extent, endeavor to produce them as often as he has the
> power, and dares venture to use it. (p. 16)

Place explains that the aim is not drunkenness but the continuous
'buzz' of half-drunkenness, which still inures workers to their
tedious tasks. He describes this state with remarkable clarity:

> Absolute drunkenness is not, however, in all cases, necessary for
> the production of pleasurable ideas; an approximation to drunk-
> enness is, to many, a much more pleasureable state than absolute
> intoxication, and many seek stimulation with liquor, so as to
> 'muddle' themselves, a term well known and well understood by
> the working people: 'he is muddle,' or 'he muddles,' is the
> common expression for that state which produces a pleasant
> delirium, somewhat analogous to the effects of opium, as de-

scribed by several who have become habitual users of the drug. (p. 17)

The two-martini lunch and the pub 'lunch' from eleven to one still produce this 'pleasant delirium' or 'muddle'.

Place believes that education has improved the lives and hopes of working men during his own lifetime, but he notices with fury, especially in his *Defense of the People against J. S. Buckingham and the Committee* (1834) that the upper classes still single out the occasional drunken working man or woman who makes a spectacle on the streets and blame the whole class for one. Meanwhile the upper classes do their drinking in clubs and home banquets where no one can see them falling down. These higher classes are now the ones that are drinking gin, accounting, in his view, for the increase in the consumption of spirits from 1817 to 1828. Place's analysis of the central role of class in the assessment of British drunkenness anticipates Friedrich Engels's *Condition of the Working Class in England*, written fifteen years later.[56] The difference is that Francis Place writes as a self-educated man from within the working classes, and as a former heavy drinker himself, well aware of the temptations, despairs and feelings of the labourer. His outrage is personal and passionate, but nevertheless closely analytical: he can see from the inside what it feels like to be a drunk; at the same time he can see the workers as the middle classes see them.

As Francis Place occupied a pivotal point in the many concerns of the period from drunkenness to penal reform, and corresponded with figures as diverse as the labour reformer Thomas Hardy, the economist David Ricardo, and Mary Shelley's half-sister Claire Clairemont's brother, spanning classes even as they were moving apart in their 'unhappily progressive alienation',[57] so, too, Basil Montagu (who wrote to Francis Place about their common involvement in the fight against capital punishment for crimes without blood[58]) was a central figure of the age with a similarly difficult recovery from alcohol abuse.

This personal dimension appears obliquely in Montagu's *Some Enquiries into the Effects of Fermented Liquors, By a Water-Drinker* (1814). A friend of the Wordsworths, Coleridge, Lamb, and many other Londoners during the Georgian and Regency periods, as well as an attorney for Percy Bysshe Shelley in the custody case for his children by Harriet Westbrook, Montagu compiles his book from literary and medical sources. He aims to present passages for meditation that will keep young men from slipping down the precipice of drunkenness. He believes that families and schools have failed to provide guidance: 'The formation of habits upon which our happiness and utility must be founded are left to chance, to the customs of our parents, or the practices of our first college associates: and thus our most interesting young men are induced, from ignorance of the effects of stimulants, from the love of imitation and the fear of singularity, to take any baneful and exciting drug which the fashion of the place may recommend' (p. xvi). Of all the enticing stimulants none are more alluring and ultimately more damaging, in his view, than fermented liquors.

> The gratification which they produce is immediate and exquisite: their pernicious effects are slow and remote: but if pleasure, often a deceitful guide to happiness, will deign to listen to the voice of reason: if ingenuous youth will, for a moment, suffer the enchantment by which he has so long been spell-bound to be broken, he may at least be induced to examine this gift of Circe and pause lest there be death in the cup. (p. xx)

Quoting from *Hamlet*, Robert Burton, Pope and Shaftsbury, Montagu alludes to his own earlier want of guidance, and speaks the words of warning that he wishes someone had spoken to him when he held up his 'cheerful glass, the promoter of conviviality' (p. xxiii), without recognizing 'death in the cup'.

Although Montagu's tortured biography[59] belongs in later chapters, his book provides further evidence of the widespread worry about drunkenness in the Romantic period and suggests his own nervousness about his past dissipations as he darts from Benjamin Franklin to Samuel Johnson to Dr Anthony Carlisle to Erasmus Darwin to Dr Thomas Beddoes to Jeremy Collier. Eager for material, he publishes Charles Lamb's 'Confessions of a Drunkard' without Lamb's authorization. When he must withdraw Lamb's essay, he substitutes 'The Lamentable Case of Hartley Coleridge', using privileged knowledge of Hartley's condition. The rapacity with which Montagu snatches material indicates his desperation to have other voices covering over his own, where the introduction promised a personal confession of wasted youth. While it documents Romantic drinking, Montagu's *Enquiries* is a troubled confession that refuses to confess the 'wild habits' that he or someone else excised also from his memoirs.[60]

Though never before brought together as 'Romantic' texts, these writings by Doctors Trotter, Rush, Fothergill, Lettsom, Darwin, Beddoes, Carlisle, Currie and MacNish, and social commentators Colquhoun, Dunlop, Place and Montagu, indicate that heavy drinking of spirits was perceived as a crisis in the Romantic era. These substantial investigations – *An Essay, Medical, Philosophical, and Chemical, on Drunkenness* (1788 and 1804); *Observations and Facts relative to licenced Ale-Houses* (1794); *Essay on the Abuse of Spirituous Liquors* (1795); *Zoonomia* (1801); *Hygeia* (1802); *Some Enquiries into the Effects of Fermented Liquors* (1814); *Anatomy of Drunkenness* (1825); *On Drunkenness* (1830); *Artificial and Compulsory Drinking Practices* (1839), and other writings and references to these works – demonstrate real worry about drinking during the period 1780–1830. They add a new dimension to Romanticism and fill in a gap in social history. They form another layer of context surrounding the writings of the more strictly 'literary' writers who will occupy later chapters.

Such evidence of a historical shift has been ignored for two reasons: the modern preoccupation with opium use in the period, and the popular allocation of literature about alcohol use to twentieth century American fiction. Readers who devise ever longer lists of American writers who were alcoholics – Ernest Hemingway, F. Scott Fitzgerald, Ring Lardner, Dorothy Parker, William Faulkner, John Berryman, Robert Lowell, Elizabeth Bishop, Jack London, John Steinbeck, Sinclair Lewis, John Cheever, and many others[61] – and find ever more reasons for the spiritual emptiness of 'the Alcoholic Republic',[62] as well as readers who have noted the occasional depiction of drunkards selling their children or spontaneously combusting in nineteenth century English, French, and Russian novels,[63] will be surprised by similar lists, but deeper investigations, in the Romantic era.

So, too, preconceptions about opium addiction block the possibility of seeing alcoholism in an unexpected time and place. In many critical studies Romanticism is almost synonymous with opium dreams.[64] Opium use has sometimes been thought to characterize the Romantic period, propelling 'the thrust in romanticism toward the invention of a disciplined mysticism'.[65] Indeed, the mysticism, orientalism and meditative suspensiveness of opium, its floating, spatially pulsing images, render its early stages far more pleasant and medicinal than alcohol. But De Quincey, who used both intoxicants, thought alcohol the more damaging. The dangers of opium

eating were only belatedly learned; the dangers of drink were daily
to be seen in the shaking hands of inveterate dram-drinkers. De
Quincey asserts that 'no quantity of opium ever did, or could,
intoxicate. As to the tincture of opium (commonly called laudanum) *that* might certainly intoxicate, if a man could bear to take
enough of it; but why? Because it contains so much proof spirits of
wine, and not because it contains so much opium.'[66] Many important and obscure people did take opium, often dissolved in wine as
laudanum, for whatever ailed them, from headaches to arthritis to
anxiety. Many, like Coleridge, De Quincey, Dorothy Wordsworth,
Jane Austen's mother, and William Wilberforce, began to use
opium as medicine, then discovered the expanding perceptions and
timelessness of the drug experience, and only gradually became so
addicted to it that brains, bowels and will were disrupted. In addition, many opium addicts also drank, intensifying the intoxication
by cross-addiction, and further justifying a designation of the
period as 'The Age of Intoxication'.[67] Where opium addiction is
serene and somnolent until the nightmares start, drunkenness is
fervid and vocal. Addictions to drink and drugs co-exist, and
Romantic writers in England, like modern writers in the United
States, celebrate and lament their own drinking.

3.

Within these mythical and medical contexts, Romantic literary
writers develop a variety of representations of drinking and drunkenness. They see drunkenness as a historical, sociological and
medical reality; as an illness of an ambiguously physical and spiritual sort; as a psychology of multiple selves and a philosophy of
secular hedonism; as an experiment in what can happen to the
human being from outside forces or from internal ones; and as an
expression of bodily pleasure and communal merriment.

The poles of Romantic understanding of drunkenness veer from
exuberance to disgust, as the figure of the drunkard illustrates different aspects of the human being and serves different philosophical purposes. At one pole, Goethe's young Werther, confronted by
his sober and rational rival Albert, cries out for inebriation:

"Oh you sensible people! … . Passion. Inebriation. Madness. You
respectable ones stand there so calmly, without any sense of par-

ticipation. Upbraid the drunkard, abhor the madman, pass them by like the priest and thank God like the Pharisees that He did not make you as one of these! I have been drunk more than once, and my passion often borders on madness, and I regret neither. Because, in my own way, I have learned to understand that all exceptional people who created something great, something that seemed impossible, have to be decried as drunkards or madmen. And I find it intolerable, even in our daily life, to hear it said of almost everyone who manages to do something that is free, noble and unexpected: He is a drunkard, he is a fool. They should be ashamed of themselves, all these sober people! And the wise ones!"[68]

In using the word 'Inebriation', Werther intends a multitude of modes of escape, through art, joy and drink, using alcoholic pleasure as a symbol for other kinds of release. Intoxication for Werther represents genius, bold action, defiance, expansion. Werther plays Romanticism's Pantagruel, embracing life, with his slimmer, more introspective and ironical Romantic body, but fearing that life will never satisfy his infinite thirst.

At the other pole, George Crabbe, minister, medical practitioner, and 'Malthus turned metrical romancer' who 'set[s] his ill news to harsh and grating verse',[69] catalogues and exaggerates the horrors of drunkenness in the England of 1775–1810. His first published poem, 'Inebriety' (1775), laments the ubiquity of sots:

> See Inebreity! her wand she waves,
> And lo! her pale, and lo! her purple slaves;
> Sots in embroidery, and sots in crape,
> Of every order, station, rank, and shape;
> The King who nods upon his rattle-throne,
> The staggering Peer, to midnight revel prone;
> The slow-tongu'd Bishop, and the Deacon sly,
> The humble Pensioner, and Gownsman dry;
>
> The proud, the mean, the selfish, and the great,
> Swell the dull throng, and stagger into state.

With a censorious eye Crabbe looks at a saturated society, from 'the poor Toper whose untutor'd sense,/ Sees bliss in ale, and can with wine dispense', to the jovial vicar, to 'the stumbling Charmer as she falls'.[70] Crabbe's 'The Borough' (1810) classifies kinds of drinks, groups of drinkers and the places where they drank. In 'The Parish Register I' (1807) he scrutinizes the family of Sot, Cheat and Shrew, and notes the screams of the beaten wife and ragged children.[71] In 'Hester' he imagines the confession of the harlot who drinks from disgust at the demands of her trade:

> Then first with the seducing Cup
> I tried to steel my Breast,
> To keep expiring Courage up,
> And lull Dispair to rest.
> [...]
> And hence with Liquors strong we heat
> The Brain till fear is flown,
> The Ruffian in his Mood to meet,
> With Spirit like his own.[72]

In Letter XI of 'The Borough' he categorizes the strata of inns by social class and in Letter XVI describes the process by which Benbow 'with Wine inflated' lost his father's possessions and ended in the Alms-House.[73] As a doctor and a clergyman Crabbe watches 'inebriety' debase patients and parishioners; he registers the dark side of Romantic drinking.

With more sympathy but similar dismay, Percy Bysshe Shelley sees that the Dionysian myth has withered away, leaving besotted workers, empty, spiritless shells. In 1817 in 'An Address to the People on the Death of the Princess Charlotte', he understands why the poor are debauched in a kingdom ruled by an 'old, mad, blind, despised, and dying King' (as he calls him in the sonnet 'England in 1819') and his profligate, publicly drunken sons:

> In the manufacturing districts of England discontent and disaffection had prevailed for many years; this was the consequence of that system of double aristocracy produced by the causes before mentioned. The [factory laborers], the helots of luxury, are left by this system famished, without affections, without health, without leisure or opportunity for such instruction as might counteract those habits of turbulence and dissipation produced by the precariousness and insecurity of poverty.[74]

Shelley, abstemious in drink, may have had a greater interest in Dionysianism than has been previously suspected,[75] but he knows that in his own lifetime it has ceased to signify freedom.

Subsequent chapters of *Romantic Bacchus* unfold the many meanings of the drunkard as Romantic poets and prose writers look back to the exultant drinking of antiquity and the Renaissance, and also forward to the guilt, fragmentation, self-disgust and fear of irrationality that pervade modern drunkenness. Enmeshed in biography, psychology, medicine, history, sociology, myth and literary tradition, the Romantic drunkard stands as a complex figure for human risk and also degradation.

2

Romantic Homage to the Dionysian Burns: Wordsworth and Others

Up Scotland! who only drunky sexy Burns
producing, which returns.
          – John Berryman (1964)

The publication in the years 1786 and 1787 of three editions of Robert Burns's *Poems, chiefly in the Scottish Dialect* provoked sudden and surprising fame in London as well as in Edinburgh, and almost immediate revelations of Burns's drunkenness and ribaldry.[1] Even while he was lionized as a rustic genius by lawyers and critics in Edinburgh salons, tongues wagged about his personal excesses. Enthusiasts of the simple ploughman poet were shocked by songs about sex and whisky and by raucous behaviour acceptable among the rich but unsuitable for an upstart exalted by his betters. When in 1796 the 37-year-old Burns died of rheumatoid endocarditis (which in fact may have been held in check by his drinking), his early death was widely blamed on dissipation.[2] In the *London Chronicle*, 28–30 July 1796, an obituary notice, frequently reprinted, described the waste of Burns's nights 'in those haunts of village festivity, and in the indulgences of the social bowl, to which the Poet was but too immoderately attached in every period of his life', claimed that 'his talents were often obscured and finally impaired by excess', and that his dissipation heartlessly left impoverished a wife and five children, with a sixth on the way.[3] A year after Burns's death, Robert Heron coyly admitted in his memoir, 'it is true that he did not always steadily distinguish and eschew the evils of drunkenness and licentious love; it is true that these, at times, seemed to obtain even the approbation of his muse.'[4]

Burns's drunkenness, well-known in his own milieu, was pub-
licized throughout Great Britain in James Currie's 1800 account
of his life, accompanying the first complete edition of Burns's
works. Dr Currie speaks frankly about Burns's increasing drunkenness after he enters the social and intellectual scene in
Edinburgh:

> accustoming himself to conversation of unlimited range, and to
> festive indulgences that scorned restraint, he gradually lost some
> portion of his relish for the more pure, but less poignant pleas-
> ures, to be found in circles of taste, elegance, and literature. The
> sudden alteration in his habits of life operated on him physically
> as well as morally. ... He saw his danger, and at times formed
> resolutions to guard against it; but he had embarked on a tide of
> dissipation, and was borne along on its stream.[5]

Currie traces the poet's progressive decline: Burns is 'seduced' by
the tables of gentlemen of Nithsdale, whose parties, celebrated in
his poem 'The Whistle', 'inflamed those propensities which temperance might have weakened, and prudence ultimately suppressed'
(p. 198); then, moving to Dumfries and turning to strong liquors,
'his irregularities grew by degrees into habits' (p. 205); toward the
end of his life, 'perpetually stimulated by alkohol [sic] in one or
other of its various forms, the inordinate actions of the circulatory
system became at length habitual' (p. 217).

> His temper now became more irritable and gloomy; he fled from
> himself into society, often of the lowest kind. And in such
> company that part of the convivial scene, in which wine increases
> sensibility and excites benevolence, was hurried over, to reach
> the succeeding part, over which uncontrouled passion generally
> presided. He who suffers the pollution of inebriation, how shall
> he escape other pollution? (p. 221)

Trying to euphemize Burns's condition even in this first edition
(though more so in later editions to accommodate Wordsworth's
objections to his demeaning of genius), Currie nevertheless presents a painful portrait of a disintegrating, possibly even violent,
drunkard, whose family again and again forgave him. Currie ends
his biographical account with a warning to men of genius to avoid
excesses of drink, since they are, by virtue of the very genius that

glorifies them, prone to heightened sensibility, indolence, and diseases of the mind (p. 248).

The Scot John Dunlop, writing about the Burns legend in 1839, forty-three years after Burns's death, takes Burns's drunkenness for granted. He cites numerous poems indicating that 'Scotch Drink' was his tenth muse, and believes that the Scottish passion for strong drink exceeds that of other nations. 'The gentle and elegant effusions of Anacreon, in praise of the dissipation of Greece, might almost be denominated "Temperance Rhymes" when put into contrast with the fierce and inexorable excess that alone receives the meed of praise from the Scottish Bard.'[6] But Dunlop blames the customs of Scotland for Burns's decline, for who can resist 'that savage hospitality that knocks a man down with strong liquors', as Burns himself calls it. Dunlop uses Burns as his main example of the dangers of such customs, even as Burns reinforced those customs with his poems:

> Indeed, although it would be dishonest to extenuate personal guilt, yet in one sense it may be affirmed, that it was the land he lived in that made Burns a drunkard; and no evil consequent has reacted upon its antecedent with more unlimited and pernicious sway, than has the intemperance of Burns upon his own people. The great frequency in this author's work of an obsequious and laudatory allusion to inebriation exhibits in no small degree the extraordinary and fatal good will that this national sin experiences in the general from the inhabitants of North Britain. (p. 96)

Drunken poet and drunken country reciprocally drove each other to greater drunkenness. Environment and the individual will are perniciously intertwined. Burns's many poems in praise of drink inspired and corrupted his contemporary admirers.

To offset this dissolute influence, later biographers have tried to deny Burns's drunkenness and thus to restore his simple, pure reputation. Ignoring the many poems praising drink and drinkers in the first editions of the poetry, and in the longer 'Tam O'Shanter', 'Death and Doctor Hornbook', and 'Tam Samson's Elegy and Epitaph', they censor from letters and memoirs evidence of Burns's wild behaviour. As Alan Bold quips, Currie's 'infamous judgement on Burns ... so outraged modern Burns scholars that they have gone to the other extreme and made the often-plastered saint an almost teetotalitarian figure.'[7] This prudish suppression of information has been mocked in a review of a 1992 biography. Calling for 'More Dirt, Less Deity', Pat Rogers addresses the issue of Burns's drinking:

> The author tries all he knows to undo the impression [that Burns is a drunken, dissipated character], even though a [well-known] letter begins, "I recollect something of a drunken promise yesternight. ..." Evidence is drawn from far and wide to show that Burns cannot have been an alcoholic ... [But] although Burns was able to restrict his drinking for long periods, he was from abundant other evidence a very heavy drinker at times ("Occasional hard drinking is the devil to me"). Hence the juvenile and humiliating escapades he was sometimes led into.

Rogers urges some future biographer to 'embrace the grovelling as well as the soaring, the pie-eyed as well as the prim, the lecherous wastrel as well as the good homekeeping body who did a solid career stint in the Excise and turned up sober to the Volunteers.'[8]

Whatever biographers may wish to see or not to see, Burns's love of drink is unavoidable in the poems. The volumes are steeped in praise of whisky:

> Inspiring bold *John Barleycorn*!
> What dangers thou canst make us scorn!
> Wi' tippenny, we fear nae evil;
> Wi' usquebae, we'll face the devil.[9]

Burns extolls tavern life:

> Leeze me on Drink! it gies us mair
>   Than either School or Colledge:
> It kindles Wit, it waukens Lear,
>   It pangs us fou o' Knowledge.
> Be't *whisky-gill*, or *penny-wheep*,
>   Or oniy stronger potion,
> It never fails

('The Holy Fair', XIX; *BP*, 1, 134–5)

He imagines the Doctor's drunken hallucinations in 'Death and Doctor Hornbook: A True Story' (*BP*, 1, 79):

> The Clachan yill had made me canty,
> I was na fou, but just had plenty;

letters are sprinkled with quotations from Burns and praise for
poets who sometimes sound like him.

Acting quickly, perhaps in response to the obituary cited above
urging benevolence to the impoverished family, the 24-year-old
Coleridge contributed a poem to a volume designed to gather
money for Burns's widow and children. The poem, 'To a Friend
who had declared his intention of writing no more poetry', was
addressed to Lamb and echoed Milton's *Lycidas* in an appropriate
elegy for a fellow poet. Coleridge's poem asks,

> Is thy Burns dead?
> And shall he die unwept, and sink to earth
> Without the meed of one melodious tear?
> Thy Burns, and Nature's own beloved bard,
> Who to the 'Illustrious of his native Land
> So properly did look for patronage.'
> Ghost of Maecenas! hide thy blushing face!
> They snatch'd him from the sickle and the plough –
> To gauge ale-firkins.

(CCP, 159, ll. 17–24)

The Burns myth leaps full-grown from Coleridge's head: Burns
abandoned by his countrymen; nature's bard left to starve by rich
Scotch merchants and aristocrats who corrupted his innocence and
encouraged his dissipation, laughing as he cracked open nine-
gallon barrels of ale. Into his outrage Coleridge weaves quotations
from Burns's own expressions of exploited genius, initiating an
intertextual dialogue among poets who pay homage to each other's
works, echoing and criticizing each other's phrases.

The admiration of these young Romantic poets for a pleasure
seeker, the creator of the famous drunkard 'Tam O'Shanter' and of
drinking songs about whisky and willing Caledonian women,
signals a new ideal of the poet: a rude and earthy rustic, worn by
farming a hard land and ruined by the rich; a revolutionary demo-
crat expressing Jacobin sympathies; a spontaneous artist; an outspoken wastrel in a Pharisaical age; a reincarnation of Dionysus,
Pantagruel, and Falstaff. The convivial, passionate Burns was the
type of the Romantic artist, in part because he was a drunk. Living
the ancient ideal of the inspired drunkard, he also looks ahead to
twentieth-century singers who risk their sanity to create their
songs, like Jim Morrison of 'The Doors', who drank whisky to

invent and to perform, and who proclaimed himself 'Dionysus'. As contemporary followers of Morrison visit the *cimetière de Père Lachaise* in Paris, covering the grave with relics and dionysian ivy, so Romantic poets also made the pilgrimage to Burns's grave in Dumfries, a spot of earth radiating power.

Whereas Lamb and Coleridge pour out their admiration immediately and embrace the Burns model in their own often drunken behaviour, as we shall see in later chapters, Wordsworth's response is more ambivalent. The Burns legend is far more important to him than the tangential notice it has received for influencing a few poems and verse forms in the *Lyrical Ballads*. Wordsworth's thoughts about the possibly altered states of mind in which insights arrive or poetic composition occurs often revolve around Burns. They range from 1787 or 1788, the year at Cambridge when he gets drunk in Milton's rooms, to 1803–6 when he and Dorothy visit Burns's grave and begin to brood on its meaning, to 1816, when he writes a defence of Burns's inspired drunkenness, to 1819, when he finally publishes his long-revised 'Benjamin the Waggoner'. Between the early experience of clouding his mind with fumes of wine and the castigation of himself in the 1805 *Prelude*, Book III; the 1803–6 anguish over Burns's dissipated death and failure to guide his sons, to the sympathy with Benjamin and then with Burns's courage in exploring his irrational depths, Wordsworth tacks and veers through difficult waters of poetic enthusiasm and the problem of artificially heightening it. Artificially inducing such states by wine is a moral problem, arising from a belief that pleasure and inspiration should be 'natural', and perhaps a psychological one, reflecting the fear of self-loss that Wordsworth's childhood traumas may have imbedded, and also a professional one, in that Wordsworth seeks to sustain a long and ambitious career. Burns forms for Wordsworth the core of a series of meditations on pleasure, on human sorrow, and on poetic enthusiasm.

Burns forces the at first anxious and then deliberately austere Wordsworth to consider his own ideas about pleasure and wildness, on the one hand seeking 'the elementary forms of pleasure' and on the other holding himself back from self-abandon.

'Pleasure' is a word that appears often in the *Lyrical Ballads*, in the two prefaces to them, and in the versions of the *Prelude*. Usually pleasure is peaceful, suspended and passive. It is associated with breezes, mildness, the presences of nature and absorbed participation in its rhythms. It is gentler than joy, more organic; indeed, very often it comes to the passive child or boy as a 'drinking' in; often it is mentioned as occurring in the past, as a 'former' or 'unremembered' pleasure.[13] Sometimes it becomes a 'stealthy' pleasure, aroused by surreptitious or rapacious acts, of stealing nests or ravaging enclosed nut groves. When Wordsworth states that the poet should represent 'the grand elementary forms of pleasure', he includes the forms of nature that press upon his mind, the bird song he loves, the rhythms of metrical verse, sexual pleasure (explicitly noted in the Preface) and maternal love, which for Betty Foy, too, comes as a drinking in, when she 'a drunken pleasure quaffs / To hear again her idiot boy.'[14] Pleasure is 'natural' for Wordsworth; it should flow in on the feelings or along the blood without being sought; it is 'the pleasure which there is in life itself'.[15] It is essential to the 'native and naked dignity of man', which Wordsworth equates, by apposition, to 'the grand elementary principle of pleasure, by which he knows, and feels, and lives, and moves'.[16]

These are high claims for pleasure, yet to seek pleasure actively is to violate it. If the human being 'knows, feels, lives, and moves' by pleasure, and sympathizes with others only by pleasure (a strange notion), how can the person sit still and wait for it if it is slow to come, and refrain from actively seeking or artificially stimulating it? If pleasure comes through sensations, is it cheating to apply 'gross stimulants' to sharpen or blunt the receptive senses?[17] For the blood does not always flow 'with its own pleasure', nor does excess of pleasure come upon us always as or with a 'weight'.[18] Cultivating 'gross and violent stimulants' blunts the mind's sensitivity to the natural flow of pleasure, a violation that Wordsworth believes is frequent in his own depraved age, with men living in cities, seeking the artificial stimuli of crowds, theatres, street scenes, and drinking spots to recapture the lost pleasure that ought to come of its own.

As in the stealthy pleasures of boyhood, Wordsworth once violated the natural flow of pleasure when he visited Milton's rooms at Christ's College, Cambridge. The violation of the sacred, temperate grove of natural genius is a remarkable moment in Wordsworth's career as a poetic competitor. He is shocked by it himself. It is perhaps to this event that A. E. Housman refers when he says 'Cambridge has seen many strange sights. It has seen Wordsworth drunk; it has seen Porson sober.'[19] In Book III of the *Prelude* (1805) Wordsworth tells Coleridge about his 'empty noise and superficial pastimes' at Cambridge, and about 'a treasonable growth/ Of indecisive judgements that impaired/ And shook the mind's simplicity' (ll. 211–13; 214–16). This unnatural self, not his true being, is the one to blame for the crass ravage of Milton's 'innocent nest':

> Among the band of my compeers was one,
> My class-fellow at school, whose chance it was
> To lodge in the apartments which had been
> Time out of mind honored by Milton's name –
> The very shell reputed of the abode
> Which he had tenanted. O temperate bard!
> One afternoon, the first time I set foot
> In this thy innocent nest and oratory,
> Seated with others in a festive ring
> Of commonplace convention, I to thee
> Poured out libations, to thy memory drank
> Within my private thoughts, till my brain reeled,
> Never so clouded by the fumes of wine
> Before that hour, or since.

(Prel. III, 304–7)

His brain reels with the artificial stimulus of wine poured by a group of young males as libation to the temperate bard – a gross stimulant that violates Milton's principles and essence. Wordsworth sees in retrospect his low self scurrying away, his gown hitched up, 'with shallow ostentatious carelessness'. He apologizes for his 'vague and loose indifference' both to Milton and to Coleridge, the imaginary listener to his memories, who at least would understand his 'weakness':

>   Empty thoughts,
> I am ashamed of them; and that great bard,
> And thou, O friend, who in thy ample mind
> Hast stationed me for reverence and love,
> Ye will forgive the weakness of that hour,
> In some of its unworthy vanities
> Brother of many more.

(Prel. III, 322–5)

Is this moment of drunkenness a moment of abandon, pleasure, wildness, defiance? Why did Wordsworth retreat from it so cravenly, feeling his personality 'rotted as by a charm'?

This one moment of being overcome by the fumes of wine – never repeated – tells us much about Wordsworth's feelings about pleasure and his fear of it. Commentators have wondered why he seems to avoid ecstatic self-loss, to fear being overwhelmed by irrational forces, or by the blank void of the sublime, or by death anxiety.[20] Balancing his faith in play as the foundation of adult creativity with his disapproval of frivolous dissipations, as Willard Spiegelman reveals, Wordsworth shuns social idleness as a waste of self.[21] In this college episode of group drunkenness, Wordsworth is sickened by his violation of the spirit of Milton.

To clarify this unusual drunken moment Mary Jacobus sets it in the context of Wordsworth's reading of Milton. She shows that Wordsworth in *The Prelude* borrows Milton's vocabulary of Dionysianism to reject wild fervour: 'drinking to Milton's memory takes on an aspect at once sublime and Bacchic – inebriated with his poetry while disrespectful of Milton's own temperance.'[22] Milton expresses his 'terror of Bacchic orgies' in Book VII of *Paradise Lost*:

But drive far off the barbarous dissonance
Of Bacchus and his revellers, the race
Of that wild rout that tore the Thracian bard
In Rhodope, where woods and rocks had ears
To rapture, till the savage clamour drowned
Both harp and voice … (ll. 32–7)

Similarly, in his own Book VII Wordsworth rejects the 'short-lived uproar' of his 'glad preamble', fearing that he, too, might be torn to pieces and his voice submerged in a savage clamour. Like Milton, he rejects Dionysian possession. Instead of continuing in the rapturous mode of 'barbarous dissonance', Wordsworth chooses to respond to 'a little band, / A quire of redbreasts… minstrels from the distant woods' (*Prelude* 1805, VII, ll. 4, 6, 7, 23–5). After his intemperate celebration of the poet of temperance, Wordsworth replaces Comus's drunken revellers with robins and the steadily flowing river Derwent. Wordsworth sets behind him the temptations and terrors of libations, the reeling brain, and the short-lived uproar of Dionysian inspiration and wildness. The disgust with his own violation of Milton's room steadies him, and colours his views of other poets who seek artificial stimuli to intensify their poetic power. Where Milton's example is positive, Burns's fate is a negative influence on Wordsworth's rejection of Dionysianism;

however, he will return in 1816 to the problem of poetic wildness and risk, with a very different view.

Burns's poems ask Wordsworth to think about human frailties as partially self-imposed, and lead him to see the sorrows of his closest friends in this perspective. In response to Burns's early death, which occurred just when Wordsworth was dedicating himself to poetry and refusing to compromise his calling with ordinary forms of livelihood, he meditates in short and long poems and in prose on the difficulties of being a poet and a man, torn by divided impulses of pleasure and pain. This sympathy with Burns, or with the idea of Burns, provoked an unusual aspect of Wordsworth: a dionysian Wordsworth at odds with his usual image. This sympathy was possible because Burns was dead, and thus the point – that risk and wildness are finally dangerous – is already, safely, made.

Wordsworth's exploration of the Dionysianism of Burns spans almost twenty years, beginning with his adaptation of key principles and techniques from Burns in 1798 and moving through the late 'Letter to a Friend of Burns' in 1816. In 'Resolution and Independence' of May 1802 Wordsworth identified with the 'miserable reverses' of the young poets Thomas Chatterton (who died of tuberculosis and addiction in 1770 aged 17) and Burns, 'who walked in glory and in joy / Following his plough, along the mountain-side'. In these two tragic figures he saw himself potentially, and all other poets who risked their sanity to create art:

> By our own spirits are we deified:
> We poets in our youth begin in gladness,
> And thereof come in the end despondency and madness.

> (*PWW*, 1, 553, ll. 47–9)

Significantly, a phrase from the second line – 'We Poets in our Youth' – becomes the title of Eileen Simpson's memoir of John Berryman, Delmore Schwartz and Robert Lowell, three twentieth-century poets whose alcoholism destroyed them. Wordsworth recognizes the interconnection of creative and destructive elements in the impassioned poet, suggesting in the word 'thereof' that heights of 'gladness' precipitate almost inevitably a plunge to despondency and madness in the exultant and fragile poetic spirit.

Wordsworth's wonder at the mysterious conjunction of creativity and destructiveness is intensified on his Scottish walking tour a year after the composition of 'Resolution and Independence', where he contemplates his predecessor's death. His poems about Burns or modelled on Burns's poems show his struggle to come to terms with the Dionysian exultation and the Dionysian *sparagmos*, the tearing apart in sacrifice, the ancient myth which in the figure of Burns took on human form, and which Wordsworth steeled himself to avert. In the figure of Burns Wordsworth explores the connection between creativity and drunkenness with far more tolerance than he allows his own drunken contemporaries.

To Burns's grave, a spot of holy ground, came Wordsworth in August 1803 with his sister Dorothy. (Coleridge, who had accompanied them this far, stayed alone in his room at the inn, suffering from his own addictions. He records that the Wordsworths spent the morning of 18 August 'in visiting Burns's House & Grave'.[23]) Wordsworth paid homage to one of the three major influences on the voice, forms, and theory behind his *Lyrical Ballads* (1798),[24] to the Highland poet who had inspired or validated his theories that 'low and rustic life' provide good soil for 'the essential passions of the heart'.[25] Burns preceded Wordsworth in popularizing the rough highlands, in praising mountains, simple mountain people and rustic singers, and in using the ballad form. But Wordsworth's homage was shadowed with sad knowledge of Burns's dissipation. Currie's revelations of sottishness and ribaldry violated the sanctity and power of Burns's memory, tainting his greatness with a smutty middle-class censoriousness and condescension.

Lament for 'the heart riven' pervades the three beautiful elegies and warnings inspired by the blustery visit to Burns's grave, elegies that show Wordsworth at his most humane, profound and poignant, and that, nevertheless, are rarely studied. In the first poem inspired by this visit – 'At the Grave of Burns, 1803: Seven Years after his Death' – the poet 'shivers' at the physical, final, earthly death of the poet under the soil. He is fearful of the vapours breathed from the grave, and of the weight of dark thoughts. He addresses the dead poet as 'Spirit fierce and bold' as if warding off the magical hauntings of Scottish weird sisters:

> I shiver, spirit fierce and bold,
> At thought of what I now behold:
> As vapours breathed from dungeons cold
>   Strike pleasure dead,

So sadness comes from out the mould
　　Where Burns is laid.

And have I then thy bones so near,
And thou forbidden to appear?
As if it were thyself that's here
　　I shrink with pain;
And both my wishes and my fear
　　Alike are vain.

Off weight – nor press on weight! – away
Dark thoughts!

　　　　　　　(*PWW*, 1, 587, ll. 1–14)

The poet Wordsworth evades the suffocating weight of mortality
by turning to praise the dead man's poems, weaving into his
tribute quotations from Burns's verse, as Coleridge also had woven
the hero's voice into his own. Wordsworth stresses Burns's
influence on his own boyhood decision to become a poet. The
affinities between himself and Burns multiply: Burns taught him
'How Verse may build a princely throne / On humble truth' (ll.
35–6); Burns and he inhabited the rugged northern margins of
Britain and knew similar mountains; they were neighbours and
might have been friends; they might at this moment be talking together 'where gowans blow', with Burns now 43, had he lived, and
Wordsworth just 11 years younger. The poet chokes back this realization of how close in age they would have been:

　　　　　　　But why go on? –
　　Oh! spare to sweep, thou mournful blast,
　　　His grave grass-grown. (ll. 58–60)

Seeing beside Burns's grave the recent grave of Burn's young son
prompts the poet to seek consolation. The dead boy, at least, is safe,
'Harboured where none can be misled, / Wronged, or distrest'
(ll. 69–70). Unlike the living brothers addressed in a later poem, this
son of Burns will not be tempted by bad influences; he will not,
like his father, be 'Checked oft-times in a devious race' (l. 74).
Wordsworth ends the poem imagining Burns's heavenly ascent
hymned by Seraphim.

　　Having written the poem and exalted his troubled hero,
Wordsworth nevertheless continues to brood around the spot of time
that is the grave, for he has created too easy an ending, an unearned

apotheosis. He resumes his meditation in 'Thoughts Suggested the Day Following, on the Banks of the Nith, near the Poet's Residence', for the weight of the 'Dark Thoughts' could not be so easily conjured away nor the dungeon vapours dispersed by 'ritual hymn'. In a sentence of stunning elegance and intricacy, the second poem opens in frank recognition of Burns's own waste of himself:

> Too frail to keep the lofty vow
> That must have followed when his brow
> Was wreathed – 'The Vision' tells us how –
>   With holly spray,
> He faltered, drifted to and fro,
>   And passed away.

(PWW, 1, 590, ll. 1–6)

As Wordsworth himself in the experience recorded in the 1805 *Prelude* (Book IV, ll. 341–4) took vows to dedicate himself to a high poetic calling, also feeling himself 'wreathed' 'with holly spray' in an Apollonian luminosity or a Dionysian ecstasy (or with 'vine leaves' as Hedda Gabler will call the inspired state in Ibsen's play about the destruction of a brilliant alcoholic thinker), so Burns, too, promised a similar single-minded dedication in his poem 'The Vision', making a vow to the Scottish Muse who granted him a vision of Scottish history and crowned him with holly (ll. 20–2). But Burns, unlike Wordsworth, was unable to keep his 'lofty vow', 'drifted to and fro', and slipped away. This failure and its complex causes overwhelm Wordsworth and his sister Dorothy (now acknowledged as the fellow pilgrim beside him at the grave) with a sorrow relieved only by a deliberate turning ('Enough of sorrow, wreck and blight' [l. 19]) toward Burns's moments of artistic creation (ll. 20–4), his 'varying' influence on their own youthful sensibilities (ll. 25–30), and his emblematic position as a natural genius (ll. 37–42). Despite his human frailties, 'Deep in the general heart of men / His power survives' (ll. 47–8) – phrases that W. H. Auden will adapt when he works a similar transcendence for the vagaries of W. B. Yeats's biography and politics: 'poetry' 'survives': 'In the deserts of the heart / Let the healing fountain start.'[26] Wordsworth's sympathy for his errant poetic predecessor goes even further, however: for Burns's frailty is shared not only by fellow poets but also in one way or another by all human beings, and Wordsworth speaks with Hamlet's wisdom – 'Use every man

after his desert, and who shall scape whipping?' (II, 2, 516–17) –
when he concludes his elegy:

Sweet Mercy! to the gates of heaven
This Minstrel lead, his sins forgiven;
The rueful conflict, the heart riven
    With vain endeavour,
And memory of Earth's bitter leaven,
    Effaced forever.

But why to Him confine the prayer,
When kindred thoughts and yearnings bear
On the frail heart the purest share
    With all that live? –
The best of what we do and are,
    Just God, forgive!

(PWW, 1, 592, ll. 55–66)

Even this sense of shared human suffering does not chase away
the dark thoughts and vapours exhaled from Burns's grave. Worry
about Burns's children (sparked by the fresh grave of Burns's 'safe'
son beside him) persists over the next three years and emerges in
the poem 'To the Sons of Burns, after Visiting the Grave of their
Father', composed between early September 1805 and 21 February
1806. In her *Recollections* (for 18 August 1803) Dorothy Wordsworth
reveals that the topic has a peculiar importance to them both: 'The
grave of Burns's son, which we had just seen by the side of his
father, and some stories heard at Dumfries respecting the dangers
his surviving children were exposed to, filled us with melancholy
concern, which had a kind of connexion with ourselves' (cited n. to
PWW, 1, 657).

This 'kind of connexion with ourselves' is, I suspect, their 'melancholy concern' for the sons of their dear friend Coleridge – Hartley
and Derwent – who, with their mother, lived near and sometimes
with them in Grasmere. For Burns's drunkenness reminds them of
Coleridge's drunkenness (as they understood it), and the danger to
Burns's sons reminds them of the similar danger to Coleridge's
sons; simultaneously, Coleridge's fate alerts them to Burns's, and
Coleridge's sons' prospects alerts them to Burns's sons' prospects.
The specific nature of this connection is noted by Mark L. Reed in
his *Chronology* for 18 August 1803: 'W, DW, STC depart Dumfries,
pass by Burns's farm Ellisland, reach the Brownhill inn, where they

pass the night. W, DW walk out after dinner, talk of Burns, STC's family, Burns's family in terms afterwards reflected in W's "To the Sons of Burns."'.[27] In 'To H.C., Six Years Old' from March–June 1802, Wordsworth had already prophesied a painful life for Coleridge's first born, Hartley. Now, with Coleridge's more and more pronounced addiction to drugs and alcohol, his illness and isolation during the trip to Burns's grave, his departure in 1804 for Malta in order to heal himself, and his consequent abandonment of his children, ten-year-old Hartley's fate seemed even more hopeless than it had when 'To H.C.' was composed. Thus the ever-mysterious questions – how do sons escape their father's heredity and influence and avoid the fatality of a father's self-destructive behaviour and despair? – troubled William and Dorothy Wordsworth during this period in regard to the sons of two profligate poets, Burns and Coleridge. For, throughout, the examination of Burns is shadowed by the nearer figure of Coleridge, who is destroying himself in similar ways even as Wordsworth writes.[28] It is possible, too, that yet another drunken father with a troubled son came to their minds: Basil Montagu, whose drunkenness William Wordsworth had shielded in their shared London rooms in 1795, and whose son, also Basil, William and Dorothy had rescued from him and raised in Dorset.[29]

In the third poem in the Burns sequence Wordsworth's heart turns 'trembling' from father to sons, recognizing their more than usual burden in their father's 'Nature' and his 'name'.

> Through twilight shades of good and ill
> Ye now are panting up life's hill,
> And more than common strength and skill
>   Must ye display;
> If ye would give the better will
>   Its lawful sway.
>
> Hath Nature strung your nerves to bear
> Intemperance with less harm, beware!
> But if the Poet's wit ye share,
>   Like him can speed
> The social hour – of tenfold care
>   There will be need;
>
> For honest men delight will take
> To spare your failings for his sake,

Will flatter you, – and fool and rake
  Your steps pursue;
And of your Father's name will make
  A snare for you.

(PWW, 1, 658, ll. 7–24)

In addition to the fame and popularity that their father's name will
bring them, and the offers of drink in the old tradition of Scottish
hospitality (which Dunlop criticizes), the boys may also have inherited some of the personal sensitivity of their father. Will their
nerves be strung so as to resist intemperance, or will they require
whisky to soothe those nerves? Will their wit soar with a few
drinks? Will they need those drinks to 'speed the social hour'?
What power will their 'better will' have over their weaker will in
the psychomachia of their lives? Wordsworth begs them to avoid
the social, convivial, raucous, witty and brilliant aspects of their
father's nature and behaviour, and to choose instead his simple
aspects of cottager, mountaineer and ploughman, to imitate his
independent, generous and brave side, but to remember the early
grave and its reasons. But how can any child so pick and choose
from his father's nature?

Although in later years Wordsworth often sounds smug in the
face of Coleridge's self-destruction, as when he told Basil Montagu
that Coleridge was 'a rotten drunkard' 'rotting out his entrails with
intemperance', he looks at Burns's fate with anguish at human suffering. As epigraph to his poem to the sons of Burns he quotes the
first line of Burns's 'A Bard's Epitaph':

Is there a man, whose judgment clear,
Can others teach the course to steer,
Yet runs, himself, life's mad career,
  Wild as the wave;
Here pause – and through the starting tear,
  Survey this grave. (56)

This stanza reveals Burns's power over Wordsworth in its use of
the epitaph itself; for Wordsworth imitates the poem in 'A Poet's
Epitaph' in *Lyrical Ballads* (1798), praises the form in his *Essay on
Epitaphs* (1810),[30] uses Burns's verse form with its four iambic
tetrameter lines broken by two short lines of trochee and iamb,
heavy and abrupt with sorrow, and suffuses the poem with sadness

before 'Life's mad career'. Wordsworth loves and honours Burns, and weeps for him.

In the same years that Wordsworth was writing and revising the poem to the sons of Burns, 1806–7, he swelled his meditation on Burns's self-destructive genius by writing a long narrative poem, 'Benjamin the Waggoner', which can be seen as an adaptation of Burns's much quoted tale, 'Tam O'Shanter'. Both are stories about drunkards, a topic expected in Burns, but surprising in Wordsworth, though Wordsworth acknowledges in a veiled reference in 'Home at Grasmere' that his pastoral community in the Lakes can be occasionally interrupted by fierce voices, 'Debased and under profanation', 'Issuing when shame hath ceased to check the brawls / Of some abused Festivity', and Dorothy earlier notes that the Queen of Patterdale 'had been brought to drinking by her husband's unkindness and avarice'.[31]

Of 'Benjamin the Waggoner' Wordsworth recalls that the first version was 'thrown off under a lively impulse of feeling' between 1 January and 14 January 1806, when he felt 'inspirited'. He repeatedly revised the poem through 1812. This four-part tale in iambic tetrameter vigorously recounts the drunken ride of Benjamin, whose good intentions are waylaid by the lure of a tavern on a cold and wet night. Plot and description closely resemble 'Tam O'Shanter', where the hero also rides drunkenly through a hallucinatory and demonic landscape, where the cosy tavern is a shelter in the storm, and where animals (a single horse for Tam; eight wagon horses, an ass and a sensitive growling mastiff like Christabel's for Benjamin) sympathize with their drunken masters.[32] Nor is this Wordsworth's only use of 'Tam O'Shanter' as a model: Elinor Shaffer has demonstrated the substantial influence of its form on Wordsworth's early poem 'A Night on Salisbury Plain' (1793), where warlocks and witches, a murdered child, a hanged woman, and coffins recreate Tam's drunken hallucinatory journey.[33]

In 'Benjamin the Waggoner', however, Wordsworth greatly complicates Tam's simple and riotous journey. 'Benjamin the Waggoner' is four times as long as 'Tam' and has many more characters and voices, including a drunken sailor, his wife, her baby, and some on-lookers. It catalogues the tempting inns of the Grasmere and Wythburn area, including the inn that was called 'Dove and Olive-bough' in former days, and is now called 'Dove Cottage', where dwells 'a simple water-drinking bard' (l. 60), as Wordsworth coyly names his teetotal self in the poem.

In part by means of the multiplication of perspectives, Wordsworth examines Benjamin's reasons for drinking and, despite his own abstemiousness as a 'water-drinker', shows much sympathy for the drunkard. This complexity is brushed aside by Keats's friend John Hamilton Reynolds in his parody of the poem, which makes it almost interchangeable with 'Peter Bell' and 'Simon Lee' in foolish redundancy.[34] But Wordsworth does seem to be trying to understand the inward motivation of a character whose springs of action are very different from his own. He depicts Benjamin's kindness to others and his reluctance to drink:

> I trespassed lately worse than ever –
> But Heaven will bless a good endeavor;
> And, to my soul's delight I find
> The evil one is left behind.[35]

He shows how Benjamin's resolve is broken by the force of the storm and the invitations of the sailor:

> And Benjamin is wet and cold,
> And there are reasons manifold
> That make the good, tow'rds which he's yearning,
> Look fairly like a lawful earning.

> (ll. 312–15)

Wordsworth describes the ebullience of the foaming tankards and steaming bowl. In the tale within the tale, the sailor recreates the dangers of the battle of the Nile, as in Plate 3, 'old Nilers' roar and drink. The jolly sailor's infectious patriotism rouses Benjamin to 'A deep, determined, desperate draught!':

> "A Bowl, a Bowl of double measure,"
> Cries Benjamin, "A draught of length,
> To Nelson, England's pride and treasure,
> Her bulwark and her tower of strength!"

> (ll. 421–4)

Wordsworth describes the rapture 'still mounting to a higher height' (l. 467), the 'enraptured vision' (l. 476), the 'mutual exaltation; / Rich change, and multiplied creation!' (l. 483), and 'the turbulence of glee' (l. 490) of the drunkards as they stagger through the mountain passes. For a water-drinker, Wordsworth describes their hangovers with surprising accuracy:

And, after their high-minded riot,
Sickening into thoughtful quiet;
As if the morning's pleasant hour
Had for their joys a killing power.
They are drooping, weak, and dull. ...

(ll. 654–8)

While expressing sympathy for the causes of drunkenness, Wordsworth multiplies the damaging consequences. Instead of the horse merely losing his tail as in 'Tam O'Shanter', Benjamin loses his job, fired by a furious employer who sees through Benjamin's tardy efforts to appear sober, a reflection perhaps of the new working code of the industrial era, which demanded precision and alertness. Wordsworth laments the loss of Benjamin to the community, since, drunk or sober, he helped the homeless and desolate.

Wordsworth's understanding of the complex springs of drunkenness may arise from close readings of such philosophical and humane Burns poems as 'Address to the Unco Guid, or the Rigidly Righteous', or 'Epistle to a Young Friend', which urge tolerance for the incomprehensible resistances, weaknesses and excesses of human character. Wordsworth writes that Burns's 'Ode to Despondency I can never read without the deepest agitation.'[36]

Wordsworth's 1819 dedication of 'Benjamin the Waggoner' to Charles Lamb brings this sympathy into his circle of friends. Why should Wordsworth dedicate his only narrative about a drunkard to one of the notorious drunkards of the Romantic era? The reasons are complex. For one, Charles Lamb was an idolator of Burns, and both he and Wordsworth associated 'Benjamin the Waggoner' with 'Tam O'Shanter', and loved them both. When Wordsworth had just finished 'Benjamin the Waggoner' in 1812 he travelled to London and recited it on 22 May to Coleridge (whose impressions of the poem, heard soon after their estrangement, can only be imagined), the Morgans, Charles and Mary Lamb, and others; a week later Henry Crabb Robinson records that he talked 'very finely on poetry. He praised Burns for his introduction to Tam O'Shanter – By bringing together all the circumstances which can serve to render excuseable what is in itself disgusting – Thus interesting our feelings and making us tolerant of what would otherwise be not endurable' (Betz, p. 21). The connection between the two poems is clear to others as well: after hearing 'Benjamin the Waggoner' Crabb Robinson praises it: 'This is in the spirit of Kindness and indulgence Wordsworth praises in Burns Tam O'Shanter.' Only in 1819 did Wordsworth publish 'Benjamin the Waggoner', after much encouragement from Lamb, who liked it much better than 'Peter Bell' because of its 'spirit of beautiful tolerance' (cited Betz, p. 3). In thanking Wordsworth for the dedication to him – which Wordsworth said he delayed out of 'timid scruples' – , Lamb hints at his deeper reasons for liking the poem:

> Methinks there is a kind of shadowy affinity between the subject of the narrative and the subject of the dedication – but I will not enter into personal themes – else substituting ******* **** for Ben, and the Honble United Company of Merchts trading to the East Indies for the Master of the misused Team, it might seem by no far fetched analogy to point its dim warnings hitherward – but I reject the omen –. … (*LL*, 7 June 1819)

Seeing the intricate connections among the real drunkards – Burns and Lamb – and the real Water-Drinker Wordsworth, and the fictional drunkards Tam O'Shanter and Benjamin, Lamb seems to feel that Wordsworth knows and sympathizes with him. Despite Wordsworth's egotism and self-importance, Lamb senses in this poem a return to an earlier humbler self. With the asterisks disguising the letters of his own name, Lamb sees himself as Wordsworth sees him, or imagines he does so; he makes the connection between Benjamin's cruel boss and the merchants of the East India Company who control his own life; he sees the warning, but stoutly rejects the prediction of failure. In this poem Wordsworth has returned to the love of simple troubled humanity, and the waterdrinker who can depict the joys of the tavern is once again a friend.

As a water-drinker, Wordsworth struggles with Burns's career in relation to those of Lamb and Coleridge, who may also have sensed a shadowy affinity with Benjamin. This struggle to understand a dangerous way of living is one aspect of his own complicated feelings about pleasure and poetic inspiration. Wordsworth's brief experiment in submitting to Dionysian fervour in Milton's rooms re-emerged in 1816 when he rushed to defend Burns from the censures of ordinary people, Pharisees, who called the 'noble, free, and unexpected' (to use Werther's terms) Burns 'drunkard and fool'.

Wordsworth's 'Letter to a Friend of Burns' (1816), written a year after the final version of 'Benjamin the Waggoner' but published before it, suggests that Burns's person, his real and his invented selves, his drunkenness and his greatness are closely connected in Wordsworth's mind. The vituperation of this letter aroused public outcry, because Wordsworth insisted that Burns, like himself, was at the mercy of uncomprehending critics. His rage against these critics (Hazlitt describes him as a dog fixing his teeth in the *Edinburgh Review*, growling, shaking it, leaving it covered with 'the drivelling slaver of his impotent rage'[37]) and his allegiance to his fellow poet against them, transformed Wordsworth's ideal of the poet, for even a dissolute poet is better than a carping critic. Where the Preface of 1800 had called the poet 'a man speaking to men', here the 'privilege of poetic genius' is to 'catch ... a spirit of pleasure wherever it can be found.' The poet has the licence to cultivate excess in the search for Dionysian rapture:

> The poet, trusting to primary instincts, luxuriates among the felicities of love and wine, and is enraptured while he describes the fairer aspects of war: nor does he shrink from the company of the passion of love though immoderate – from convivial pleasure though intemperate – nor from the presence of war though savage. ... (*WProse*, 3, 124)

Once again it is 'Tam O'Shanter' that best represents Burns's vast experience of human nature. From reading it, Wordsworth recognizes 'that genius is not incompatible with vice and that vice leads to misery – the more acute from the sensibilities which are the elements of genius – .' Burns's power to write 'Tam O'Shanter' suggests the value of the genius's search for experience even if it involves savouring vice:

> Who, but some impenetrable dunce or narrow-minded puritan in works of art, ever read without delight the picture which he has drawn of the convivial exaltation of the rustic adventurer, Tam o'Shanter? The poet fears not to tell the reader in the outset that his hero was a desperate and sottish drunkard, whose excesses were frequent as his opportunities. This reprobate sits down to his cups, while the storm is roaring, and heaven and earth are in confusion; – the night is driven on by song and tumultuous noise – laughter and jest thicken as the beverage improves upon the palate ... – and, while these various elements of humanity are blended into one proud and happy composition of elated spirits, the anger of the tempest without doors only heightens and sets off the enjoyment within.

No narrow-minded puritan this water-drinking poet who takes such glee in the story of the 'desperate and sottish drunkard'! The straight road of virtue will not lead to inspired art; but where does this leave Wordsworth himself? Wordsworth turns his scorn on the sober puritan, whoever he may be:

> I pity him who cannot perceive that, in all this, though there was no moral purpose, there is a moral effect.
> > "Kings may be blest, but Tam was glorious,
> > "O'er a' the *ills* of life victorious."
> What a lesson do these words convey of charitable indulgence for the vicious habits of the principal actor in this scene, and of those who resemble him! – Men who to the rigidly virtuous are objects almost of loathing, and whom therefore they cannot serve!
>
> (*WProse*, 3, 124)

Defending Burns against the moralistic outcry brought on by Currie's revelations of drunkenness, Wordsworth heightens his early idea that poetry is 'the spontaneous overflow of powerful feelings' and omits its qualifying emphasis on long and deep thought.[38] Perhaps influenced by Coleridge's praise of Burns's genius in the 1812 *Friend*, where he cites the lines about snow on the water from 'Tam O'Shanter', lines that Byron also cites two years later,[39] Wordsworth has intensified his idea of genius. Now the poet's powerful feelings are no longer spontaneous, but are deliberately sought in the depths of life, in a Faustian risk. Wordsworth's Dionysian Burns plunges into extreme passions, for imagination and passion are bound to suffering:

> The poet, penetrating the unsightly and disgusting surfaces of things, has unveiled with exquisite skill the finer ties of imagination and feeling, that often bind these beings to practices productive of so much unhappiness to themselves, and to those whom it is their duty to cherish.

Daring to destroy himself for the sake of art, Burns is the 'authentic' poet whose words are testimony to his 'personal suffering' (*WProse*, 3, 126). This strangely twentieth-century praise of authenticity and personal revelation suggests Wordsworth's anticipation of confessional poetry by Robert Lowell, John Berryman, and other contemporary alcoholic poets.

As much as Wordsworth admires Burns, and transforms his theories of poetry in order to defend him, he nevertheless must acknowledge that Burns fails to be of the first rank. He falls short because of his uncontrolled 'propensities':

> It is probable that he would have proved a still greater poet if, by strength of reason, he could have controlled the propensities which his sensibility engendered; but he would have been a poet of a different class: and certain it is, had that desirable restraint been early established, many peculiar beauties which enrich his verses could never have existed, and many accessary influences, which contribute greatly to their effect, would have been wanting. (*WProse*, 3, 125)

When Wordsworth suggests that a sober Burns would have been 'a poet of a different class', he is speaking of levels of epic greatness that only he and Milton, both water-drinkers, could reach in a post-Shakespearean age. Long-range thinking about their careers kept them temperate, with their eyes on future glory. Burns, a poet of sensibility on a slightly lower level, speaks from his suffering self 'confessions' that take 'the shape of a prophecy!' (126). But in the long run, prudence may win the day; in some complex displacement, this conclusion is also a rebuke to the risky, wild and self-destroying Coleridge.

Wordsworth gauges his own performance in relation to Burns's ambiguity. Not the first or last to watch a fellow writer dissipate his talents, Wordsworth observes Burns as Samuel Johnson lamented Richard Savage, who enacted Johnson's suppressed desire to throw himself away but lacked Johnson's will to save himself by abstinence, or even to struggle with his drunkenness as Boswell, another shadow figure, did.[40] Like Savage and Burns (though Burns created a body of admired work, while Savage bitterly raged), Richard Brinsley Sheridan (as we will see in Chapter 7) also stood as a disputed warning figure of drunken creativity.

Assessing will-power and self-indulgence in persons and careers, Wordsworth sees his friends Montagu and Coleridge in relation to each other and as shadows of Burns. When he returned a self-disgusted wreck from Paris, Wordsworth had seen first hand 'the wild habits' and 'dissolute ways' of Basil Montagu,[41] the illegitimate son of the dissolute Earl of Sandwich and a singer named Martha Ray, who was murdered by a lover when Basil was nine.

Although Montagu's memoirs are suspiciously ripped at the confession of youthful drunkenness, his situation was so desperate that
he let the impoverished Wordsworth siblings raise his son and lend
him £900 of their legacy, not repaid until years after he achieved
his later respectability.[42] While the Wordsworths do not mention
any drunkenness, William calls him 'poor Montague' and Montagu
never ceased to believe that Wordsworth saved him. Montagu's
horror of drinking precipitated the quarrel between Coleridge
and Wordsworth in 1810;[43] it also caused his own quarrel with
Coleridge, who tried to serve wine to a guest in Montagu's dry
Bedford Square home.[44] His *Enquiries into the Effects of Fermented
Liquors, By a Water-Drinker* (1814), cited in Chapter 1, shows his
strong opinions. His zeal (including trying to reform such drunkards as Coleridge and Coleridge's son) struck some companions as
comical. Coleridge describes Montagu's new teetotalism in a letter
to Josiah Wedgwood:

> there is a zeal, an overacted fervor, a spirit of proselytism that
> distinguishes these men from the manners, & divides them from
> the sympathies, of the very persons, to whose party they have
> gone over. Smoking hot from the Oven of conversion they don't
> assort well with the old Loaves. So much of Montague; all that I
> know, & all, I suspect, that is to be known. (*CCL*, 1, 568)

Southey suspects a deep character flaw, calling Montagu 'a cracked
pitcher, spoiled in the making, and treacherous because of the
flaw'.[45] But Wordsworth remains more loyal to Montagu than to
any others, because of their early association when they were both
bereft, and because Montagu, unlike Coleridge, reformed. He
confides to him Coleridge's troubles, visits Bedford Square, and tol-
erates Montagu's wife, while closer friends drop away. Montagu is
prudent; Coleridge, 'a rotten drunkard'; and Burns a troubling
threat to his own values.

In the 'Letter to a Friend of Burns', the paragraph elevating prudence above wildness enrages William Hazlitt, whose own heavy
drinking after Napoleon's defeat had endangered his life and
whose moderate sobriety after 1818 bespoke a miracle of will.
Hazlitt ignores the transformation of Wordsworth's image of Burns
the rhapsode in the earlier pages of the essay, and focuses on
Wordsworth's own inability to let himself go, to live 'in a state
of intellectual intoxication', to experience pleasure or 'animal

I stacher'd whyles, but yet took tent ay
          To free the ditches;
An' hillocks, stanes, an' bushes, kenn'd ay
          Frae ghaists an' witches.

He sings the ballad of 'The Whistle', about Scottish 'Bacchanalians'
downing bumpers and bottles. He toasts his drinking companions;
he rollicks through choruses in the voices of imagined drunks:

We are na fou, we're na that fou,
   But just a drappie in our ee;
The cock may craw, the day may daw,
   And ay we'll taste the barley bree.

("Willie Brew'd a Peck o'Maut", *BP*, 1, 476–7)

He thinks back on his debauched life and laments in 'A Bard's
Epitaph' that 'thoughtless follies laid him low, / And stain'd his
name!' In letters as well as poems he acknowledges and laments
his hard drinking. His nightly seat at the Globe Inn in Dumfries has
been preserved as a shrine.[10] Given this prevalence, it is all the
more remarkable that generations of biographers after Currie have
sought to deny his drunkenness, as Pat Rogers perceives, 'because
of a reluctance to consider the ways in which Burns's creative self
depended on his immersion in the destructive elements of his own
personality.'

For a Romantic age characterized by its celebration of genius, the
very recent wildness of Burns significantly recalled ancient traditions of Dionysian poetic fervour and its destructive force. Just how
much wildness was necessary in the genius? What chance of greatness had the poet who did not risk his sanity? Burns's fame and
fate posed these questions sharply.

Burns's 'irregularities' (to use the euphemism of his defender,
Maria Riddell, and of Jane Austen mockingly in *Sanditon*[11]) had a
major influence on the poets of the next generation, the geniuses of
the age to come, an influence comparable to Young Werther's, who
also praised inebriation and passionate extremes. In England the
young poets Charles Lamb, Samuel Taylor Coleridge and William
Wordsworth, eager for innovative models, followed Burns's career
closely. Already in 1787 when he was 17 Wordsworth took his
sister's friend Jane Pollard's advice and read Burns, just as the first
editions came to press.[12] When Burns died, Lamb, then aged 21,
wrote Coleridge that Burns was 'the god of my idolatry'. Lamb's

existence', or to throw away his 'peculiar *sang froid*, circumspection, and sobriety.' Lecturing at the Surrey Institution in 1818, Hazlitt tears this paragraph of Wordsworth's essay to shreds, asserting that Wordsworth of all people should be sympathetic to the opposite calls of the Muses and the Excise, that 'from the Lyrical Ballads, it does not appear that men eat or drink, marry or are given in marriage', and that Wordsworth's cold and calculating nature is entirely opposed to Burns's vital gusto; where Charles Lamb would have understood Burns and written a far better defence of him, Wordsworth never could, for '[h]e is repelled and driven back into himself, not less by the worth than by the faults of others. His taste is as exclusive and repugnant as his genius. ... It is because so few things give him pleasure, that he gives pleasure to so few people.'[46] This is devastating criticism of a poet whose earliest experiments had aimed at giving and evoking pleasure.

Byron touches just this difference between Burns and Wordsworth in a March 1814 letter to another hard-drinking Scot, James Hogg, where, as Pat Rogers notes, 'he assaults the Lake Poets as tea-drinkers'. These two tea-drinking Lake Poets are presumably Wordsworth and Southey, since Coleridge lived in London at the time and Byron knew him to be 'drunken'.

> I doubt if either of them ever got drunk, and I am of the old creed of Homer the wine-bibber. Indeed I think you and Burns have derived a great advantage from this, that being poets, and drinkers of wine, you have had a new potation to rely upon. Your whisky has made you original.[47]

Like Hazlitt, Byron attacks Wordsworth for prudence and the repression of joyful spontaneity. For Coleridge, too, Wordsworth comes to embody prudence and self-protection, as he notices a film rise up to cover his moral eye.

Two years after Wordsworth's furious letter defending Burns, and bristling with rage at his own critics – all those sober puritans who do not understand the ecstasies of the poet – (a letter that would have surprised Byron, though there is no record that he read it and could therefore modify his contempt for 'Turdsworth'[48]), the young John Keats made his own pilgrimage to the grave of Burns (1818). He, too, pays homage to Burns in poems, 'On Visiting the Tomb of Burns', 'Ah! ken ye what I met the Day', 'This mortal body of a thousand days', and 'There is a joy in footing slow across a silent plain'.

Doubling back on our narrative, and showing the parallel careers of Wordsworth and Keats, these poems recreate roughly the pattern of Wordsworth's three poems at Burns's radiant, Dionysian grave: the horror at the early death of an unusually lively body; the consolation in art; the imitative homage to 'Tam O'Shanter'; and, in Keats's case, the recognition of his own similar fate.

For Keats, as for Wordsworth, the visit to Burns country is also a recognition of the centrality of drink to the Burns legend. Aileen Ward reports that in Ayr at Burns's birthplace Keats 'tasted his first whisky – "very smart stuff it is" – and learned how to make a toddy, "very pretty drink, & much praised by Burns."'[49] He refers to drink and drunkenness as part of his homage: In 'Ah! ken ye what I met the day' he imagines a visit by the drunken Tam:

> Young Tam came up an' eyed me quick
>   With reddened cheek –
> Braw Tam was daffed like a chick,
>   He could na speak.

(KCP, p. 271, ll. 33–6)

He describes his own drunkenness when visiting Burns's room, like Wordsworth's in his visit to Milton's room: 'My pulse is warm with thine old barley-bree'; his own 'Fancy is dead and drunken at its goal'; he can 'gulp a bumper to thy name' ('This mortal body of a thousand days,' ll. 5, 8, and 13). The commercialization of Burns's cottage, and again its association with drink, brought home to Keats the fragility of Burns and his vulnerability to exploiters in death as in life. In Ayr he and Brown 'lingered on the bridge which Tam O'Shanter crossed, then walked on to Burns's cottage in the nearby village of Alloway, which they found turned into a whisky shop. ... An old man who had known Burns was there ready to spin anecdotes and drink a glass with any visitor who happened by, and he filled Keats with unaccountable rage' (Ward, p. 199). Stuart Sperry has written movingly about Keats's struggle to assess the truth about a genius who is personally sordid, miserable and impoverished.[50]

But drink is only the prelude to death in Burns's case; the contemplation of Burns's early death and unfulfilled career catches the 22-year-old Keats in his own deepest fears. In the first sonnet, 'On Visiting the Tomb of Burns' the blank, pale landscape obliterates the human memorial. Burns as poet and as man has vanished in earth and sky, and is called back only as the poem closes:

Burns! with honour due
I have oft honoured thee. Great shadow, hide
Thy face – I sin against thy native skies.

(*KCP*, 266)

The second sonnet makes more precise the association of his own expectation of early death with Burns's early death. Specifically, he believes he will live only three years longer, so his mortal body is 'This mortal body of a thousand days' that now fills up a space in Burns's room where Burns himself no longer exists. The space he occupies will also soon be empty. Burns's body, that is now in the grave, had been full of dreams and ignorant of approaching death; but Keats's temporary body, though it can still stamp on Burns's floor and open window-sashes, making noise and changing the view and thus having more of an effect on the world than a shade has, foresees its own non-existence. Keats drinks to his fellow spirit among the shades, 'pledging a great soul', realizing that such a quickly consumed toast is all the fame that either young poet can hope for. Like Burns, he expects to die early, his work unfinished. Ward shows that this encounter with the shade of Burns is a moment of self-recognition: 'It struck Keats with a terrible irony that he should be sitting there in Burns's own house, drinking the whisky Burns loved, looking out on the hills of his beloved Ayrshire – that on this summer evening he should be alive and Burns dead. ... Keats found himself staring at the prospect of his own death, less than three years ahead' (Ward, p. 200). He tries to forget the weight of these dark thoughts by drinking 'toddy without any Care', as he writes to Reynolds. Struggling to be jaunty, he bids adieu: '"Tell my friends I do all I can for them, that is drink their healths in Toddy"' (cited Ward, pp. 200–1).

While Keats's own drinking and drinking-songs will be the subject of a later chapter, his participation in the Romantic fan-club of the dissipated genius Burns reveals a continuity in the movement centred in alcoholic inspiration and fatality. Burns was the model, the forerunner, dazzling Wordsworth, Coleridge, Lamb, Hazlitt, Keats and Byron with his greatness and self-destructive daring, but at the same time rousing their pity and terror at the dark side of drunkenness. He is a flesh and blood figure for the double power of Dionysus. Like the bibulous Homer, the vinous Propertius and Catullus, the tavern-seeking Ben Jonson and cronies, or the intoxicated poets of the late nineteenth century,

Burns generated a cult of wildness, risk and self-loss. Ignored were his fellow poets, Kit Smart and John Clare, who lived out their days in madhouses in part because of excessive drinking. Burns may have taught drunken bravado and drinking verse to his idolators, but he himself was influenced by the drinking patterns of the hard-drinking era from 1780 to 1830 when many poets and ordinary men and women felt themselves swept away in the newly self-conscious 'disease' of dissipation.

3

Fragmented Persons: Charles Lamb, *John Woodvil* and 'The Confessions of a Drunkard'

"The barometer of his emotional nature was set for a spell of riot."
– James Joyce, "Counterparts", *Dubliners*

Attitudes toward heavy drinking change at the end of the eighteenth century. We have seen that doctors and social observers noticed the heavy drinking of the poor because of their greater concentration in cities and around industries, and that doctors began to call this drinking a disease and to lament it not just for groups but also for individual cases. We have seen Dr Currie examine at length Burns's drunkenness where fifty years before it would scarcely deserve mention and two hundred years before would rouse laughter, as the transformation of the drunkard Christopher Sly in Shakespeare's *Taming of the Shrew* sets the tone of the actions to come. Dating the moment of change is difficult, but the contrast between Samuel Johnson (who willed himself to stop drinking) and James Boswell (who tried, but could not) points the way:[1] inward struggle, powerlessness and guilty awareness subtly deepen the problem of drunkenness.

The moment when heavy drinking begins to be perceived as a disease seems to coincide with an increased self-awareness and introspection, a shift that many readers associate with Romanticism.[2] A new kind of self-consciousness encourages a propensity to examine the uncertain discontinuities of body and mind, to see the inner being as a subject of inquiry, and to stress its susceptibility to outside forces. Such introspection in turn leads to a discourse of medicine and addiction, which participates in the cross-fertilization of vocabularies among philosophy, psychology and physiology.[3] To be sure, self-awareness did not begin abruptly, nor does its application to the specific inward struggles of heavy drinking begin all at once,[4] but a change is nevertheless discernible.

This self-awareness about drinking is part of a larger interest in fractures within the person in the philosophical and psychological writing of the eighteenth century. Eighteenth-century philosophers of consciousness such as Hume, Hartley and Kant probed the question of personal coherence and aggravated an already widespread uncertainty about the dissolving or dissipating self. Their uncomfortable discoveries, sometimes referring directly to the effects of alcohol on the transformed personality, add to the trembling sensitivities of the age, which register the barometer of the emotional state and are helpless against it. These discoveries can be seen in action in the writings of Charles Lamb, who saw all too painfully their application to himself.

For Charles Lamb's lifelong drunkenness was an often dangerous response to his own and his sister's insanity, to the sometimes unnerving presence of Coleridge, Hazlitt, and other heavy-drinking companions, and to an uncertainty about his own identity that was given a terminology by eighteenth-century sceptics. This drunkenness allowed him to feign other selves, to be a buffoon or a child when he needed to vent his rage. As an outlet for hidden selves it had a purpose for him similar to his writing: for in his essays and drama he could play with voices, vary his being, escape the tedium of his workaday duties. But where writing kept him sane or dispersed the insanity, drinking sometimes threatened to engulf his consciousness. Lamb's remarkable ability to watch, record, and even celebrate his own disarray is evident in essays and letters about his personal fragmentation and need for drink, and in the disjointed tragedy *John Woodvil*, the study of an alcoholic who destroys his father in the inadvertence of drunken oblivion.

I.   THE PHILOSOPHICAL CONTEXT FOR INTROSPECTION

Boswell's fellow Scot David Hume, convivial and sanguine on the surface, may have been the philosopher most responsible for encouraging and giving reasons for the sense of fragmentation and fragility of personal being at this time. Hume's 'bundle theory of personality' disturbed and engaged Joseph Butler, Thomas Reid, Immanuel Kant, Friedrich Schelling and Samuel Taylor Coleridge, and continues to rouse contemporary Anglo-American philosophers, some to a delight in porous personal boundaries, like Derek Parfit, others to anxiety.[5] Hume's position is precisely stated in *A Treatise of Human Nature*, I, 4, 6:

> But self or person is not any one impression, but that to which our several impressions and ideas are suppos'd to have a reference. If any impression gives rise to the idea of self, that impression must continue invariably the same, thro' the whole course of our lives; since self is suppos'd to exist after that manner. But there is no impression constant and invariable. ... [Because our impressions constantly change or suspend their operations,] I may venture to affirm of the rest of mankind, that they are nothing but a bundle or collection of different perceptions, which succeed each other with an inconceivable rapidity and are in a perpetual flux and movement.[6]

In a Heraclitean flux rivers, ships, vegetables, animals, selves, moods and opinions change moment by moment; any continuity is only (oh, great *only!*) the work of imagination.

But Hume's seemingly 'personal' response to his discovery is often overlooked, though it follows in the next chapter. This response is hardly as jovial and amused as one would expect from one of Hume's self-assured and easy nature; indeed, it is an expression of 'existential shipwreck':[7]

> Methinks I am like a man, who having struck on many shoals, and having narrowly escap'd shipwreck in passing a small frith, has yet the temerity to put out to sea in the same leaky weather-beaten vessel, and even carries his ambition so far as to think of compassing the globe under these disadvantageous circumstances. ... [The thought of my errors and perplexities] makes me resolve to perish on the barren rock, on which I am at present, rather than venture myself upon that boundless ocean, which runs out into immensity. ... I am first affrighted and confounded with that forelorn solitude, in which I am plac'd in my philosophy, and fancy myself some strange uncouth monster, who not being able to mingle and unite in society, has been expell'd all human commerce, and left utterly abandon'd and disconsolate.[8]

Alone on a tossing ocean of impressions 'ever-varying', Hume believes that we make ourselves up: any connections we find come
from our own imaginations, and are then subverted by it. This precarious self-invention provokes anxiety and even paralysis: 'Where
am I, or what?. ... I am confounded with all these questions, and
begin to fancy myself in the most deplorable condition imaginable,
inviron'd with the deepest darkness, and utterly depriv'd of the use
of every member and faculty.'[9]

This fragility of being, which Hume may just be imagining
or feigning for the moment, before his mood shifts and he dines
and is 'merry with friends', is one of Hume's many legacies to
Romanticism: he invents the anxious philosopher clinging to his
rock, gazing at the obtuse people who go on as if they have continuous identities to live in.

David Hartley intensifies Hume's theme of ever-varying flux by
giving it a physical dimension. The shifting impressions become
bodily vibrations, or what he calls vibratiuncles, coursing and
pulsing in the brain. More specifically, he asks how chemical substances like opiates or wine alter the already altering consciousness,
or suspend it altogether. Hartley's self-consciousness is 'felt along
the blood'. By adding alcohol and opium to Hume's 'bundle
theory', he increases its volatility and uneasiness, and incidentally
may entice young enthusiasts to experiment with his science of
mind, as Coleridge, Sir Humphry Davy, and Tom and Josiah
Wedgwood eagerly did. He describes the vibrations and associations of consciousness as heightened by wines; 'the vivid Vibrations
excited by the Wine, or Aliment, will illuminate all the Impressions,
and add Strength to all the Motions. The same thing is observed of
Opiates, in those who take them frequently.' While this temporary
state suspends almost pleasantly the continuity of being, more permanent 'alienations of mind' disrupt 'in great measure, that
Consciousness which accompanies our Thoughts and Actions, and
by which we connect ourselves with ourselves from time to time'.
Hartley examines the continuum between the pleasantly vivid
sense of a continuous self sustained by wine or opium and the
gradual movement into madness that breaks the connection with
past selves.

Acknowledging that 'it is impossible to fix precise Limits, and to
determine where Soundness of Mind ends, and Madness begins',
Hartley examines the erroneous judgements of children, idiots, and
people suffering from dotage, drunkenness, deliriums, fixed ideas,

violent passions, melancholy and madness. In his section 'Of Drunkenness', his vibrations in the blood contribute to an understanding of the transforming powers of wine. He begins by recognizing the original impetus of pleasure, and then turns to watch the wine reaching the stomach, surging through the brain, and thence descending through the blood to the staggering limbs:

> The common and immediate Effect of Wine is to dispose to Joy, i.e. to introduce such Kinds and Degrees of Vibrations into the whole nervous System, or into the separate Parts thereof, as are attended with a moderate continued Pleasure. This it seems to do chiefly by impressing agreeable Sensations upon the Stomach and Bowels, which are thence propagated into the Brain, continue there, and also call up the several associated Pleasures that have been formed from pleasant Impressions made upon the alimentary Duct, or even upon any of the external Senses.

He imagines how wine rarefies the blood, distends the veins and sinuses, compresses the medullary substance, and eventually brings on palsy. 'The pleasant vibrations producing this Gaiety, by rising higher and higher perpetually, as more Wine is taken into the Stomach and Blood-vessels, come at last to border upon, and even to pass into, the disagreeable Vibrations belonging to the Passions of Anger, Jealousy, Envy, &c. more especially if any of the mental Causes of these be presented at the same time.' Drunkenness often causes the other alienations of mind, deliriums, fixed passions and madness.[10]

Hartley's introduction of the body's action into the transformation of personal identity seems to increase the sense of alienation of the person from his parts. The body goes on with its rising and falling vibrations while the consciousness observes it or intermittently observes nothing. Changes occur, associations make their connections, passions rise, paralysis sets in, and the self knows little of what is happening to it. Who is responsible for this coursing blood and its strange transformations? By focusing on drunkenness as one of the main kinds of alienation of mind, and the cause of several others, Hartley not only entices his readers to see for themselves, but also expresses one aspect of the spirit of the age, the concern with intoxication, personal dislocation and oblivion.

The very word 'dissipation' gains its present meaning only in the mid-eighteenth century. The earlier meanings of 'to dissipate' had been neutral and scientific, as 'to scatter, disperse, disappear, dispel, reduce to atoms, or dissolve'. *The Oxford English Dictionary* traces the gradual change to mean 'distraction of the mental faculties or energies from concentration on serious subjects: at first often with colourless sense ... but later implying the frittering away of energies ... and thus gradually passing into sense 6', which is, 'the waste of the moral and physical powers by undue or vicious indulgence in pleasure; intemperate, dissolute, or vicious mode of living. ...' In a 1788 sermon on 'Dissipation', John Wesley observes the new meaning of the word: 'We hear of the still increasing dissipation ... [T]he word ... was hardly heard of fifty years ago ... And yet it is so in every one's mouth that it is already worn thread bare, being one of the cant words of the day.'[11] This narrowing of the word to the specific meaning of drunkenness has an end point where the history of the word's meaning suddenly reverses itself. In F. Scott Fitzgerald's 1931 story 'Babylon Revisited' the hero Charlie Wales 'suddenly realized the meaning of the word "dissipate" – to dissipate into thin air; to make nothing out of something.' The narrow meaning widens back out again to embrace evaporations physical, moral and spiritual.

The 'dissipating' person became a frightening notion during this period. It made the person the object of scientific scrutiny like atoms or oxygen or other physical substances that dissolved and left only atmospheric traces of themselves. As the word 'dissipation' could be applied to dispersing elements and also to personal disintegration due to alcohol, so, too, the word 'dissolute' came in this period to mean both dissolving particles and dissolving psychological centres, also due to alcohol. Empirical science took as its subject not only objects but also subjects, examining them both with a microscopic scrutiny.

So much is *dissipation* 'in every one's mouth', as Wesley puns, that even the sober Kant addresses the joy and pain of drunkenness when he returns at the end of his life to his final effort to refute Hume's 'bundle theory' of the person. In *Anthropology from a Pragmatic Point of View* (1797), he studies 'what man as a free agent makes, or can and should make, of himself.' In the first paragraph he states decisively that the human being is a person and not a thing, and he seems to assume the efficacy of his earlier arguments in *Critique of Pure Reason* (1781) and in *Fundamental Principles of the Metaphysic of Morals* (1785). Beginning 'On Self-Consciousness' he writes:

> The fact that man can have the idea 'I' raises him infinitely above all the other beings living on earth. By this he is a *person*; and by

virtue of his unity of consciousness through all the changes he may undergo, he is one and the same person – that is, a being altogether different in rank and dignity from *things*, such as irrational animals, which we can dispose of as we please.[12]

But this personal agent can also choose to inhibit or weaken his senses and transform his own behaviour. He can arouse his imagination and enter ecstatic states by using intoxicants. Drunkenness, Kant writes, 'is an unnatural condition in which we cannot order our sense representations by laws of experience, insofar as this is caused by drinking to excess.' Drinking excessively may also lead to being 'beside oneself', to being 'gay, noisy, talkative, and witty', to being candid and forthright. But, in either the negative or the positive case, the drinking person is not the same person as the original person who says 'I'. 'While he is drinking, can we really explore the temperament of a man who is getting drunk, or his character? I think not. Alcohol is a new fluid mixed with those flowing in his veins and a new neural stimulus, which does not reveal his natural [temperament] more clearly but introduces another one.' This self-transformation is akin to poetic furor and *raptus*.[13] Indeed, the person may say 'I' and thus be a person, but at another moment he may imagine he is a different 'I' and be that person, often because of a new liquid that is flowing in his old veins. Kant destabilizes his argument for the integrity of the person here by mentioning drunkenness, as he does also in the *Metaphysic of Morals* by mentioning dependencies (as of wives on husbands, debtors on creditors). Even Kant is powerless against the notion that none of us is the same from one moment to the next: moment by moment we dissipate in time and space; we dissolve in a swirl of physical and temporal particles.

II.   LAMB'S FRACTURED IDENTITIES IN ESSAYS AND POEMS

The disturbing power of these queries into the instabilities of personal identity can be seen infiltrating many Romantic speculations. Charles Lamb was not immune to their unsettling reminders. Although he was not as theoretically metaphysical as his boyhood friend Coleridge, whom he described in the courtyard of Christ's Hospital School discoursing on philosophy like the 'young Mirandula', Lamb's essays give hints that, either on his own or through long conversation with Coleridge ('you taught me some smattering of [metaphysic]')[14] he had struggled with the general outlines of Hume's bundle theory, Hartley's sense of the fluid self moving in and out of forms and transformed by alcohol, and Kant's troubling efforts to affirm free agency.

Lamb had personal reasons for knowing the truth of Hume's observer on the desolate rock: his sister Mary's recurrent episodes of madness; the 'day of horrors', 22 September 1796, when she murdered their mother and wounded their father with a carving knife; his long life of repressing his own desires and ambitions in order to care for his sister and senile father, supporting them with hard work on the British East India Company ledgers. In addition, and surely in part because of these life circumstances, Lamb was one of the notorious drunkards of the London scene during the Romantic era, a distinction he shared with Richard Brinsley Sheridan, Richard Porson, Charles James Fox, William Pitt and the Prince Regent, among many others.

Lamb's anxious fragility and his severe alcoholism required a series of constructed behaviours and voices to present to the outside world in place of the well-known scandal of the family legend and his own image, dark, timid, stuttering and staggering. His invented selves are creative adjustments to sorrow; they might be called lies or denials but they are also ways of surviving. Very rarely the bare face of pain is revealed, as in 'The Confessions of a Drunkard', but then the mask of mockery is quickly raised to deny what has been glimpsed. Lamb's one 'tragedy', *John Woodvil*, his essay 'The Confessions of a Drunkard', and related essays, letters and poems provide a glimpse into the crumbling chasm of Romantic personal identity, deepened by intoxication.

Only recently has the underlying sorrow and panic of Lamb's life been acknowledged. Gerald Monsman has shown that beneath the antic disposition of the invented voice of 'Elia' lies a single fact, the murder that is never mentioned: 'The essence of Lamb's persona is the absence of any explicit narrative of that pivotal "day of horrors" which nevertheless everywhere informs the contours of Elia's essays. Elia is the result of Lamb's having confronted an emotional catastrophe and turned that primal horror back upon a host of other moments and memories forged by loss, each enriched and deepened emotionally by the others.'[15] Monsman sees the murder as a chasm beneath errant behaviour, a chasm that gives the many voices of Elia and Lamb a desperate and hollow ring. In an extended metaphor from the Egyptological studies developing in this period as a result of Napoleon's conquest and Nelson's reconquest of the Nile, Thomas McFarland describes this hidden truth beneath layers of Lamb's fictions: the essays themselves 'are the chambers of an Egyptian pyramid designed to delude the curious into thinking the tomb is empty; and the false guide, Elia, continually assures us, whimsically, that there are no bodies here. Nevertheless, many of the rooms do contain bodies, not publicly exhibited in stately crypts, but concealed under the floor. ... Each essay has a subtext of desperation.'[16]

Although Monsman and McFarland are certainly correct in pointing to the murder as the major absence in the writing, the gap that destabilizes the person shaping his defences above it, it should not be forgotten that less than two years before Mary's outbreak of rage at her invalid mother who 'met her caresses ... with coldness and *repulse*' and preferred her neglectful older son (*LL*, I, 52), Charles himself had spent six weeks in the Hoxton Madhouse, as he writes Coleridge on 27 May 1796:

> Coleridge, I know not what suffering scenes you have gone through at Bristol, – my life has been somewhat diversified of late. The 6 weeks that finished last year & began this your very humble servant spent very agreeably in a *mad house at Hoxton* – . I am got somewhat rational now, & *dont bite any one*. But *mad* I was – & many a vagary my imagination played with *me*, enough to make a *volume* if all *told* – (*LL*, I, 3–4)

This rarely recognized episode of incarceration preceded his sister's violence, and suggests that his madness began at a much younger age than did hers. But already in this letter written three months after the event, Lamb covers the episode in a cheerful voice to amuse his friend, keeping up his humour about not biting anyone, while suggesting that the brief reference has a *volume* behind it, a book of causes, a heft of trouble. Referring often in letters to the insanity of others such as Charles Lloyd and William Cowper, and praying often to be preserved from insanity, Lamb somehow, in an amazing tribute to his will, controlled his madness so that he could bear his responsibilities at work and continue to protect his older sister from the law and a permanent incarceration in a public madhouse.[17]

Charles Lamb's own madness has been overshadowed by his sister's periodic frenzies, which he learned to see coming when she was overstimulated, as by the visits of the intense and manic

Coleridge, who 'would almost make her dance within an inch of the precipice' and was sometimes begged to leave. As she teetered 'on the brink of madness', her brother, too, felt vulnerable: 'a careless and a dissolute spirit had advanced upon *me* with large strides' (*LL*, I, 127). But Lamb's own madness could not have been banished permanently by any act of will. It emerged and was released through his frequent drunkenness, a drunkenness that allowed him to speak free of his stuttering, a speech defect that Winifred Courtney has shown to be rooted in very early neurosis and resultant hostility.[18] Drunkenness gives him freedom; ventriloquizing gives him a different person's voice. Though alcohol usually exacerbates psychosis, in Charles Lamb's case it seems to have vented it, and allowed him, as Samuel Johnson said wisely, 'to lose [him]self, to throw [him]self away', and, with the old self discarded, to imagine new selves.

Thus, the bodies of parents are not the only ones under the floor. Lamb's own madness and his alcoholism are hidden beneath the surface also.

Lamb responds to the fragmentation of personality suggested by Hume, Hartley and other associationists in an intensely personal rather than theoretical way. Hume's ever-varying being, uncertainty and fragility is a lived reality for Lamb; he feels the buffeted solitude of Hume's 'uncouth monster', the fragility of the leaky vessel in the tossing ocean. 'I am completely shipwreck'd. – My head is quite bad. ... I almost wish that Mary were dead', he writes to Coleridge on 12 May, 1800 (*LL*, 1, 67, 203), revealing his frustration with his obligations, so persistent and unending, his hostility and his hangover. A number of essays and letters describe inner divisions that cause anxiety and panic and subtly connect these underlying uncertainties with Hume's 'bundle theory of personality'. In 'Imperfect Sympathies' he alludes to the theory by admitting, 'I am a bundle of prejudices... the veriest thrall to sympathies, apathies, antipathies.'[19] In 'New Year's Eve' he regrets the loss of his past self. He may love his early self, the self he was as a child, but believes that 'no one whose mind is introspective – and mine is painfully so – can have a less respect for his present identity than I have for the man Elia. I know him to be light, and vain, and humoursome; a notorious * * *; addicted to * * * *; ... a stammering buffoon.' (The asterisks veil the words 'sot' and 'wine', as in Chapter 2 they veil his identification with the drunkard Benjamin the Waggoner in his acceptance of Wordsworth's dedication of the poem.) This new self is a 'stupid changeling of five-and-forty', far from the heroic boy he was, or believes himself to have been: 'From what have I not fallen, if the child I remember was indeed myself, – and not some dissembling guardian, presenting a false identity' (*LCW*, 27). Beneath these anxieties of the changing self is the greatest change, death, that 'alteration', that 'new state of being' that 'staggers me'. New Year's Eve prompts him to rebuke that master terror, allied to 'cold, numbness, dreams, perplexity', and to cry, 'out upon thee, I say, thou foul, ugly phanthom!. ... thou thin, melancholy *Privation*, or more frightful and confounding *Positive!*' (*LCW*, 28).

A persistent undertow of uncertain personal identity rumbles through assorted essays. In 'The Old and New School Master' Lamb examines professorial role-playing, and the many ways that teachers must by virtue of their positions submerge their identities. One person's power can also absorb another's. Alluding perhaps to the power of his dear friend Coleridge over both his sister and himself, he remarks, 'Too frequent doses of original thinking from others, restrain what lesser portion of that faculty you may possess of your own. You get entangled in another man's mind, even as you lose yourself in another man's grounds' (*LCW*, 49). While this self-loss is often destructive, Lamb feels himself spreading in and out of other selves. Pretending to be a friend of the 'late Elia', he plays with 'natural' selves and 'affected naturalness' and praises Elia's novelistic ability to 'imply and twine with his own identity the griefs and affections of another – making himself many, or reducing many unto himself' (*LCW*, 135). In 'The Convalescent', he describes the multiple selves of the self-pitying invalid: 'He makes the most of himself; dividing himself, by an allowable fiction, into as many distinct individuals, as he hath sore and sorrowing members' (*LCW*, 165). Lamb's concern with changing and feigned identities makes him sympathize with temporarily invented selves, a sympathetic openness that has been called 'feminine'.[20] Of a beggar who pretends to have a family he entreats,

"It is good to believe him. If he be not all that he pretendeth, *give*, and under a personate father of a family, think (if thou pleasest) that thou hast relieved an indigent bachelor. ... You pay your money to see a comedian feign these things, which, concerning these poor people, thou canst not certainly tell whether they are feigned or not" (*LCW*, 107).

Honour the lie, he counsels, as an imaginative performance.

But if feigned selves perform on the stage, on the street, and in drawing-rooms, empty selves may lurk inside, selves battered by impressions, made frantic. In addition to nervousness about fluid identities, an underlying panic resounds in the strange 'Chapter on Ears', where the narrator is frenzied by a cacophony of musical harmonies that he cannot follow: 'I have sat through an Italian Opera, till, for sheer pain, and inexplicable anguish, I have rushed out into the noisiest places of the crowded streets, to solace myself with sounds, which I was not obliged to follow, and get rid of the distracting torment of endless, fruitless, barren attention!' He is oppressed by 'empty instrumental music', terrified by the obligation to fill up the sounds; he cites Robert Burton on 'the infernal plague of melancholy' that seizes him and terrifies his soul. 'I stagger under the weight of harmony, reeling to and fro at my wit's end' (*LCW*, 37–8).

This panic of incomprehensible sound may be related to the 'Witches and Other Night Fears' that terrorized his childhood, and seem still to haunt him. Lamb discerns a kind of personal continuity in his own past patterns of anxiety. 'The night-time, solitude, and the dark were my hell' (*LCW*, 59). Long before the terrible crisis that split his life in half, the young Charles Lamb suffered from 'nervous terrors':

> Parents do not know what they do when they leave tender babes alone to go to sleep in the dark. The feeling about for a friendly arm – the hoping for a familiar voice – when they wake screaming – and find none to soothe them – what a terrible shaking it is to their poor nerves! (*LCW*, 59)

He speaks of the 'sweats for which the reveries of the cell-damned murderer are tranquillity'. And where do these horrors come from in the nightmares of children who have not yet lived to see real terrors – 'that strange thing, an infant's dream,' as Coleridge called it in 'Frost at Midnight'? Lamb forecasts Carl Jung in pronouncing that these 'Gorgons, and Hydras, and Chimaeras dire' do not come '*ab extra*', 'but they were there before. They are transcripts, types – the archetypes are in us, and eternal.' Not only does he anticipate the Jungian 'archetype' but also the Freudian 'anxiety': for he perceives that 'These terrors are of older standing. They date beyond body... .' This kind of fear 'is strong in proportion as it is objectless upon earth.' Is this a core of his own fearful person, or a general human response persisting in a *spiritus mundi*?

Lamb and Coleridge have surely felt similar free-floating anxieties, for he quotes from Coleridge's 'Rime of the Ancient Mariner' to catch this objectless dread that rises from within:

> Like one that on a lonesome road
> Doth walk in fear and dread,
> And having once turn'd round, walks on
> And turns no more his head;
> Because he knows a frightful fiend
> Doth close behind him tread.

He defends this poem against Wordsworth's criticisms precisely because the mariner 'undergoes such *Trials*, as overwhelm and bury all individuality or memory of what he was. – Like the state of a man in a *Bad dream*, one terrible peculiarity of which is, that all consciousness of personality is *gone*' (*LL*, I, 266; 30 Jan. 1801); he is 'hurt and vexed' that Wordsworth cannot see a psychological truth so essential and profound. In the poem 'Hypochondriacus' he recounts the experience of being haunted in dreams by spectres:

> By myself walking,
> To myself talking,
> When as I ruminate
> On my untoward fate,
> Scarcely seem I
> Alone sufficiently,
> Black thoughts continually
> Crowding my privacy;
> They come unbidden,
> Like foes at a wedding,
> Thrusting their faces
> In better guests' places,
> Peevish and malcontent,
> Clownish, impertinent,
> Dashing the merriment ...

(*LCW*, 524–5)

These irresistible black thoughts are Diaboli, Hobgoblins, Lemures, Night-riding Incubi, and a series of mythic figures that originated in a mind teetering on paranoia and projecting its fears in myths.

They assault him like the foul fiends do 'Poor Tom a Bedlam', whose madness is only feigned.[21]

The *Essays*, in ventriloquizing voices often called playful, bitter-sweet, maudlin or nostalgic, glimpse a persistently troubled being taking multiple forms as a terrified child, an adult bristling with resentment and hostility, a boy-man who fears the *'toga virilis'* (*LCW*, 137), even as he bears more responsibilities than most men, certainly than his elusive brother John, who rarely visited and never sent money to help in the care of his father, aunt and sister, and who was one of the most fervent advocates of sending Mary to a permanent public madhouse, while he fastidiously built up his private collection of paintings. Masking rage, Lamb keeps in his memory the many stages of past selves that form an elusive core of his person.

Evasions and ventriloquisms are methods by which Lamb covers his sufferings and his desires. When he praises Hogarth, for instance, he is using him as a screen for defending his own disjunction of surface and depth. Vicarious and intensely personal is Lamb's attention to Hogarth's *Gin Lane* and *Rake's Progress*, which depict alcohol abuse and madness. Lamb identifies with Hogarth, for he, like Lamb himself, may 'appeal chiefly to the risible faculty', but beneath the surface reaches to 'the very heart of man, its best and most serious feelings' (*LCW*, 309). Praising the *Rake's Progress*, Lamb reveals his intimacy with the madhouse in his own and his sister's experience. He notes that Hogarth does not cheapen the Rake's final madness with 'face-making', but shows 'grief kept to a man's self, a face retiring from notice with the shame which great anguish sometimes brings with it, a final leave taken of hope, the coming on of vacancy and stupefaction, a beginning alienation of mind looking like tranquillity' (*LCW*, 313). His Rake is grand like King Lear, not histrionic like Timon of Athens. Lamb sympathizes not only with the sorrow of becoming mad but also with a tragic artist who is called 'inferior and vulgar' because of his laughing surface. Against contemporaries who relegate Hogarth to a rank lower than Sir Joshua Reynolds, Lamb angrily defends Hogarth, who like Shakespeare can mix 'merriment and infelicity, ponderous crime and feather-light vanity' (*LCW*, 315). He insists that Hogarth, when he depicts the contemporary horrors of Gin Lane with its 'diabolical spirit of frenzy', its buildings reeling as if drunk (quoting his friend Coleridge standing by his side at the exhibition [*LCW*, 312]), is 'not a mere buffoon' (*LCW*, 315). Himself a great giggler and mocker, he loves artists who can create and understand fools, who hide pain under a mask.

Ventriloquizing again, and combining his frolicsome voice with his friend Jem White's in a joint production dear to his heart, *The Original Letters, Etc., of Sir John Falstaff and his Friends* (1796), Lamb and White don ribald drunken masks. Writing together in high spirits Lamb and White (the heroic Jem White who annually feasted chimney-sweeps during St Bartholomew's fair) imagine the cravings for more and more drink of the fat knight; here they can confess their own love of drink while speaking in the giddy, rather archly archaic voice of this well-known sack-drinker; under cover of his prodigious capacity they can also participate in such consumption. They imagine the knight's voice:

> "Yes, I have had the Spinster's ring – I was sous'd into the Thames, and wrung by mine host's scullions; cramp'd twixt hand and hand like a rinc'd doublet. – I had thought my swoln belly were but a mass of congealed sack, beverag'd, indeed, with a slight smack of distillation from the poppies of the drowsy God; but I was out, villainously mistaken – I had more bucket-water than sack: and for distillation, I'm a knave an there hath been a scruple of it in my whole system for a matter of eight and forty hours."[22]

The voice allows White and Lamb to play the gross drunkard from a free-wheeling Renaissance; they seem to be giggling as they write. In the varied voices of these essays, then, we hear the terror of personal instability and the desperate laughter that derides it.

III.   ALCOHOL, MASKS AND ERRANT BEHAVIOUR

If we add to Lamb's terrors and inner divisions his excessive 'partiality for the production of the juniper-berry',[23] we are faced with a miraculous balancing act. For on the upswing gin releases Lamb's manic, raucous, sometimes silly and childlike aspects, and on the downswing it leaves him sick and maudlin, thus adding two more unsettled persons to accommodate inside his being. When he is carousing in a jolly frame of mind, he raises his glass in frequent healths. So, in the essays an occasional *topos* is the valedictory toast. At the end of 'New Year's Eve', for instance, appropriately, he dismisses the sanctimonious speakers on tombstones and calls for

'Another cup of wine'. After reciting Cotton's poem 'The New Year', he asks his reader, 'do not these verses ... fortify like a cordial, enlarging the heart, and productive of sweet blood, and generous spirits, in the concoction?' Reading poems and drinking wine are both forms of imbibing that warm his heart. Book and bottle, metonymies for different kinds of absorption that serve a similar purpose in Shakespeare's *The Tempest*,[24] solace Lamb from his fear of death. He shouts again, 'And now another cup of the generous!' (*LCW*, 30). Like Robert Herrick (whose 'Farewell to Sack' he imitated in 'A Farewell to Tobacco') he toasts the dead. Where Herrick in 'Trust to Good Verses' raises larger and larger vessels to his poetic predecessors (Homer, Horace, Catullus, Propertius, etc.) and by downing them feels himself flushed and giddy,[25] so Lamb bids farewell to the subjects of some of his essays, eager to reward himself with celebratory draughts. His terror of music is soothed by 'a draught of true Lutheran beer' (*LCW*, 38); in 'All Fool's Day', donning his motley, he summons, 'Fill us a cup of that sparkling gooseberry – we will drink no wise, melancholy, politic port on this day' (*LCW*, 39); he promises 'bumpers' to many known fools. Celebrating Isola's twenty-first birthday he begins, 'Crown me a cheerful goblet' (*LCW*, 537).

This sportive drinking is one joy in his celibate life, part of what Fred V. Randel calls his 'extraordinary verbal preoccupation with food and drink'.[26] Promising the kind of bibulous pleasure depicted in Plate 4, he invites Thomas Manning to London: 'you shall drink Rum, Brandy, Gin, Aquavitae, Usquebagh, or Whiskey a nights – & for the after-dinner-Trick I have 8 Bottles of genuine Port which mathematically divided gives 1 1/7 for every day you stay, provided you stay a *week*' (11 Aug. 1800; *LL*, 1, 223). Manning's invitation to him offers corresponding temptations: 'The very thoughts of your coming makes my keg of Rum *wobble* about like a porpoise & the liquor (how fine it smells!) goes *Gultch squlluck* against the sides for joy.'[27] Lamb seems to cherish his image of a drunk, rebuking Coleridge for calling him 'gentle hearted Charles' and recommending, instead, more truthful adjectives – 'drunken dog, ragged-head, seld-shaven, odd-ey'd, stuttering, or any other epithet which truly and properly belongs to the Gentleman in question – ,' especially since he has 'been getting drunk two days running' (14 Aug. 1800; *LL*, 1, 224). He loves the 'cheerful glass' and even the imagining of it. One of his most elaborate fancies, in imitation of his subject, is the feigning of drunkenness at the poor table of Captain Jackson, a genius of life, who, 'steeped in poverty up to the lips, [can] fancy himself all the while chin-deep in riches.'

> Wine we had none; nor, except on very rare occasions, spirits; but the sensation of wine was there. Some thin kind of ale I remember – "British beverage," he would say! "Push about, my boys"; "Drink to your sweet-hearts, girls." At every meagre draught a toast must ensue, or a song. All the forms of good liquor were there, with none of the effects wanting. Shut your eyes, and you would swear a capacious bowl of punch was foaming in the centre, with beams of generous Port or Madeira radiating to it from each of the table corners. You got flustered, without knowing when; tipsy upon words; and reeled under the potency of his unperforming Bacchanalian encouragements. (*LCW*, 170)

The contagious imagination of Captain Jackson fills the stomachs and intoxicates the hearts of his guests; 'tipsy upon words', Captain Jackson teaches Lamb how to invent the rapture of life if he have it not.

In composing this very paragraph, rich in the glow of festivity, Lamb shows that he learned Captain Jackson's lesson, in writing as also perhaps in squeezing out daily pleasures from the stone soup of his life. He imbibes, he toasts, he celebrates, he joins his companions in The Salutation and Cat or in Feathers, he cheers up when he reads of Falstaff and Benjamin the Waggoner, his doubles, or sees Hogarth's Gin Lane and Beer Street. He sings childish songs and cannot contain his merriment: 'Bacchus we know, and we allow / His tipsy rites.'[28] In this phase he forgets the absence of love and the weight of duties.

This joyful side of Lamb's alcoholism is noticeable in Benjamin Haydon's narration of the immortal dinner party of 28 December 1817. The party began with Wordsworth, Keats, Lamb and Thomas Monkhouse, 'a merchant of Budge Row', and later added Joseph Ritchie, an explorer soon to die in Libya, and John Kingston, a deputy comptroller of the Stamp Office.[29] Haydon focuses on Lamb's behaviour: 'Lamb got excessively merry and witty, and his fun in the intervals of Wordsworth's deep & solemn intonations of oratory was the fun & wit of the fool in the intervals of Lear's passion. Lamb soon gets tipsey, and tipsey he got very shortly, to our infinite amusement', getting more tipsey by the moment as he proposes 'healths' to Voltaire and Newton. Between dozes, Lamb

wakes up to insult the comptroller, a pompous head of the stamp
department lording it over Wordsworth because of his stamp
department connection. Haydon recalls:

> The Comptroller went on making his profound remarks, and
> when any thing very *deep* came forth, Lamb roared out,
>> Diddle iddle don
>> My son John
> Went to bed with his breeches on
> One stocking off & one stocking on,
>> My son John.
> The Comptroller laughed as if he marked it, & went on; every
> remark Lamb chorused with
> Went to bed with his breeches on
>> Diddle iddle on.
> There is no describing the scene adequately.

Lamb had to be dragged into an adjoining paint room to quiet him,
though he continued to insult the Comptroller: 'Who is that fellow?
Let me go & hold the candle once more to his face –

> My son John
> Went to bed with his breeches on –

& these were the last words of C. Lamb. The door was closed upon
him.' Jollity and hostility are intertwined: the childishly assaultive
hostility defends Wordsworth against an administrative boor ignorant of poetry but smugly glib about it, a type hateful in both their
jobs; elsewhere the hostility is less loyal. 'Diddle diddle dumpling'
is also his drunken refrain at a party at Mrs Proctor's, where he had
to be carried around.[30] His regression to nursery rhymes may allow
his fury an acceptable, boyish outlet.

The love of drink, which drew Lamb to appreciate Wordsworth's
'Benjamin the Waggoner', as we saw, and elicited Wordsworth's
dedication of that poem to him because of his 'affinities' with
Benjamin, was not always joyful. The other side of gin-drinking
creeps up on him, first in incompetence, then in unseemly wildness,
and finally in fury and barely controlled violence.[31] Many letters
record drunken episodes and apologize for outrageous behaviour.
To Thomas Manning (Feb. or March 1801) he writes, 'Last Sunday
... as I was coming to town from the Professor's inspired with new
rum, I tumbled down and broke my nose. I drink nothing stronger

than malt liquors' (*LL*, 1, 276–7). A month later he writes Manning, 'I am afraid I must leave off drinking' (*LL*, 2, 3). In mid-August, he apologizes for irreverence and folly at Walter Wilson's party, reminding him (perhaps by way of sharing the blame) that 'you knew me well enough before, that a very little liquor will cause a considerable alteration in me' (*LL*, 2, 11). A letter of 14 June 1805 to Dorothy Wordsworth reveals the tension building between himself and Mary when her madness approaches: 'irritable and wretched with fear ... I constantly hasten the disorder ... She lives but for me; and I know I have been wasting and teasing her life for five years past incessantly with my cursed drinking and ways of going on' (*LL*, 2, 169). Mary, who herself liked brandy and water with Sarah Stoddart, urges Charles to drink water with her; he expresses his reluctance in a letter to Dorothy Wordsworth in Autumn 1810: 'Must I then leave you, gin, rum, brandy, aqua-vitae, pleasant jolly fellows? Damn Temperance and he that first invented it! – Some Anti-Noahite.' These drinks, with their wistful names, are his friends; he clings to them; he conspires with them against his sister's rule.

Mischievously or even maliciously, Lamb incriminates Coleridge to Dorothy. He describes Coleridge as a sleek Bacchus, downing goblet after goblet, just at the time when Coleridge is rumoured to be mourning the rupture of his friendship with the Wordsworths (*LL*, 3, 62). Lamb implies that the drunken merriment of their much older friendship continues to provide pleasure despite Coleridge's break with these late-comers. Indeed, by 20 October 1811, Coleridge's presence in London as an available drinking partner has endangered Lamb's health, for Coleridge in a letter to John Rickman blames himself for visiting Lamb too often and too early, though he thinks that Hazlitt's visits are even more destructive. He sees 'what Harm has been done', and observes Lamb's patterns: Lamb is 'contented with Porter' until he gets a Pipe; then 'the unconquerable Appetite for Spirit comes in with the Tobacco' (*CCL*, 3, 340; letter 833). To William in 1814 Lamb confesses, 'I write with great difficulty, and can scarce command my own resolution to sit at writing an hour together. I am a poor creature, but I am leaving off gin' (*LL*, 3, 125). In June 1828 he describes to Reverend H. F. Carey the vicious circle of drinking and hangovers which spun him on its wheel:

There is a necessity for my drinking too much ... at and after dinner; then I require spirits at night to allay the crudity of the weaker Bacchus; and in the morning I cool my parched stomach with a fiery libation. Then I am aground in town, and call upon my London friends, and get new wets of ale, porter, etc.; then ride home, drinking where the coach stops, as duly as Edward set up his Waltham Crosses. (EVL, p. 734)

Years of occasional drunkenness build to his later condition, 'the destruction he is rapidly bringing on himself' (EVL, p. 818) by his 'insuperable proclivity to gin' (EVL, p. 790). After a scene at the Cary's home he cravenly moans: 'I protest I know not in what words to invest my sense of the shameful violation of hospitality which I was guilty of on that fatal Wednesday'; he describes his 'burning blushes' and 'hiccupped drunken snatches of flying on the bats' wings' (EVL, p. 1024, for October 1834). He apologizes to Jacob Vale Asbury for being carried home, like Ariel, 'on a bat's back' (EVL, p. 767).

Lamb's biography reveals many of the dissipations and fractures of personal identity that Hume believes we all experience. Beneath the regular surface of life as a clerk at the East India Company, perched from ten to four on his high stool and metamorphosing into the wood of his desk, as he fantasizes in 'The Superannuated Man' (*LCW*, 173), promoted regularly up the bureaucratic scale, lurked a deep voice saying 'I would prefer not to', but far less rational and deliberate than Melville's disenchanted Bartleby. Like his even more degenerate scrivening heir, James Joyce's Farrington, in 'Counterparts', the story that provides the epigraph to this chapter, he must sometimes have yearned for the warmth of the public house on a rainy evening, and have erroneously penned 'the said Bernard Bodley be' so that the page had to be recopied.[32]

One of the persistent arguments for denying that Lamb had a drinking problem is his keeping regular hours at the East India Company. If he were a drunk, argues David Cecil, for one, why was he not impaired in his tedious but exacting work?[33] Lamb answers this question himself in his description of the drunkenness of his co-worker, Tommy Bye. To his drinking companion Thomas Manning, Lamb describes this 'man and madman' (nine years older than himself) whom he has known for 27 years:

He was always a pleasant, gossiping, half-headed, muzzy, dozing, dreaming, walk-about, inoffensive chap; a little too fond of the creature – (who isn't at times?); but Tommy had not brains to work off an over-night's surfeit by ten o'clock next morning;

and unfortunately, in he wandered the other morning drunk with last night, and with a superfoetation of drink taken in since he set out from bed. (28 May 1819).

Lamb in high spirits describes Bye's stagger, his indigo face, his laughter, and the on-the-spot termination of his job of 36 years. The trick is always to sober up by ten and not to drink in the morning. Lamb chuckles at Tommy Bye getting caught and ruined (is this laughter, too, a screen for horror at the ruthlessness of his employers and the precariousness of his own position?), but he shows that he knows the method and makes sure to use it.

Though the word 'alcoholic' is never used, Lamb's biographers report frequent episodes of drunkenness.[34] E. V. Lucas gives numerous reports of Lamb's being 'overcome'; he names Ralph Fell and John Fenwick as the drunken companions who first encouraged Lamb to drink, and who continue to lure him to nights of excess (EVL, p. 245). Crabb Robinson records seeing Lamb getting very drunk and believes the 'Confessions of a Drunkard' 'will hardly be thought so near a correct representation of a fact as it really is' (EVL, p. 407). Several references in Crabb Robinson's diaries indicate that Lamb's health declines when he stops drinking,[35] suggesting a dependence so severe that it has obliterated his own natural functioning. Though Mary begs him to 'be a good boy', and in that phrase indicates her infantilization of her ten years younger brother, the middle-aged Charles continues to pour the gin. Katherine Anthony has found that Lamb's drunkenness was so excessive that he was put in the stocks in a little village outside of London when he was 34 (fictionally recalled perhaps in 'Reflections in the Pillory' in 1825[36]); Anthony argues that Lamb died from a wound that developed into 'erysipelas', incurred when drunkenly stumbling.[37]

These incidents hardly add up to Carlyle's charges, virulently describing the 57-year-old Lamb as 'a confirmed, shameless drunkard [who] asks vehemently for gin and water in strangers' houses, tipples til he is utterly mad, and is only not thrown out of doors because he is too much despised for taking such trouble with him. Poor Lamb! Poor England, when such a despicable abortion is named genius!' (EVL, p. 787). But they do suggest that in a life filled with duties to others and deficient in freedoms, romantic attachments, and travel, Lamb released his demons in alcohol and that it is fair to call him an alcoholic, even if sometimes a charming one.

IV: *JOHN WOODVIL* AND 'CONFESSIONS OF A DRUNKARD':
      ALCOHOLIC FICTIONS AND FRAGMENTED SELVES

In the context of his own admitted and observed drunkenness, and
of his madness, night terrors, and feelings of vulnerability and doubleness, it is significant that two of Lamb's most ambitious works
reveal how drunkenness splits apart an already dissolving 'personality'. His play, *John Woodvil: A Tragedy* (1797–1801) dramatizes this
fragmentation from the outside and inadvertently; his long essay,
'Confessions of a Drunkard' (1813), analyses it from the inside and
with a steady gaze. Both works show in theme, in voice, and in skit-
tishness of purpose that drink magnifies personal fragmentation.
Like Basil Montagu, but brilliantly and artfully, Lamb reveals his
alcoholism in the fractured surface of his evasions.

A pecularity of the critical study of Romantic drama is an almost
total silence about Lamb's play. Though never produced, the play
demonstrates the Romantic revival of the Renaissance, the
Romantic concern with the English Revolution in its parallels with
the revolutions in the Romantic era, the Romantic interest in the
theatrical representation of psychological states, and the Romantic
identification with a Hamlet-like introspection about the failure of
action.[38] *John Woodvil*, set in Devonshire during the Restoration,
imitates a 'medley' of *King Lear* and *As You Like It*, and, like Lamb's
and White's later letters of Falstaff, mimics a Renaissance language.
Originally entitled 'Pride's Cure', it features an erring Cavalier hero
whose drunkenness leads him to betray his Puritan father Sir
Walter and brother Simon, who hide from Royalist persecution in
Sherwood Forest, and to reject his childhood sweetheart Margaret.
Begun in 1797 in the excitement of a visit to Coleridge and
Wordsworth, whose early pantheism influences Simon's love of the
natural world, it was submitted to Drury Lane in 1802 and rejected.
The play, precisely because of its failure, tells much about the
dangers to dramatic representation of the Romantic breakdown of
coherent selfhood, especially when drunkenness further disrupts
continuity of thought and action. Lamb seems to recognize the
dangers of submerged autobiographical elements when in the
Preface to the *Last Essays of Elia* he asks, 'how shall the intenser
dramatist escape being faulty, who, doubtless, under cover of
passion uttered by another, oftentimes gives blameless vent to his
most inward feelings, and expresses his own story modestly?'
(*LCW*, 135).

Drunkenness pervades the play in a variety of moods and has fatal consequences.[39] Drinking is the central activity of lower and upper classes. John Woodvil's servants, like Goneril's retinue, waste the father's patrimony, toast each other, promise to 'be fuddled anon', to 'topple off' their seats, 'to blab out secrets', and to drink quarts in the morning like 'beasts'.[40] They are berated as 'foul excrescences' by the retainer Sandford:

How oft in old times
Your drunken mirths have stunn'd day's sober ears,
Carousing full cups to Sir Walter's health? –
Whom now ye would betray.

On a higher social level John Woodvil's friends revive a Restoration libertinage after Puritan repression. They, too, volley witticisms, mocking the water-drinking self-denial of the previous regime. A 'Drunken Man' sings, 'Ale that will make Grimalkin prate', and quips: 'At noon I drink for thirst, at night for fellowship, but, above all, I love to usher in the bashful morning under the auspices of a freshening stoop of liquor.' He sings, 'Ale in a Saxon rumkin then, makes valour burgeon in tall men' (*LCW*, 435). In honour of the Restoration of Charles II, says John Woodvil, 'Now Universal England getteth drunk / For joy' (*LCW*, 436). Still drinking in Act 3, the cavaliers sing, jest and down their twenty bumpers each.

But even in the midst of cavalier 'dissipation', John Woodvil describes the natural intoxication of the poet, whose enthusiasm arises in the brain without the external stimulus of alcohol. His ideas resemble Wordsworth's rejection of gross stimuli in the 'Preface to the *Lyrical Ballads*', and anticipate Coleridge's remarks about the intoxication of creativity in the *Biographia Literaria*. Woodvil tells Lord Lovel,

your poet-born hath an internal wine, richer than lippara or canaries, yet uncrushed from any grapes of earth, unpressed in mortal winepresses... . It is denominated indifferently, wit, conceit, invention, inspiration, but its most royal and comprehensive name is *fancy*.

Lovel asks, 'And where keeps he this sovereign liquor?' Woodvil answers:

Its cellars are in the brain, whence your true poet deriveth intoxication at will; while his animal spirits, catching a pride from the
quality and neighbourhood of their noble relative, the brain,
refuse to be sustained by wines and fermentations of earth.
(*LCW*, 443)

Despite his appreciation of such autonomous inspiration, Woodvil
himself is not such a water-drinking poet. Instead, he drinks constantly, shifting his moods and personalities as the alcohol dictates.
He is many men, and no one. In one mood, toasting the king, he
drinks until he becomes witty and ecstatic:

We have here the unchecked virtues of the grape. How the
vapours curl upwards! It were a life of gods to dwell in such an
element: to see, and hear, and talk brave things. Now fie upon
these casual potations. That a man's most exalted reason should
depend upon the ignoble fermenting of a fruit, which sparrows
pluck at as well as we! (*LCW*, 444)

'Ravished', flushed with 'madness', John Woodvil 'soliloquises':

My spirits turn to fire, they mount so fast.
My joys are turbulent, my hopes show like fruition.
These high and gusty relishes of life, sure,
Have no allayings of mortality in them.

Drink makes him too intense, too wild, too divine to endure mere
human life. 'Too hot' and 'o'ercapable', he wants 'adversity' 'To
take these swellings down' (*LCW*, 444). In another abrupt shift of
'personality', he yearns for calamity to dash his drunken flights. He
chooses the unworthy Lord Lovel as his friend and for no reason
tells him where his father and brother lie hidden, an arbitrary disclosure that will become the 'Calamity' that he seeks 'to take these
swellings down', again to change himself.

The unpredictability of Woodvil as a dramatic character is
directly tied to his drinking, whether he is irritable, bitter, poetic,
exalted or dejected. Waking with a hangover, he gradually realizes
what his drunken other self has done:

A weight of wine lies heavy on my head,
The unconcocted follies of last night.
Now all those jovial fancies, and bright hopes,

Children of wine, go off like dreams.
This sick vertigo here
Preaches of temperance, no sermon better.
Some men are full of choler, when they are drunk;
Some brawl of matter foreign to themselves;
And some, the most resolved fools of all,
Have told their dearest secrets in their cups.

(*LCW*, 449)

The realization of his drunken indiscretion comes too late to save his father: without a word the father's heart breaks at the knowledge of his son's betrayal, recreating in disguised form the murder of a parent that lies at the heart of Lamb's pain.

Though John Woodvil recognizes that imaginative activity can feel like intoxication, his drinking does not foster art. For drink has become such an obsession with him that he is alienated from his natural feelings of love and loyalty to his exiled father and brother, and so cynical that Margaret must flee from his jeers. He is lost in a calculating, coarse indifference, but in his cups still yearns for friendship. He is never the same 'person' from minute to minute. His desperation for friendship and his indiscretion, too drunk to realize what he is saying, cause his father's death. Although John Woodvil is finally healed by Margaret's assertion that his was a 'mistake' and not a 'crime' (an early example of the 'I'm okay, you're okay' attitude toward personal responsibility) and by a sudden eruption of religious sentimentality, he bears the guilt of having betrayed his father and brother in a night of boozing. His well-founded remorse vanishes with drunken memory and shifting selves.

While the play recreates an atmosphere of festive singing and group drinking, it indicates the irrevocable danger of loss of consciousness and free agency as the drunken hero says he knows not what and disjoins himself from his 'true' nobility. From the divine heights of drunkenness he swoops to self-loathing for his indirect role in his father's unexplained death, and just as suddenly, with Margaret's return, feels forgiven and hopeful, hearing the bells of Ottery St Mary's church (strangely, the church of Coleridge's childhood and marriage).

The shifts in John Woodvil's moods and attitudes are irrational and abrupt, his character discontinuous, the swerves unmotivated. These discontinuities may be caused by the hero's drunkenness, which removes the consistent springs of moral action, by the author's interest in personal fragmentation and multiple selves, by the author's 'discontinuous and abrupt mind' (in De Quincey's phrase), or by the author's 'inability to construct dramatic plots and to handle characters'.[41] Themes of corrupting friends, loyal younger sons and treacherous older ones, women who gently rescue and nurture, guilt for drunken misbehaviour, uncertain personal identities, and parent-murder connect the 'tragedy' with Lamb's biography in a disguising fiction set in an earlier revolutionary time.

John Woodvil, uncertain of his values or his voices, trying on poses of indifference, aestheticism, remorse and salvation, forgetful of treacherous deeds committed in oblivion, is just the sort of tragic hero to emerge in the wake of Hume's pulverization of personal integrity and the resulting doubt about responsibility for a previous self's actions. He is an appropriate tragic hero to arise from an alcoholic sensibility, attempting to represent such a sensibility in fragmented action. Does Lamb know what he is doing or can he not help himself?

When the failure of his tragedy led Lamb to acknowledge having 'no head for play-making', he used a very different form a decade later to explore the lure and danger of drunken congeniality, fragmentation of personality, betrayal, and maudlin collapse. He feigned 'a confession', written as if from the depths of self-disgust. The 'I' of the 'Confessions' will show the alcoholic 'person' split, surprised by his own deeds, pitying himself for doing them, a skittish Woodvil seen from 'within'.

'Confessions of a Drunkard' sits at the centre of the great *lacuna* that Monsman and McFarland note in Lamb's writing. But the 'Confessions' are encircled with ironic recantations. Ashamed at Gifford's reference to the truth of this essay in *The Quarterly Review*, Lamb defends himself in the *London Magazine* of 1822, nine years after the first publication of the 'Confessions'. In involuted phrases that may in themselves bespeak lying, he says that these 'Messieurs' have added 'from their peculiar brains, the gratuitous affirmation, that they have reason to believe that the describer (in his delineation of a drunkard, forsooth!) partly sat for his own picture.' 'The truth is', prevaricates Lamb, that this essay is a parody of 'Edax on Eating', a humorous confession of an obese glutton, which does not reveal personal truth about the slim author. To further disassociate himself from the essay, Lamb pretends to suspect that 'a contemporary ... has perversely been confounded with him.' This remote alter ego, imitating another acquaintance, intends to write 'a better paper – of deeper interest and wider use-fulness — ... out of the imagined experiences of a Great Drinker.' Not only is the author many times removed and the essay imaginary, but it is also ironic; it compresses in one imaginary figure all the drunks ever known:

> Accordingly, he set to work, and, with that mock fervour and counterfeit earnestness with which he is too apt to over-realize his descriptions, has given us – a frightful picture indeed, but no more resembling the man Elia than the fictitious Edax may be supposed to identify itself with Mr L. its author. (*LCW*, 366)

The author screens himself in lies, but admits some personal involvement in one of these imaginary personae: 'We deny not that a portion of his own experiences may have passed into the picture; (as who, that is not a washy fellow, but must at some times have felt the after-operation of a too-generous cup?) but then how heightened! how exaggerated!' Hostility against 'washy fellows' grows as the author turns on the 'Quarterly slime, brood of Nilus, watery heads with hearts of jelly spawned under the sign of Aquarius, incapable of Bacchus, and therefore cold, washy, spiteful, bloodless'. He threatens to take revenge on these bloodless water-drinkers in a later spoof, to be entitled 'Confessions of a Water-Drinker', a sly reference to Basil Montagu's 1814 volume.

The brilliant 'Confessions of a Drunkard' nevertheless exists, and stands as one of the deepest and most instructive analyses of how alcoholism begins, how it feels, and how impossible it is to cure.

Lamb (under his many screens of denial, ventriloquism and masks) directs his essay to the 'sturdy moralist' who refuses to understand that the person addicted to alcohol cannot simply will himself to stop, as a pilferer or a liar can, for his body and soul are both wholly engaged in the addiction. He calls for compassion, and begs the sturdy moralist, 'Trample not on the ruins of a man.' He wishes him to bear in mind how difficult it is to begin to stop: 'what if the whole system must undergo a change violent as that which we conceive of the mutation of form in some insects? what if a process comparable to flaying alive be to be gone through?' This man crying 'aloud, for the anguish and pain of the strife within him', he admits is himself (whoever that may be in the tangle of *personae*, voices, masks and lies). 'It is to my own nature alone I am accountable for the woe that I have brought upon it.' While he bravely tries to take responsibility for his own deeds, the nature he blames is multiple and shifting, the accountability difficult to pinpoint.

That nature is in itself a cause for pity. Unlike ordinary people, drunkards are timid, weak, nervous, easily lured to drink by fellows with 'robust heads and iron insides'. Drunkards need 'some artificial aid to raise their spirits in society to what is no more than the ordinary pitch of all around them without it'. Students of alcoholism recognize in these opening pages the self-abasement, isolation, depression and self-pity of the alcoholic, who tries to take the blame but ends by blaming others. Here he points the finger at a boisterous crowd of drunks who encouraged him to be 'a professed joker', despite the 'natural nervous impediment in my speech!' For their applause he compromised his values:

> to be spurred on to efforts which end in contempt; to be set on to provoke mirth which procures the procurer hatred; to give pleasure and be paid with squinting malice; to swallow draughts of life-destroying wine which are to be distilled into airy breath to tickle vain auditors; to mortgage miserable morrows for nights of madness; to waste whole seas of time upon those who pay it back in little inconsiderable drops of grudging applause, – are the wages of buffoonery and death.

Crowds of social drinkers may lure the drunkard at first, but the substances themselves unleash their own power, causing a progressiveness in the disease. The narrator charts his descent from malt liquor to thin wines to those 'juggling compositions' of 'mixed liquors', until he sees himself enslaved like a figure in 'a print after Correggio' in whose face can be seen 'a Sybaritic effeminacy, a submission to bondage, the springs of the will gone down like a broken clock'. He describes the intricate twining of drunkenness, guilt, and drunkenness as 'the sin and the suffering co-instantaneous, or the latter forerunning the former, remorse preceding action – all this represented in one point of time.'

The narrator's aim is to prevent young men from repeating his downward slide into 'the black depths'. He wishes the youth to

> look into my desolation, and be made to understand what a dreary thing it is when a man shall feel himself going down a precipice with open eyes and a passive will, – to see his destruction and have no power to stop it, and yet to feel it all the way emanating from himself; to perceive all goodness emptied out of

him, and yet not to be able to forget a time when it was otherwise; to bear about the piteous spectacle of his own self-ruins.

This Miltonic vision of the fall down a precipice is complicated by
the double vision of the alcoholic, who slips into a sea and help-
lessly watches himself drown, as if he were an outside observer,
split off, and conscious of his own unconsciousness. This self-
observing disintegration occurs in fictional alcoholics in the
decades following the publication of Lamb's essay, in the husband-
narrator in Poe's 'The Black Cat', for example, and in Marmeladov
in Dostoyevsky's *Crime and Punishment*, Chapter 2, who watches
himself repeatedly transgress, and yearns for the punishment
which will allow him to begin again.

When Lamb writes, 'The waters have gone over me', and
describes a drowning and falling sensation, he uses metaphors
that many others have used for the helplessness of alcoholism.
Dr Thomas Trotter believes that the 'habit, carried to a certain
length, is a gulph, from *whose bourne no traveller returns*'; he traces 'a
gradation in the vice' where the drunkard feels himself falling as it
were in the scale of being' (Trotter, pp. 5, 177). Dr Robert MacNish
describes the gradual decline from charm to unsteadiness. To the
drunkard's 'distorted eyes all men, and even inanimate nature
itself, seem to be drunken ... Houses reel from side to side as if they
had lost their balance; trees and steeples nod like tipsy Bacchanals;
and the very earth seems to slip from under his feet, and leave him
walking and foundering upon the air' (MacNish, p. 43). Charles
Dickens describes the gulf into which drunkards plunge, some by
misfortune but most by their own wills: 'by far the greater part
have wilfully, and with open eyes, plunged into the gulf from
which the man who once enters it never rises more, but into which
he sinks deeper and deeper down, until recovery is hopeless.'[42] A
recent writer has described 'the liquidity of drunkenness': 'a
drunk's world is hopelessly fluid, now rocking us gently, now
breaking over us with blind and cruel force.'[43]

In Lamb's view, as for many modern observers of alcohol abuse,
there is 'no middle way betwixt total abstinence and the excess
which kills you', because 'the pain of self-denial is all one.' Alcohol
comes to replace the original personality; without alcohol, the self
becomes a void. In such a state, the alcoholic is only 'himself' when
he is drunk, or, as Lamb puts it, *'reason shall only visit him through
intoxication.'* More elaborately than in his other references to multiple and shifting selves, Lamb analyses the alcoholic metamorphosis

of the person: 'it is a fearful truth, that the intellectual faculties by repeated acts of intemperance may be driven from their orderly sphere of action, their clear daylight ministries, until they shall be brought at last to depend, for the faint manifestation of their departing energies, upon the returning periods of the fatal madness to which they owe their devastation. The drinking man is never less himself than during his sober intervals. Evil is so far his good.' He or the person he once was has been replaced by a phantom being, a shape shifter; he has ceased to be an agent, and has become passive, buffeted, reactive.[44] The allusion to Milton's Satan, whose first wrong choice precipitates his inevitable doom as he leaves behind him his remaining angelic traces, is a fitting Romantic reference point for this analysis of the self-inflicted destruction of the originally healthy personality, pulled apart by the watching consciousness, the defiant will and the disgusted conscience, in a freely chosen enslavement.

Extreme dividedness may be a distinctive element of the 'alcoholic personality', that is, the personality distorted by alcohol rather than the personality susceptible to it in the first place. Gregory Bateson argues 'that the "sobriety" of the alcoholic is characterized by an unusually disastrous variant of the Cartesian dualism, the division between Mind and Matter, or, in this case, between conscious will, or "self," and the remainder of the personality.' One part of the personality of the alcoholic is challenged to prove its power over the other, and thus to risk drinking, as if the drinking is 'outside' of the person. The mind takes the risk exactly when 'success begins to appear probable.' Bateson explains that 'the element of "bad luck" or "probability" of failure places failure beyond the limits of the self. "If failure occurs, it is not *mine*."' In an alcoholic personality alcoholism is imagined to be outside the self, and threatening or invading the self, but is instead at the core of the total personality, 'an alcoholic personality which cannot conceivably fight alcoholism by "self-control",' or will.[45] Lamb has anticipated Bateson in many aspects of his analysis, especially in his recognition of the total transformation of the alcoholic's personality, even when he is sober.

Lamb's essay concludes with a description of the narrator's present broken state, paralysed with fear, fancying discouragement to impede every pursuit, unable to act or muster interest even in his favourite books, lying and betraying his friends, suffering shame and deterioration. Impotence and maudlin self-pity shatter the essay itself into small bits, the paragraphs get shorter and shorter, more and more disconnected, and less and less conclusive. The pages seem to be damp with maudlin tears leaking from shallow wells: 'The noble passages which formerly delighted me in history or poetic fiction, now only draw a few weak tears, allied to dotage. ... I perpetually catch myself in tears, for any cause, or none. It is inexpressible how much this infirmity adds to a sense of shame, and a general feeling of deterioration.' 'I am a poor nameless egotist', he cries, speaking truly of the alcoholic's self-involved pathos and indicating in the oxymoron that the evaporating nameless self is still ironically self-involved.[46] He adds a whiff of Swift's narrator at the end of 'A Modest Proposal' when he assures his reader he has nothing to gain, 'no vanity to consult', by these Confessions. He has exposed his frailties to warn his readers to stop before they turn into some poor being like himself. Who am I? asks the writer, whose act of writing asserts that he still exists. Does 'he' know what is 'true' about the lost self he laments? Is he the same 'I' who dreaded lying in darkness as a child or who dreaded unseen spectres tracking him in the road? Is this the 'I' of John Woodvil, bewildered by postures, betraying his loved ones, forgetting that he did so, and then pitying his own confusion?

Deny its importance as Lamb may, the essay illuminates the subject of alcoholism as a progressive and persistent disease. In its complex analyses it also illuminates Romanticism for its self-consciousness, its confessional outpourings even when ringed with irony, its turbulence and passion, its recognition of the nearness of 'despondency and madness', its self-referential metafictional forms, its recurrent use of Satanic images from Milton, especially ones of plunging and falling, its interest in the replacement of selves by supernatural beings.

Although the essay owes much to Montaigne's self-mocking search for an 'I', it also trembles with the philosophical uncertainties set in motion by Hume, Locke and Hartley, and with the corresponding uncertainties of Lamb's personal sorrows. Uncontrolled drinking is one of them, which generates its own lies, denials and evasions in a dense style that after Lamb we also see in such fictive alcoholic confessions as Sherwood Anderson's 'I'm a Fool' and F. Scott Fitzgerald's 'The Crack-Up', devious truth-tellings that laugh at their own ingenuities, pretending to tell the truth as they invent excuses for lying. Don Birnum, drinking dark bourbon as he looks through the mirroring glasses in the bar in Charles Jackson's

Lost Weekend, similarly mocks his own aspirations to write his story, even as the story vanishes into the reflecting brown and glass air of his drunken musings.[47] Indeed, like these modern fictions, Lamb's 'Confessions' pretend to be confessions but turn around to deny their reality; very different is F. Scott Fitzgerald's supposedly confessional 'The Crack-Up'. In both cases the drinking 'I' denies his drinking, but in Lamb's the possibly false text is intact; in Fitzgerald's the text is shot through with falsity, including ascribing the drunkenness to substitute figures while claiming to tell the truth. Both texts are invented to contain some of the self-loathing, imagined or exaggerated, that also suffuses the voice of Sherwood Anderson's mendacious narrator of 'I'm A Fool', who ends by asserting that he should not help keep alive a fool like himself, even by lying about his own folly, or excusing his pretenses brought about by drunken bravado blamed on a posturing superior at the bar.

Thus accustomed to appreciate a surface of laughter over a depth of pain in the art of others and in his own disguises, Lamb denies that 'Confessions of a Drunkard' is anything but a jest, but, 'drunken-dog' or 'sot' (the first he asks Coleridge to use in place of 'gentle-hearted', the second he hides in asterisks), he has snuck up behind himself and told some hard truths about how drinking submerges the will and replaces it with a multitude of phantoms. Like the failed tragedy, *John Woodvil,* the essay, 'oftentimes gives blameless vent to his most inward feelings, and expresses his own story modestly.' The essay takes its place as a Romantic response to philosophical queries about ways to lose the self, to be replaced and absorbed, and to imagine possible selves that might evolve. It reveals the complex interplay between alcoholism and self-consciousness.

1. Statue of Dionysos and Hope, in Thomas Hope's galleries on Duchess Street, London, from 1796 to 1841.

2. *A doctor trying to administer medicines to a drunken, carbuncled sailor.* Coloured etching by W. Elmes, 1811.

3. *Drunken sailors round a table cheering and throwing hats in the air as man with wooden leg recounts the Battle of the Nile*. Reproduction of an etching by C.H., c.1825, after G. Cruikshank.

4. *Three men carousing beneath a mulberry tree, with a poem accompanying the image*. Etching by G. Cruikshank, 1808, after himself.

5. *Sound Philosophy: Captain Morris's drinking song illustrated by five men at a table drinking.* Engraving and etching, c. 1806.

6. *Children Grape Gathering.* Samuel Palmer, 1852.

7. *Bacchus on a chariot preceded by a drunken procession of nude men, women, and satyrs all carrying grapes.* Engraving, early 16th century, after G. Romano.

8. *Three very drunken men unaware of 'death', as a crowned skeleton, emerging from under the tablecloth.* Engraving by S. Natim, c. 1815, after W. Craig.

4

Coleridge and Alcohol: Songs and Centrifuges

Hail, Dionysos,
god of frenzy and release, of trance and visions.
I see them recede,
handsome men, beautiful women,
brains clever and bright, spirits gay and daring,
limbs tremble and shake,
caught in your divine power,
carried away on the stream of your might,
Dionysos.

> – Dudley Randall, 'Hail, Dionysos' (1966)

Coleridge's position as an example of the double experience of drunkenness for medical commentators; as the veiled substitute figure behind Wordsworth's examination of Burns; as a companion, witness and interlocutor of Lamb's giddy instabilities; and as the formative father of a notably enfeebled drunkard puts him at the centre of a Romantic network of writings about drink. His own writings on the subject take jocular, confessional, philosophical, sociological and aesthetic forms.

In this chapter Coleridge appears as an inventor and singer of drinking-songs; as a self-analysing sufferer of voluntary and involuntary excesses; as an observer of the drinking habits of impoverished groups of people; as a philosopher assessing the limits of the human being caught between divinity and animalism; as an aesthetician of Dionysian energy in verse and in drama; and as a religious thinker worried about freedom of the will.

He exemplifies the double experience of drinking described by the philosopher David Hartley (after whom he named his first son): 'the common and immediate Effect of Wine is to dispose to Joy', but too quickly 'the pleasant vibrations pass into the disagreeable Vibrations belonging to the passions of Anger, Jealousy, Envy.' He embodies the words of Thomas Taylor, a contemporary Platonist who influenced his work: 'he who lives Dionysiacally rests from labours and is freed from his bonds.' In art and life he illustrates the two sides of Dudley Randall's 'Hail, Dionysos' in the epigraph: drunkenness veering from ecstasy to illness.

I. Songs

Coleridge's art and life merge in the unregarded area of his drinking-songs. These poems reveal a wild and spontaneous Coleridge, the delight of parties and taverns, who might sit 'drinking steadily' with his fellows as in the illustration to 'Captain Morris's Celebrated Drinking Song' in Plate 4. As a writer and singer of drinking-songs Coleridge participates in an old culture of men in groups. Since his school days with Robert Allen, the LeGrice brothers, and Charles Lamb, he magnetized his cronies in tipsy evenings that Lamb wistfully recalls: 'I have been laughing, I have been carousing, / Drinking late, sitting late, with my bosom cronies.'[1] Amid the pleasures of drinking, singing and talking in the heightened enthusiasm of the tavern, Coleridge appears as one of the loudest and most frivolous, although other Romantic poets also composed drinking-songs. Tom Moore bids an imaginary companion to 'Fill the Bumper Fair', to 'Wreath the Bowl', and to 'Drink of this Cup'. Similarly imperative, Byron, on 'bladders of rhyme', calls to 'Fill the goblet again'.[2]

English public houses have a rich lore. Their furnishings welcome – velvet seats, burnished wood panels, and swivelling cut-glass windows; their lingo is arcane and amusing – names of mixtures (negus and nappy), of containers (jereboams and tankards), and of foods ('toad in the hole'); their garrulity often crosses class lines and fosters local loyalties. Taverns have long served as meeting rooms, gathering places, pay areas, lecture halls; they are refuges from cold dark lodgings, from hungry children, from nagging or despairing wives.[3] Famous taverns are associated with literature like Chaucer's Tabard Inn, Ben Jonson's Devil's Inn, Shakespeare's Mermaid Tavern, his Falstaff's Boar's Head Tavern, Lamb's and Coleridge's Cat and Salutation, and Tennyson's Cock Tavern, for the nut-brown ale of bully Britain heightens conversation, loosens words and inspires songs. Even the water-drinking William Blake imagines 'the little vagabond' yearning for the warmth of the ale-house while he shivers in church:

Dear Mother, dear Mother, the Church is cold.
But the Ale-house is healthy & pleasant & warm;

... if at the Church they would give us some Ale
And a pleasant fire, our souls to regale;
We'd sing and we'd pray, all the live-long day.[4]

The drinking-songs that sometimes waft from English taverns, or
are written as if they do, celebrate the refuge, fellowship, energy
and wit released and permitted there. These songs express the
pleasures of men in groups, who believe that they continue the
drunken dialogues of ancient *symposia*.

Drinking-songs form a subset of songs of *carpe diem*, celebrating
wine, women and song, a brief life and a merry one. Essentially
pagan, like the songs of anonymous Greek lyricists, of Anacreon,
Catullus and Propertius, of medieval students, and of Herrick,
Cowley and Rochester,[5] they relish vitality and sensuousness. This
pagan frolic may seem at first glance foreign to Romantic poets,
whose self-conscious yearnings cannot be contained in such
ephemeral forms. Yet the rarely noticed drinking-songs of Coleridge
and Keats suggest that despite their disappointments in love,
Coleridge and Keats carried on jovially at dinners and in pubs where
neither Asra nor Fanny could intrude on their masculine riot. In their
songs they recreate in rhythms a warmly lit scene of pleasure, fit companions for Burns, Moore, Byron, Sheridan, and other sons of Ben.

Coleridge's drinking-songs reveal not only the convivial aspect
of his nature but also his knowledge of the traditional metre and
conventions of the form. Two of these songs are tucked away in the
section called '*jeux d'esprit*' in Ernest Hartley Coleridge's edition of
the poems, two appear in letters, and one was found in the flyleaf
of a volume in Coleridge's cottage in Nether Stowey, copied out in
his daughter Sara's hand. Other drinking-songs will soon be published and will restore the antic Coleridge that his nephew tried to
purify in his mid-Victorian edition.[6] Coleridge the sober metaphysician shares the stage with Coleridge the man of pleasure, whose
social style is one of many voices in his repertoire.[7]

Brazenly, Coleridge prints two verses on drinking in the *Morning
Post* in 1801, announcing to its large readership his delight in ale.
The first, 'Song to be Sung by the Lovers of all the Noble Liquors
comprised under the name of Ale', equates drinking human beings
with drinking gods. Two voices, A and B, exchange witticisms:

A.

Ye drinkers of Stingo and Nappy so free
Are the gods on Olympus so happy as we?

B.

They cannot be so happy!
For why? they drink no Nappy.

A.

But what if Nectar, in their lingo,
Is but another name for Stingo?

B.

Why, then we and the Gods are equally blest,
And Olympus an Ale-house as good as the best![8]

Lifting their tankards, the two speakers celebrate their gleeful freedom; they are happier than gods, unless the gods are also drinking ale. The frequency of dialogue in these *jeux d'esprit* and comic poems suggests that, along with his fame as a monologuist, Coleridge's wit sparked convivial repartee. His reference to Nappy banters back in time with John Skelton, whose satirical poem 'The Tunning of Elinour Rumming' reveals Elinour brewing 'noppy ale', and with John Gay, whose 'A Ballad. On Ale' praises 'nappy Ale' as patriotic, liberating, and heavenly:

Can any taste this drink divine,
And then compare Rum, Brandy, Wine,
    Or aught with nappy Ale?[9]

Also appearing in *The Morning Post*, a second song trumpets a defiantly anti-philosophical Coleridge. Coleridge addresses 'Drinking *versus* Thinking' to 'My Merry men all', an audience that has widened beyond his cronies to include the readership of the paper. The singer rejects philosophy, imagining that old Nick will ferry it across the Stygian Lake, and chooses merriment:

Away, each pale, self-brooding spark
That goes truth-hunting in the dark,
    Away from our carousing!
To Pallas we resign such fowls –
Grave birds of wisdom! ye're but owls,

And all your trade but *mousing*!

My merry men all, here's punch and wine,
And spicy bishop, drink divine!
    Let's live while we are able.
While Mirth and Sense sit, hand in glove,
This Don Philosophy we'll shove
    Dead drunk beneath the table!

The singer and his friends banish the search for truth, Athena, and her owl, in favour of drink and present delight; they shove philosophy under the table in a reversal of Coleridge's usual philosophical role.

Carousing the night away, Coleridge writes drinking-songs when he is supposed to be grieving for his lost friendship with Wordsworth and when he is on the verge of death. In April 1811, soon after the quarrel with Wordsworth, he imitates a drinking-song by Schiller and designs it for music by the composer John Whitaker, whose wine party of the previous night inspired this song. Like the two previous drinking-songs, it summons bibulous Greek gods to join the praise of drinking and to suggest the olympian highs of drunkenness; here the verse form is more complex than the others, lofty in tone and syncopated in metre:

Hah! – we mount! On their pinions they waft up my soul!
    O give me the Nectar!
        O fill me the Bowl!

    Give, give [h]im the Nectar!
    Pour out for the Poet!
        Hebe! pour free!
Moisten his Eyes with celestial Dew,
That STYX the detested no more he may view,
But like one of us Gods may conceit him to be!
Thanks, Hebe! I quaff it! IO PAEAN, I cry!
    The Wine of the Immortals
        Forbids me to die.[10]

Two voices again resound: the poet's and the answering god's; wine raises the drinker to a divine state as ale did; it deifies the drinker and banishes death. Exclamations and capitalizations signal the poet's inspired enthusiasm.

Two examples of earlier drinking songs demonstrate the generic type, and show Coleridge's familiarity with its distinctive features. References to the drinking of the gods keep alive a traditional *topos*, as seen in two anonymous songs from 1713 set to music by Corelli. The first, illustrated with a miniature of Hogarth's *Very drunken Party*, begins:

> Since Drinking has Pow'r for to give us Relief,
> Come Fill up ye Bowl, & a Pox on all Grief;
> If we find that won't do, we'll have such Another, –
> And so we'll proceed from one Bowl to ye Other,
> Till like Sons of Apollo, we'll make our Wit soar,
> Or in Homage to Bacchus fall down on ye Floor.
>
> Apollo and Bacchus were both merry Souls,
> They Each of them lov'd to top off their Bowls;
> Then let's try to show ourselves Men of Merit,
> By toasting those Gods in a Bowl of Good Claret ...

Another song is illustrated with a man on a donkey:

> Bacchus, assist us to sing thy great glory;
> Chief of the Gods, we exult in thy story. ...
> Wine's first projector,
> Mankind's protector,
> Patron to topers,
> How we adore thee! ...
> Friend to the muses, a whetstone to Venus;
> Herald to pleasures, when wine wou'd convene us.[11]

Many of these songs were recorded and reinvented by the theatrical writer Charles Dibdin (1745–1814) in his four volumes of songs (1803), which attest to the popularity of the form during the Romantic period. Coleridge is easy in these metres and themes, freed from personal anguish into an impersonal role of masculine revelry.

Moving from the delight of gods to social reality, Coleridge versifies admonitions to the poor in an 1832 letter to Green. He urges the 'Useful Classes' to avoid filth, alcohol and groups, so as to ward off a powerful Asiatic cholera. In Coleridge's giddy phrasing, the disease becomes a 'new-imported Nabob, from the Indian Jungles, his Serene Blueness, Prince of the Air'.

To escape Belly-ache
Eat no plums nor plum-cake!
Cry, Avaunt, New Potato!
And don't get drunk, like old Cato!
And beware of dys Pipsy,
And there*fore* don't get tipsy!
For tho' Gin and Whisky
May make you feel frisky,
They're but Crimps for Dys Pipsy.

(CCL, 3, 917–18)

Sounding manic with tipsiness himself, Coleridge urges the poor not to 'live in Styes that would suffocate Sows!'

However, for people of his own class, women as well as men, he encourages 'Hot Drams', as a song recorded by his daughter in the flyleaf of the 1834 edition of his *Poetical Works* reveals. The poem, 'Fireside Anacreontic by Samuel Taylor Coleridge in a mad mood', was titled by Sara Coleridge after her father's death.

Come damn it, Girls, don't let's be sad,
    The bottle stands so handy;
Drink gin, if brandy can't be had,
    But if it can, drink brandy,
And if old Aunts, oh! d— their chops,
    In scolding vent their phthi sick,
    Drop in of Laudanum thirty drops,
And call it opening physic.
For it opens the heart and it opens the brain,
And if you once take it, you'll take it again,
Oh! Jacky, Jacky, Jacky, Jacky Dandy
Laudanum's a great improver of Brandy.[12]

Quite apart from Coleridge's remarkable openness about his drinking and drug-taking, and his humour about it in what was then 'mixed company', Coleridge discloses a playful self familiar to his friends and perhaps not distasteful to his family. Annotating Lamb's copy of Beaumont and Fletcher in 1811, he calls attention to the Drinking Song in 'The Bloody Brother', which begins,

Drink to day and drown all sorrow,
You shall perhaps not do it to morrow.

Best while you have it use your breath,
There is no drinking after death.

As if carrying on his dialogue with Lamb, and showing his expertise in this field, Coleridge adds, 'This is the original of the excellent Song, "Punch cures the Gout, the Colic, and the Phthysic" / the Imitation is an Improvement.' George Whalley identifies this song as 'Come, Landlord, Fill a Flowing Bowl', anthologized 'in *The Frisky Songster* (which Coleridge used as early as 1798)'.[13]

The Coleridge who tossed off drinking-songs and *jeux d'esprit*, his casual, humorous by-blows, was one Coleridge among many, but not therefore a spurious one.[14] Though one Coleridge is the prematurely elderly metaphysician, sunk for decades in gloomy meditations, mumbling about 'sumject' and 'ombject', another Coleridge is an ebullient party-goer whose antics made him legendary in Cambridge, in the dragoons, in London, or on shipboard with drunken Scandinavians sailing towards Hamburg. The term *'jeux d'esprit'* suits this aspect of his work well, as it isolates his playfulness, his high spirits, his use of ardent spirits to fuel them, and the ebullience of his spirit, if not also his interest in 'spirits' as ghosts or unseen presences.

Cultivating the buzz or high just short of total intoxication, that state of energized bliss described by Francis Place, Coleridge knew that he was one of those men who, like 'musical glasses', are best kept 'wet': 'Wine – some men=musical Glasses – to produce their finest music you must keep them *wet* –' (*CCN*, 3, 4084).

II. Antic Selves

Under the surface of these overlooked drinking-songs, Coleridge's work and life were far more drink-saturated than is usually supposed. Biographical anecdotes about his drunken antics abound. In an autobiographical letter of early 1798 Coleridge writes to Thomas Poole about his ten-week stay with his mother's brother before going on to Christ's Hospital in 1782. This uncle, a tobacconist and widower with an 'ugly and artful' daughter, 'was generous as the air & a man of very considerable talents – but he was a Sot.' Having been abandoned for good reason by his daughter, Uncle Bowden turned his affections to his ten-year-old nephew:

> My Uncle was very proud of me, & used to carry me from Coffee-house to Coffee-house, and Tavern to Tavern, where I

drank, & talked & disputed, as if I had been a man – /. Nothing was more common than for a large party to exclaim in my hearing, that *I was a prodigy*, &c, &c, &c – so that, while I remained at my Uncle's I was most completely spoilt and pampered, both mind and body. (*CCL*, 1, 388)

This early association with a sottish uncle and his fellow barflies, and the excessive praise and high expectations engendered by it, may have had a sad influence on Coleridge's later behaviour. In 1820, desperate about his son Hartley's drunkenness, Coleridge reveals that his own father, the reverend, also drank too much wine, pouring glass after glass without noticing, much like his friend Charles Lamb (*CCL*, 5, 233). At Christ's Hospital and other schools, drinking among boys was heavy during the Georgian period. Charles Lamb and the brothers Charles and Valentine LeGrice were notable drunkards; drinking in schools is described by Dr Thomas Beddoes in *Hygeia*, as we saw in Chapter 1, and also by Charles Kingsley in *Alton Locke*, written in 1850 but looking back to conditions at the end of the previous century.

Letters to his older brother George at the time of Coleridge's disgrace at Jesus College, Cambridge, suggest that drink may have prompted Coleridge to flee to the dragoons. Though Coleridge may be dramatizing his bad behaviour to abase himself before the righteous and responsible George, and thereby to obtain funds from him, he calls his first two college years 'Debauchery', and 'uproar of senseless Mirth'; he admits that 'for the whole six weeks that preceded the examination' I was almost 'constantly intoxicated'; after 'wild carelessness' he 'lived in all the tempest of Pleasure'. Having escaped from debt and vice by enlisting (though 'quartered' above a 'pot-house' to nurse a fellow recruit with small-pox, a lodging which hardly helped him moderate his drinking), he now wishes to expiate his 'follies'. Wallowing in self-disgust he moans, 'My whole life has been a series of blunders.' He speaks more guardedly of his 'Imprudences', and claims to have dropped all past acquaintances 'solemnly & forever'. Yet he continues to frequent the ale house, sings songs like many a Georgian gentleman about the 'intoxicating Bowl', and, like many an undergraduate then and since, brags about how drunk he is while composing this letter: 'I am *drunk*', underlined and inked out by the recipient or by some later censor.[15] When he returns from his military adventure to college, he pretends penitence but in fact is even more prodigal than before. As

Richard Holmes summarizes, 'He had become one of the wild men of his university generation, and people waited to see what he would do next.'[16]

From Germany, writing warmly to his wife in 1799, Coleridge compares a German bacchanalian evening with his bacchanalian nights at Cambridge, implying as he writes that Sara knows about his own earlier debaucheries:

> Such an evening I never passed before – roaring, kissing, embracing, fighting, smashing bottles & glasses against the wall, singing – in short, such a scene of uproar I never witnessed before, no not even at Cambridge. – I drank nothing – but all, except two of the Englishmen, were drunk – … I thought of what I had been at Cambridge, & of what I was – of the wild & bacchanalian Sympathy with which I had *formerly* joined similar Parties, & of my total inability now to do aught *but meditate*. (*CCL*, 1, 476)

It is hard to imagine the festive Coleridge declining drink and meditating alone at such a party. He tells Sara he has not joined the drinking, nor taken 'wine or fermented liquors now for more than 3 months', but Sara may represent the 'more serious eye of mild reproof' here, as she did already in the last verse paragraph of 'The Eolian Harp'. The Bacchanalia of Cambridge, like the Salutation and Cat tavern in London with Lamb, are touchstones of community, freedom and pleasure. The exuberant man whom Dorothy Wordsworth first saw bounding down a pathless field and leaping over a gate would not give up these pleasures easily.

Like zestful youths everywhere, especially in a hard-drinking culture of taverns and punch parties, but perhaps with slightly more than usual insistence, Coleridge frequently mentions gin, brandy and intoxication. He rollicks in a 'flying Waggon' with a bottle of gin; he drank too much wine at a card club to join Joseph Cottle and Dr Beddoes for dinner; he wonders if God is 'an eating, drinking, lustful God'; he tells Cottle that he has caught the 'Brandiphobia' from drinking too much 'smuggled spirits' and Southey that his 'Monody on the Death of Chatterton' might have been written by a man 'first suckled by a drab with milk & Gin'. He shows self-knowledge in telling Poole, 'Strong liquors of any kind always & perceptibly injure me.'[17]

Coleridge's 'long alcoholic evenings in the tavern snug' with Lamb are the stuff of legend.[18] In the months following his departure from

Cambridge, and at stolen times thereafter, he and Lamb lived in a 'continuous feast' in the 'heaven' of the Salutation and Cat.[19] These exultant phrases of Lamb's correspond to Coleridge's drinking-songs comparing taverns to Olympus and drinkers to Greek gods. Lamb's own drunkenness Coleridge records often, and Lamb sometimes glories in Coleridge's, as when he writes, 'You, for instance, when you are over your fourth or fifth jorum, chirping about old school occurrences, are the best of realities.'[20] With a jorum defined as a large drinking bowl or pitcher, or, figuratively, 'a large quantity',[21] Coleridge on the fifth one might certainly be chirping.

Records from later life illustrate that Coleridge's frolicsome drinking does not end with his youth, that his gaiety persists despite longer intervals of self-destructive intemperance. In 1811, when he is in London recovering from his quarrel with Wordsworth over Wordsworth's calling him 'a rotten drunkard', 'rotting out his entrails with intemperance', he is not as despondent as he would like Wordsworth to think he is. An instructive letter written jointly by Mary and Charles Lamb to Dorothy and William Wordsworth suggests that the Lambs feel that Coleridge belongs to them when he is drinking. The Lambs make clear to the Wordsworths that Coleridge is happier in London than he was in the years of isolation in Grasmere. Lamb's long-standing belief that Coleridge sacrificed his own vitality to idolatry of Wordsworth lurks in the submerged possessiveness of this letter. Mary opens the theme by doubting Dorothy's view that Coleridge is ill and needs to be 'cured' by Dr Carlisle: 'We have had many pleasant hours with Coleridge, If I had not known how ill he is I should have had no idea of it, for he has been very chearful. But yet I have no good news to send you of him, for two days ago, when I saw him last he had not begun his course of medicine & regimen under Carlisle.' Charles's description is even more taunting:

> Coleridge has powdered his head, and looks like Bacchus, Bacchus ever sleek and young. He is going to turn sober, but his Clock has not struck yet, meantime he pours down goblet after goblet, the 2d to see where the 1st is gone, the 3d to see no harm happens to the second, a fourth to say there's another coming, and a 5th to say he's not sure he's the last. (*CCL*, 3, 61–2)

Mary and Charles love him the way he is, wild and exuberant; they do not wish to reform him. They delight that Coleridge defies the 'washy' water-drinkers in the north, as well as in London, where

Basil and Mrs Montagu (whom Coleridge calls 'Fool and Fiend' [*CCL*, 4, 950]) and Dr Carlisle, who had to 'play second fiddle' to Coleridge 'at a Wine Party', as Coleridge boasts (12 Sept. 1814; *CCL*, V, 950), are the Wordsworths' agents of reform.

Even at sixty Coleridge is antic. David Perkins cites William Jerden's memories of the whirling poet: 'On one occasion Coleridge, after much claret, threw a glass through the window pane and then took aim with a fork at a wine glass placed on a tumbler. His roseate face was "lit up with animation, his large grey eye beaming, his white hair floating, and his whole frame, as it were, radiating with intense interest, as he poised the fork in his hand, and launched it at the fragile object."'[22] In 1825, commenting on dosages of milk and wine in antiquity, he notes with delight that years before he had prescribed three glasses of Devonshire clotted cream and wine to Robert and Edith Southey and thus succeeded in curing their seven years of infertility.[23] Thomas Hood and others who heard him talk recall his radiance, his levity, his almost manic glee.[24]

Is it any wonder that 'pleasure' is a frequent term in Coleridge's lexicon? He uses it at crucial junctures in his definitions of art and poetry because for him the acts of creating, reading, listening, and figuring things out are physical pleasures akin to the physical pleasure of drinking. The sensation of singing or creating is a motion, 'Like tipsy Joy that reels with tossing head.'[25] 'The immediate object of poetry is the communication of immediate pleasure'; in the act of writing lines of verse, the poet experiences a distinctive power that seems to arise from within: it is 'that pleasurable emotion, that peculiar state and degree of excitement that arises in the poet himself in the act of composition'.[26] Coleridge's definitions ripple with physicality, excitement and immediacy. As it does for Wordsworth, pleasure for Coleridge courses along the blood. But for Coleridge pleasure is not peaceful or gentle; rather, it rouses, speeding the pulse, stimulating to excitement whether as rapidity of movement, of perception, or of thought. Intoxication intensifies vision, as he notes in August 1800, looking from Mount Skiddaw,

> The poet's eye in his tipsy hour
> Hath a magnifying power.
> [...]
> His eyes can see
> Phantoms of Sublimity.

(CCN, 1, 791)

Metre's effect on verse he compares to the action of wine on conversation and on action: it tends 'to increase the vivacity and susceptibility both of the general feelings and of the attention', produces 'the continued excitement of surprize' and 'the quick reciprocations of curiosity still gratified and still re-excited', and stirs the reader or listener to intense attention (whether warranted by content or event or not). Metre, like wine, lifts, stirs and intoxicates.[27] Metre surges through the pulses and weights of words as alcohol surges through the blood and excites it: this artificial augmenting or heightening is the fundamental connection between inebriacy and poetry; it is the core of Coleridge's Dionysianism.

The effect of intense poetic metre is physical for Coleridge, and points to Coleridge not as a theorist of difficult concepts such as imagination so much as a craftsman who experiences creative moments as pleasurable highs, and who applies this exhilaration to spoken harangues, scintillating discussions, theatrical improvisations, recitations, inspired composing, conversation 'mantling like Champagne'.[28] When he understands, or connects, or sees deeply, or suddenly pours out a series of stanzas that work, he feels intoxicated as by wine. This feeling is pleasure, and when life is good he seems to feel it often.

III. The Divided Being

However, excessive drinking also brings him pain. Many contemporary readers have paid attention to Coleridge's opium addiction as it developed from 1800 to a severe decade of anguish, finally to moderate, but never end, in his years under the Gillmans' care. But Coleridge's excessive drinking was more noticeable than his opium-eating to himself and to his own contemporaries, even in a hard-drinking age. Friends and doctors blamed the brandy he took along with opium, and the wine in which he dissolved it, for his poor health and indolence. In two studies of his opium bondage, Molly Lefebure, emphasizing his drug addiction as it falsifies his every thought and feeling, often omits the concurrent references to spirits.[29] In looking at his drinking of spirits in order to redress the balance, we must bear in mind that Coleridge was taking pints of laudanum (that is, tincture of opium dissolved in wine) at the same time.

Coleridge worries about drinking in himself and for his friends; he comments on drunkenness in the society around him; he thinks about how drunkenness undermines the will and fractures the whole person as an effective agent; he anticipates the temperance movement as a possible solution for himself and others; he explores the ambiguity of drinking with a wisdom known to the ancients. All of these aspects of the drinking experience from joyful to suicidal, on personal, sociological, psychological, practical and mythological levels, appear in his writings and suggest that he knew well Dionysus' double power.

For many years he seems to have worried more about his drinking than about his drug-taking and he begins worrying about it far earlier. For example, he writes to Sara on 14 November 1802, 'I am fully convinced, & so is T. Wedgewood, that to a person with such a Stomach & Bowels as mine, if any stimulus is needful, Opium in the small quantities, I now take it, is incomparably better in every respect than Beer, Wine, Spirits, or any *fermented* Liquor – Nay, far less pernicious than even Tea. – *It is my particular Wish, that Hartley & Derwent should have as little Tea as possible – & always very weak, with more than half milk'*, a heavily underscored warning against tea for his sons that is painfully ironic in view of Hartley's later dissolution. Of himself he soon boasts, 'I sacredly abstain from Tea ... likewise as sacredly from all wine, spirits, & fermented liquors. If I am at any time very languid ... I prefer ether in small quantities with camphorated Julep, or half a grain of opium, to wine or spirit.' As addicted to opium as he is in the months before his departure for Malta, he still believes that opiates are much better for him than spirits, exclaiming to Southey, 'O dear Southey! my Health is pitiable – so mere a Slave to the Weather. In bad weather I can not possess Life without opiates – & with what aversion I take them, tho' I can not hitherto detect any pernicious Effect of it – nothing certainly compared with the effect of Spirits.'[30]

Like De Quincey in his *Confessions of an English Opium-Eater*, Coleridge blames wine and spirits for illness and outrageous behaviour, believing that opium is the 'guardian genius, the Remedy or Palliative of Evils', not realizing until 1814 that opium produced most of the evils it was supposed to be curing.[31] Like De Quincey, he believes that inebriation calls up the brutal part of man's nature, whereas opium summons the serene, exalted, divine part. In arguing that it is the wine in which opium is dissolved that causes intoxication, not the opium itself, De Quincey spins out for pages his contrast between alcohol and opium:

crude opium, I affirm peremptorily, is incapable of producing any state of body at all resembling that which is produced by

alcohol. ... The pleasure given by wine is always rapidly mounting, and tending to a crisis, after which as rapidly it declines; that
from opium, when once generated, is stationary for eight or ten
hours: the first, to borrow a technical distinction from medicine,
is a case of acute, the second of chronic, pleasure; the one is a
flickering flame, the other a steady and equable glow. But the
main distinction lies in this – that, whereas wine disorders the
mental faculties, opium, on the contrary (if taken in a proper
manner), introduces amongst them the most exquisite order, legislation, and harmony. Wine robs a man of his self-possession;
opium sustains and reinforces it. Wine unsettles the judgement,
and gives a preternatural brightness and a vivid exaltation to the
contempts and the admirations, to the loves and the hatreds, of
the drinker; opium, on the contrary, communicates serenity and
equipoise to all the faculties, active or passive. ... In short, to sum
up all in one word, a man who is inebriated, or tending to inebriation, is, and feels that he is, in a condition which calls up into su-
premacy the merely human, too often the brutal, part of his
nature; but the opium-eater ... feels that the divine part of his
nature is paramount.[32]

Up until 1814 (when he decisively blames 'this dirty business of
Laudanum'[33]) Coleridge would agree with De Quincey that wine is
disruptive, enraging and extremist. Coleridge may even have contributed his own lifelong dread of beast-like behaviour to De
Quincey's opinion that wine brutalizes the drinker.

Indeed, Coleridge is sickened by the disordered and animalistic
tendencies of his own nature that emerge when he drinks. In his
notebook of December 1804 he reviles himself for his 'involuntary
Intoxication' of the previous night: 'I in despair drank three glasses
running of whisky & water ... I verily am a stout-headed, weak-
bowelled, and O! most pitiably weak-*hearted* Animal! But I leave it,
(as I wrote it) – & likewise have refused to destroy the stupid
drunken Letter to Southey, which I wrote in the sprawling characters of Drunkenness.' Quite a number of letters apologize to hosts
of the previous night for 'my Intemperance' and vow 'entire abstinence from Spirits' in future (for example, to Daniel Stuart, 28 April
1811). He laments to J. J. Morgan about the 'hauntings of Regret
[that] have injured' him, and how he and many others have been
'driven back by repeated disappointments into themselves, there to
find tranquillity, or (too often) sottish Despondency.' Seven years
later he writes to Morgan that his destructive publishing associate

Mr T. Curtis has gossiped that he 'had often seen me intoxicated, and as he knew by the smell, with *Brandy*.' To J. H. Green from his sickbed he details what he imagines to be an abstemious diet of 'gruel with half a glass of Brandy in it, ... Mutton Chop, with a Pint of Wine, ... 2 grains of acetate of Morphine, with a small portion of the Tincture of Cardomom, & some of Battley's Liquor Cinchonae with Port Wine, so that in 3 days I probably take near two Bottle of Port Wine.' He concludes with some amazement that despite the diet 'my eyes are weak, suffused, in short to use a hateful expression, have a *sottish* wetness in them which shocks me while I am shaving.' In his notebook March 1817 he records a hang-over:

The morning after Punch-inebriation
To spit Dogs' faces in the Chamber-pot
White curly Pudel's of Froth with bladder-eyes/[34]

When he responds wittily on 4 September 1819 to Byron's calling him 'drunk' in *Don Juan*, he defines 'intemperance' as an 'elegant acquirement', whereas sottishness is solitary, continuous, disreputable, and pitiful, its overtones far more shameful than any word describing opium addiction.

Coleridge's sottish wetness and despondency are evident to John Foster, who wrote after hearing Coleridge lecture on 28 January 1815:

He is still living in a wandering, precarious, and comfortless way, perpetually forming projects which he has not the steady resolution to prosecute long enough to accomplish. His appearance indicates much too evidently, that there is too much truth in the imputation of intemperance. It is very likely he beguiles his judgement and conscience by the notion of an exciting effect to be produced on his faculties by strong fluids. I have not heard that he ever goes the length of disabling himself for the clearest mental operation, but certainly he indulges to a degree that, if not forborne, will gradually injure his faculties and health. It is probable that he is haunted by an incurable restlessness, a constant, permanent sense of infelicity. This has been augmented, doubtless, by the total deficiency of domestic satisfactions.[35]

Coleridge's dread of spirits and sometimes of all fermented liquors may arise from his physical intolerance to them, from his association of them with his sottish uncle and occasionally inebriated father, and from the general disgust occasioned by sottishness, a term that seems to be too disgusting to use. Looking at sots, he is horrified at them and at their portents for himself. In April 1805 he confides to his notebook,

> Who that lives with a continually divided being can remain healthy! And who can long remain body-crazed, & not at times use unworthy means of making his Body the fit instrument of his mind? Pain is easily subdued compared with continual uncomfortableness – and the sense of stifled Power! – O this is that which made poor Henderson, Collins, Boyce, &c&c&c – SOTS! awful Thought – O it is horrid! – Die, my Soul, die! Suicide – rather than this, the worst state of Degradation! it is less a suicide! S.T.C.[36]

The divided human being, torn between beast and angel, haunts his thoughts, prompted here by the ugly word 'SOT'.

The Wordsworths also refer with dismay to his use of gin, brandy and spirits, and mention his 'drunkenness'. Dorothy Wordsworth mentions his opium use once, but his brandy, spirits, strong stimulants and ale are a great worry during his visits in 1806, 1807 and 1809. She credits his sudden abstinence from 'Liquor' with his miraculous power to turn out issues of *The Friend* when no one believed it possible, though he still puts spirits in watered gruel to ease the 'pain in his Bowels'.[37] Southey writes to Rickman that Coleridge 'besots himself with opium, or with spirits, till his eyes look like a Turk's who is half-reduced to idiotcy by the practice.'[38] Although Wordsworth seems to have tolerated and sheltered Basil Montagu during his drunken years 1794–5, sympathizing and even taking charge of Montagu's son when Montagu could not care for him (as Chapter 2 has shown), he is less tolerant fifteen years later of Coleridge's similar 'weaknesses'. Because Montagu has become a 'water-drinker' as his *Some Enquiries into the Effects of Fermented Liquors, by a Water Drinker* (1814) will proclaim,[39] Wordsworth tells Montagu of Coleridge's drunkenness in order to warn him against taking him into his teetotal house. While the justice or cruelty of Wordsworth's behaviour has been debated at length, Wordsworth's vocabulary is specifically alcohol-related. He says that Coleridge is 'a rotten drunkard', 'rotting out his entrails with intemperance,' and that 'he was *in the habit* of running into debt at little Pot-Houses for Gin.' That Coleridge adds increasingly large quantities of opium to his wine to create laudanum is not at issue in this quarrel. It is drunkenness, or sottishness, that disgusts

Wordsworth and makes him say the terrible words that Coleridge cannot shake from his mind: that Wordsworth 'has no Hope of you'. Wordsworth's indiscretion in speaking to Montagu about Coleridge, a far dearer friend (or so Coleridge thought), and Montagu's indiscretion in revealing what Wordsworth said to Coleridge add to the tangled moral issues but do not change the central charge.[40]

Both Southey and De Quincey indicate that alcohol is at the core of the 1810 quarrel as an immediate cause, though other, deeper tensions (caused by inequalities of power, fame, prudence and love) in the friendship had been brewing for a decade. Southey writes of Coleridge's journey to London and ill-fated plan to stay with Montagu that 'Coleridge is in London – gone *professedly* to be cured of taking opium & spirits by Carlisle – *really* because he was tired of being here, and wanted to do both more at his ease elsewhere.' Southey assumes it is well-known that Coleridge takes both opium and spirits. In *Recollections of the Lakes and the Lake Poets*, De Quincey describes the folly of Montagu inviting 'a man so irreclaimably irregular as Coleridge' to stay under his roof, when Montagu 'had published a book against the use of wine and intoxicating liquors of every sort' and out of principle 'would not countenance the use of wine at his own table'. Disobeying 'the law of the castle', Coleridge invited to dinner Captain Pasley of the Engineers and 'took care to furnish [wine] at his own private cost.' As De Quincey puts it, 'bitter words ensued — words that festered in the remembrance; and a rupture between the parties followed, which no reconciliation ever healed.'[41] The conflict between the 'irreclaimably irregular' but also hospitable Coleridge and the two prudential teetotalers, Montagu and Wordsworth, went to the depths of their different natures.

IV.   Will-Maniacs

Quite apart from the positive and negative effects of drinking in his own personal experience, Coleridge attends to the drunkenness of the general population from his earliest writings to his last as part of his far-ranging involvement in the public arena.

Many of the outrages of his revolutionary time – called by one historian 'The Age of Intoxication'[42] – Coleridge describes metaphorically as 'intoxications', like terror, violence, or the lust for blood. He also describes outrages exacerbated by actual alcohol, such as savage and ignorant poor men, turned from rational beings into mobs when bribed with gin; crewmen on slave ships made heartless by alcohol and covering their sinful deeds by more alcohol; Indians, brutalized by European alcohol and European rewards for scalping; savage armies warmed and nourished by rations of rum.[43] At the base of the era's most evil violation of the laws of god and of human justice – the slave trade – lie rum and sugar: he argues that if people would boycott these unnecessary luxuries, the filthy inhuman trade in human beings would atrophy.[44] Individual politicians responsible for ineffectual or vicious policies are so drunk that they have lost feeling for their fellow man. William Pitt and Henry Dundas should be deprived of office for their dissoluteness, but Pitt especially has allowed drink to turn him into a reptile, with not even sexuality remaining to vouch for his warm-bloodedness.[45]

Coleridge's sense of the importance of alcohol, especially spirits, as a reason for contemporary brutality, whether at home, in the colonies, or on continental battlefields, is demonstrated in the speed with which he discovers two of the central analyses of drunkenness written in the mid-1790s and discussed in Chapter 1 as evidence of the new 'Romantic' awareness of the widespread danger of drink. Dr Thomas Beddoes, Coleridge's neighbour in Clifton, Somerset, and source of his experiments with nitrous oxide, analysed the damages to family and community caused by drunkenness, as we saw in Chapter 1. Coleridge cites key sentences from Dr Beddoes's *Hygeia* in a charity sermon in 1796, mentioning how 'the ignorant labourer flies to the ale-house to ... produce by poisonous liquors that tumult of the brain which supplies the place of ideas. By his drunkenness he weakens his Constitution, and exhausts his wages – his Wife and Children are exposed to all those numerous disorders which arise from cold & hunger.'[46] Dr Anthony Fothergill, whose *An Essay on the Abuse of Spirituous Liquors* also inspired Patrick Colquhoun, as we saw in Chapter 1, provides Coleridge with material for his 13 May 1796 issue of *The Watchman*. Coleridge quotes Fothergill's descriptions of the vice of dram drinking among the inferior ranks, the speedy intoxication brought on by cheap gin, 'the unspeakable misery into which this vice has plunged innumerable poor families', the loss of labour, the cost to the landed classes, and the train of diseases that follow in the wake of drunkenness. 'Drunkenness is the secret bane of society; it ruins the peace of families, destroys conjugal endearments, and strikes at the very root of population.' Coleridge agrees with Fothergill that regulation of spirits is needed, and with him advocates increasing the duty on spirituous liquors.[47] Spirits are the pandora's box that should be taxed, not beer or ale, a position that Coleridge holds to the end of his life, when he urges anti-spirits legislation along with 'universal' contributions of 'a healthsome and sound Beer' donated by a 'truly paternal' government.[48]

The issue of taxes on spirits becomes pressing in 1811 as part of discussion of the Irish question. Coleridge dined with Sir Henry Grattan when Grattan was arguing the case in Parliament for restoring the higher tax on spirits from 2s 6d to 5s 8d per gallon. Coleridge wrote Godwin, 'To sit at the same table with GRATTAN – who would not think it a memorable Honor, A red letter day in the Almanach of his Life?' If he could not sit at the table he would wait at it, so great is the man's 'true Genius, a certain *moral* bearing, a *moral* dignity'. His 'love of Liberty ... has no smatch of the *mob* in it.'[49] Despite Coleridge's many reservations about Irish and especially Catholic freedoms, he gave space in *The Courier* to an impassioned presentation of Grattan's (and also his own) arguments. This much neglected essay, 'Spirits', reveals some of Coleridge's personal meditations on the connections among alcohol, the breakdown of the will, the fractures of personality, and the pain of this persistent disease, which Fothergill thought could be instantly stopped by various self-deluding ruses like putting wax in one's glass, but which Coleridge now knows may be irreversible for nations as also for persons.

Coleridge declares that the short debate on 16 May 1811 on the duty on Spirits 'has excited more thought in our minds, and awakened a deeper interest, than many discussions which have filled all our columns'. This debate focuses his general interest in drink and irrationality on the lower classes and particularly on the Irish, where poverty, lack of education, and rage at injustice make the effects far more visible than among the educated middle classes who can disguise or keep hidden their bestial behaviour.

The 'divided being' of individual 'SOTS' endangers the public when multiplied in groups of people who have no training in self-control. He writes, 'It is well known how nearly allied to frenzy are the effects of spirituous liquors on men who have strong feelings and few ideas.' Where men of education are briefly energized by drinking spirits before their minds and bodies begin to decay, the uneducated drunkard does not experience that interlude of creative vitality; 'the same quantity renders an uneducated man, of undisciplined habits, a frantic wild beast.' Education briefly suspends the animal rages within the human being, but in the end the disintegration affects both educated and uneducated people alike. 'Nor do these effects cease with the temporary intoxication; but engender habits of restlessness, a proneness to turbulent feelings, even when the man is sober, in short, a general inflammability of temperament.' Even when the drinker of spirits is not actively drinking, his personality has been profoundly altered. Coleridge asks his readers to extrapolate this change to a whole nation that is for one reason or another more susceptible to 'the poison of spirituous drinks' than others, and in addition is metaphorically 'intoxicate[d] with another poison, a malignant hatred to Great Britain'. So strong is their rage at their English oppressors that 'a large majority of the inhabitants with the third or fourth glass of whisky "itch for a riot."'

> Reflect in short on the passion and appetite of the lower Irish for spirits, the effects of these spirits on them, and the mournfully large proportion which their numbers bear to those of the middle and higher classes – and then deduce the consequences of the poison being rendered so cheap, that a man may be mad-drunk for *threepence*!

While Coleridge assesses the relative importance of class, ethnicity, and oppression in his analysis of the Irish, he also turns his essay to general principles about the fragility of human nature, its splitness, its tendency to slide to animalism and thingness. He modulates from social and political commentary to personal psychology:

> Much injury has arisen, as well as many errors, from the indiscriminate application of the maxim, 'Things find their level.' – *Things* may find their level; but the *minds* and bodies of men do not. Drunkenness will not wheel round again to sobriety; nor sloth to industry; nor will disorderly habits and turbulent inquietude sink down again into peaceableness and obedience to laws.

Persons are not things; their illnesses cannot be instantly cured nor their wrong choices instantly reversed. Other complex forces and compulsions are at work besides reason.

In Essay XIV of the 1818 *Friend*, entitled 'Virtue and Knowledge', Coleridge explores the mysterious psychological forces that keep human beings 'vicious and miserable' even when they understand the choices before them. They see clearly what is wrong, but cannot avoid it, or clearly what is right, but cannot will themselves to seek it. This essay, originally part of the 1809–10 edition of *The Friend*, but expanded in 1818, presents 'the Sot' and 'the Prostitute' as central examples of an anti-socratic pessimism: people who know the good cannot always will themselves to pursue it. In the case of the Sot, 'the sense of impossibility quenches all will. Sense of utter inaptitude does the same.' The Sot knows for certain that poison would kill him; he is not sure that drams will do so, however slowly:

> The sot would reject the poisoned cup, yet the trembling hand with which he raises his daily or hourly draught to his lips, has not left him ignorant that this too is altogether a poison. ... why should the distance or diffusion of known consequences produce so great a difference? Why are men the dupes of the present moment?

The sot knows that ultimately his wine is also poison, but the 'disproportion of certain after-harm to present gratification' confuses him. Such uncertainty renders him 'restless';

> restlessness can drive us to vices that promise no enjoyment, no not even the cessation of that restlessness. This is indeed the dread punishment attached by nature to habitual vice, that its impulses wax as its motives wane.

Restlessness, the term applied by John Foster to Coleridge's life, and applied by Coleridge to the intrinsic cravings of all human discontentedness, takes on an impetus of its own. It does not seek; it is driven: 'its own restlessness dogs it from behind, as with the iron goad of Destiny.'[50] We can try to clarify our conceptions, we can concentrate on ideas of being, form, life, conscience, immortality, freedom, but despite these efforts at knowledge, virtue often eludes us. The will collapses. Thus, we hear again Coleridge's cry to his notebook, 'Who that lives with a continually divided being can remain healthy! ... Suicide – rather than this, the worst state of Degradation!' Coleridge, deeply saturated in the disturbing psychologies of Hume and Hartley, feels the fragmentation of his own being as Lamb did.

These two essays, 'Virtue and Knowledge' and 'Spirits', build on the formulation in a schoolboy essay on Intemperance written when

Coleridge was 14, where he 'compared the intemperate man to "a ship driven by a Whirlwind," and Temperance to "a skilful Pilot."'[51] This 'schoolboy essay', which he mentions proudly in a late letter to Green, contained these precocious and prophetic sentences:

> Alas! at the moment we contract a habit we forego our free agency. The remainder of our life will be spent in making resolutions in the hour of dejection and breaking them in the hour of passion. As if we were in some great sea-vortex, every moment we perceive our ruin more clearly, every moment we are impelled towards it with greater force.[52]

Already at 14 Coleridge predicts his own dejection and loss of free agency; already the divided being haunts his thoughts. How much more so in letters of 14 and 15 May 1814, in the midst of his most horrifying period of addiction to that 'dirty business of Laudanum' 'besides great quantities [of liquo]r', when he describes to J. J. Morgan the madness brought about by the uncontrollable dividedness of will and action:

> By the long long Habit of the accursed Poison my Volition ... was compleatly deranged, at times frenzied, dissevered itself from the Will, & became an independent faculty: so that I was perpetually in the state, in which you may have seen paralytic Persons, who attempting to push a step forward in one direction are violently forced round to the opposite.

This divided being is a hell, 'where an indefinite indescribable Terror as with a scourge of ever restless, ever coiling and uncoiling Serpents, drove me on from behind.' The more he wishes to fulfil his duties the less is he capable of doing so: 'In exact proportion, as I *loved* any person or persons more than others, & would have sacrificed my Life for them, were *they* sure to be the most barbarously mistreated by silence, absence, or breach of promise.' He looks at this divided self and begs to be 'trodden & spit upon'; 'For I am nothing, but evil – I can do nothing, but evil! Help, Help! – I believe! help thou my unbelief! –'[53]

Unable to will or choose he is no longer a person but a thing, not responsible for his most basic human behaviours, his word, his moral acts, his love. In a late notebook he clarifies this identification of drunks with things: 'that only is here called a *Person* which is in actual possession of the attributes of personality. A madman, a drunken man, &c is pro tempore a thing, and the immediate Object of Prudence, tho' for a moral end. To a madman words are not either truth or falsehood; but things used as means.'[54] Unable to speak, will or act in an intentional way, the sot forfeits his distinctly human characteristics. He can no longer judge right from wrong or truth from falsehood; he speaks lies and denies facts on the basis of his dependency. From the inside, as he perceives himself, he is no longer a self-generating person making free choices but is an animal pursuing an inappropriate craving, less than an animal in fact, moving toward being a thing. From the outside, as others see him, he is an object to care for or look out for, to deal with or to dread. Coleridge's long meditations on drunkenness engage his deepest concerns with the boundaries between persons and things and the instabilities of personal identity.[55] They resemble Lamb's 'Confessions of a Drunkard' in their discovery of the dividedness of the compulsive drunkard's mind, felt from within as a whirl of fragments.

As obliterated as the will can become, it still needs to be tested. A Christian worried about 'the wide waste of intemperance' in his country, Coleridge believes that alcohol should not be forbidden as it is in Islam, a custom approved by comparative religionists of the Enlightenment. In a late notebook he muses on the varieties of stimuli available:

> Meditating on the wide waste of Humanity effected by intemperance, the lust of intenser life from nervous excitement by physical stimulants, a sceptic, who had studied Gibbon, Voltaire, &c, with too much predilection, declared it a great ground of preference, of Mohammedanism as compared with Christianity, that Mahomet had absolutely forbidden Wine. ... Mahomet forebad wine; the faithful Followers take Opium, & smoke Bang. Is that better? ... had Christ forbidden Wine, Christians might have drunk Gin, punch, &c ... Would you have it commanded – Man shall not take into the body, by any organ, any substance that shall excite the sensations, that shall act on the nervous system? The Prohibition would include every fresh Breeze, every morsel of food that the hungry man takes. No! Religion forbids drunkenness, forbids intemperance, forbids any enjoyment of the outward creature which is not for the well-being of the Enjoyer – forbids any use that is against the true use and this places the commandment in the only sphere, in which it can effectuate

itself: in the court of Conscience. Mahomet placed it in the Court of Excise, in which the letter of the Law alone can be enforced.[56]

The weakness of the will is a terrible source of anxiety in a court of conscience. The line between the pleasurable stimulus of a breeze and the stimulus of gin, which may prove debilitating in the future, sometimes wavers. The constant testing, the failure, and the resultant guilt are torments in a protestant country devoted to free will and yet paradoxically more drunken than any other, for Coleridge has 'reason to believe that no country in God's Earth labours under the tremendous curse of Drunkenness equally with England.'[57]

Coleridge's early friend and later antagonist Hazlitt seems to have learned from Coleridge about irreversibly divided beings when he writes his famous critique of Jeremy Bentham in 1824. Drawing on phrases that may have come from Coleridge's essay 'Spirits', from the *Friend* essay, and from Coleridge's conversations, Hazlitt argues that Bentham is wrong to think human beings can be reformed by rational scientific principles and taught to will the right by sitting observed in a Panopticon. 'Criminals,' he asserts,

> are not to be influenced by reason; for it is of the very essence of crime to disregard consequences both to ourselves and others. You may as well preach philosophy to a drunken man, or to the dead, as to those who are under the instigation of any mischievous passion. A man is a drunkard, and you tell him he ought to be sober; he is debauched, and you ask him to reform; ... None of this reasoning reaches the mark it aims at. The culprit, who violates and suffers the vengeance of the laws, is not the dupe of ignorance, but the slave of passion, the victim of habit or necessity.

The charm of the life of the criminal, like that of the savage or the drunkard, 'consists in liberty, in hardship, in danger, in the contempt of death, in one word, in extraordinary excitement'. Liberty and excitement cannot be reasoned away by prudence and utility.[58] Drunkenness, like crime, is an act of liberty. Anticipating Poe's 'Imp of the Perverse' and Dostoyevsky's 'underground man', Hazlitt's drunkard or criminal defies the orderly civilization that is forced upon him and insists on his right to destroy himself as an act of free will. Gusto throws itself into life and danger; so Hazlitt, as we saw in Chapter 2, defended the 'mad, hairbrained, roaring mirth and convivial indulgence' of Burns against the prudent, dry and calculating Wordsworth; for Burns, like Coleridge and Hazlitt himself, knew that 'a man of genius is not a machine; that they live in a state of intellectual intoxication, and that it is too much to expect them to be distinguished by peculiar *sang froid*, circumspection, and sobriety.'[59]

Hazlitt's sympathy with drunkards contrasts with his personal choices. In a curious biographical contrast to the situation described in the essays on Bentham and Burns, Hazlitt himself chooses an opposite act of liberty by suddenly ceasing to be a drunkard in 1815. Stanley Jones describes him as a dishevelled, brooding, sullen alcoholic for 15 years. In 1815, despairing at the general loss of liberty with the defeat of Napoleon, 'he sank for a time into neglect, into self-abandonment, and the oblivion of drunkenness.' After Waterloo, writes Benjamin Haydon, 'he seemed prostrated in mind and body, he walked about unwashed, unshaved, hardly sober by day, and always intoxicated by night, literally, without exaggeration, for weeks; until at length wakening as it were from his stupor, he at once left off all stimulating liquors, and never touched them after.' Jones believes that Hazlitt did occasionally drink wine after this conversion, but never again harmed himself with it or presumed to preach temperance to others,[60] adhering to his principles of liberty.

But Hazlitt's power of will is unusual, and certainly not a possibility for Coleridge or for many other people on different social levels. Coleridge's preoccupation with the divided will leads him to formulate at the root of drunkenness and drug addiction a new illness: 'ideocy of will'. He shares this illness with his son Hartley and with drinkers throughout London, where chimney sweepers might steal his papers for gin: 'Half a dozen of the Books – the MSS by preference as being the heavier paper – would be off in the Soot bags to a certainty, and sold for waste paper – . Whole volumes of fervid *Mind* for glasses of ardent *Spirit*, *Worlds*, I might say of solid Intellect for mere Shooting-stars of fluid Fire! – Rainwater, and Flashes of Lightning, reconciled in Blue Ruin!'[61]

Observing this addiction and its omnivorous, morality-destroying needs, Coleridge a year before his death becomes an early believer in the new and controversial Temperance Movement. In a letter of 7 April 1833 he begs to disagree with his friend Joseph Green, who had sent away from his door a Temperance Society Man. Coleridge himself 'would have leapt forwards with content, like a key to a loadstone'. First, he argues that reasoning will not change 'the habitual Dram Drinker respecting the unutterable evil and misery of his thraldom'. Second, a new charitable institution, 'under Authority of a Legislative Act – namely, a Maison de Sante ... for Lunacy & Ideocy of the *Will*' might actually help if the patient consented to enter. In proposing such an early voluntary drying-out facility, such as our contemporary Smithers Institute, Coleridge argues,

> I am convinced, that London would furnish a hundred Volunteers in as many days from the Gin-Shops – who would swallow their glass of poison in order to get courage to present themselves to the Hospital in question – And a similar Institution might exist for a higher class of Will-Maniacs or Impotents.

He would himself be a prime candidate: 'Had such a House of Health been in existence, I know who would have entered himself as a Patient some five & 20 years ago.' He believes in addition that the new Temperance Society should be connected with the Christian churches of all denominations so that 'persons still capable of self-cure' can 'deriv[e] strength from *religion*', foreseeing the trust in a higher power and the sense of supporting community at the heart of the Alcoholics Anonymous programme.[62]

Thus Coleridge's personal highs and lows in drinking, aggravated by increasing doses of opium; his social and political observations of drinking beyond his own perimeters; his understanding of the dividedness of the mind and of the borderline between human behaviour and animal instinct; and his moral and psychological conclusions about the fragility of human nature when beset by the dualities of the drinking experience, place him in the company of Burns, the doctors and philanthropists of Chapter 1, and of Lamb in a long line of English drunkards and commentators on drunkenness.

V. Dionysian Imaginings

For Coleridge, however, the literary and artistic legacy of drink was another vibrant reality. He knew the Dionysian traditions of Greece, Rome, and Renaissance Florence; he planned to contribute narrative poems to the Dionysian tradition; he was himself a 'Bacchus, ever sleek and young', and a whirling poet who had drunk the milk of paradise. He knew both risk and rapture.

The god that drives people to a 'lust for intenser life' and simultaneously goads them from behind to destroy themselves is a powerful creative force. In an 1812 lecture on the origin of drama, Coleridge criticizes Dryden in 'Alexander's Feast' for trivializing Bacchus as a mere drinking god. He quotes,

> Bacchus, ever fair and young,
> Drinking joys did first ordain;
> Bacchus' blessings are a treasure,
> Drinking is the soldier's pleasure,

but omits the ambiguous lines that follow,

> Rich the Treasure, Sweet the Pleasure;
> Sweet is Pleasure after Pain.

Coleridge says that Dryden has made his Timotheus forget 'the God & substituted a commonplace panegyric on the Joys of drinking.' For Coleridge saw this multifaceted god as a complex figure: a hero who conquered India; a son of Jove, and thus a step-brother of Alexander, who also conquered India; more than this, 'with the ancients Bacchus, or Dionysus, was among the most aweful & mysterious Deities.' His worship operated on several levels: on the 'earthly' level, as the 'civilizer of India'; on the 'narrower and popular' level, as the 'Symbol' 'of festivity'; and, on the level of the mysteries, as 'representative of the [organic] energies of the Universe, that work by passion and Joy without apparent distinct consciousness – and rather as the cause or condition of skill and contrivance, than the result.' On this third and highest level Bacchus or Dionysus is at one and the same time a force in the universe and the upswelling of this force in the inspired artist. Genius in art, as in heroism, appears as 'something innate, and divine', that cannot be acquired by 'skill or contrivance', or even by 'art or discipline'. Instead, it appears as 'a felicity above and beyond Prudence'. In the universe at large and in the individual artist Dionysus works by 'passion and joy without apparent distinct consciousness' and also expresses himself as a god in 'all the vehement and awful passions'.[63]

Criticizing George Stanley Faber's *Mysteries of the Cabiri*, Coleridge shows his knowledge of the distinctive cries of the ancient Greek Bacchante. 'To shout Evoe', he notes, is 'the Bacchanal Hallelujah – and that the Greek Hexameter is – I invoke Dionysus, the thundering *Hurraer* – or Evoer/ the *valdisonant*

Shouter of Evoe.'[64] He underlines his own invented words: in chuckling about Chapman's Homer, he cites a 'quaint epithet' 'quaffed divine *Joy-in-the-heart-of-man-infusing Wine* ... one word, because one sweet mellifluous Word expresses it in Homer.'[65] Dionysus contains surprising inspirations, gifts of genius, moments of enthusiasm, outbursts of joy. The god is one image for the unplanned eruptions of imagination that the calculations of fancy and understanding cannot catch.

John Beer has shown that the Dionysian images merge for Coleridge with solar myths, fertility myths, myths of Isis and Osiris, and even the horned Moses of the Church of San Pietro in Vinculis in Rome.[66] In addition, Coleridge's knowledge of the mysteries comes from Plato, Plotinus, Ficino, Pico della Mirandola, Paracelsus, Boehme, Faber and Nonnus, and also from Schlegel, who likewise studied these arcane sources, often preceding Coleridge in applying their meanings to art. The Dionysian material in the Neoplatonists was readily available in Thomas Taylor's 'Dissertation on the Eleusinian and Bacchic Mysteries' (1792), which had been among Coleridge's 'darling studies' as a brilliant youth at Christ's Hospital,[67] and his love of Pico Della Mirandola had been intense enough to earn him Lamb's epithet of the 'young Mirandula'. He was thus steeped in the rapturous vocabulary of Greek and Renaissance Dionysianism from an early age. Plato's *Phaedrus* provided the topos that the blessings of madness come from the gods, and specifically those of mystics from Dionysus.[68] Pico's *Oration on the Dignity of Man* transforms Bacchus into the leader of the Muses, claims that all people wish to become the drinking companions of the gods, and extols the nectar of the gods and divine drunkenness.[69] When Thomas Taylor draws from Vergil, Olympiodorus, Plotinus, Proclus, Apuleius, Porphyry, Eusebius, Ficino and others to support his preface to the 'Hymns of Orpheus' and his 'Dissertation on the Eleusinian and Bacchic Mysteries', he extends the arena of Bacchus into multiple forms, notwithstanding his own opposition to alcohol. For Taylor, the god inspires the muses; he is nourisher, occultist, sun, blood, time, the soul of the world; he is invoked in magical 'Fumigations'; he is associated with his mother's fiery death, and with bulls, rage, violence, the vine, pleasure and fruitfulness. In the legend of his being ripped apart and boiled by the Titans, Bacchus is an image of the human soul's fall into the body and escape. As an ambiguous god he faces toward life and toward death:

Dionysus is the inspective guardian of generation, because he presides over life and death; for he is the guardian of life because of generation, but of death because wine produces an enthusiastic energy: and we become more enthusiastic at this period of dissolution.[70]

Wise as he is in this passage, Thomas Taylor expunges references to actual wine in his dissertation, and favours an ascetic spiritual drunkenness over the dissipations of real drunkenness in the fallen body. Taylor's temperance bias is confirmed in his 'Apology for those parts in the poetry of Homer, which appear in all various ways to excite the hearers to a contempt of temperance.'[71] Despite this bias, and what Coleridge judged an awkwardness of translation, Thomas Taylor was a rich mine of Bacchic rhetoric, which helped to release Romantic interest in Dionysianism, not only for the precocious Coleridge, but for Keats as well.

Indeed, Coleridge's interest in rapturous divine drunkenness led to numerous poetic plans. He had early wondered if God was an eating, drinking and fornicating god, seeming thus to yearn for a more animated and syncretic deity than the ascetic one he inherited. He plans an essay on drinking and an ode to meat and drink.[72] He notes another plan for 'The Conquest of India by Bacchus in Hexameters',[73] a poem that seems to anticipate the outline of Keats's *Endymion*, though Coleridge decides at the end of his life that it would be 'a subject of no profundity', a poem brilliant, but only of the 'fancy and the understanding'.[74]

In his plans for narrative poems Coleridge will glorify Dionysus' creative power, but also include his flaying alive of the imperfect acolytes, reconciling opposites, or at least acknowledging contrary states. Two plans, one of 1806 and one of 1808, may be versions of a single plan. The first appears elliptically: 'In the *S. of A.* [Soother of Absence] to describe Sotting allegorically, losing the way to the temple of Bacchus, come to the Cave of the Gnome, &c &c.'[75] If the protagonist of this allegorical journey is 'Sotting' personified, this plan may have been shrewdly abandoned. But it seems to be the nugget of the longer plan noted in February 1808, first discovered by John Beer. Together these two plans form a Spenserian testing of the self, seeking the temple of Bacchus, but veering from pleasurable freedom to enter a debased state, the domain of the Gnome. In the second plan, the self has expanded to include the history of human civilization:

Man in the Savage State as a water-drinker or rather Man before the Fall possessed of the Heavenly Bacchus (See Boehmen's Sophia or celestial Bride) his fall – forsaken by the [Dionysus] the savage state – and dreadful consequences of the interspersed vacancies left in his mind by the absence of Dionysus – the bastard Bacchus comes to his relief or rather the Gemini, the one *Oivas* permitted by the Dionysus – the other a *Gnome* – this pursued, in the mixt effects of the god [e.g., among the Aztecs] ... A most delightful Poem may be made of it.[76]

In her annotations to this mysterious notebook entry, Kathleen Coburn sees the potential poem as a revision of Adam's Fall. She writes, 'Before the Fall, man had Wisdom, the heavenly wine, but being forsaken by Dionysus at the Fall, he becomes a water-drinker, deprived of the inspiriting heavenly bacchic Wisdom.' Cultures that subsequently deny 'the divine wine of Dionysus', such as the Aztecs or the Turks, are 'savage', violent and prohibitive, relying on the court of excise rather than the court of conscience, as Coleridge noted of Islam. Coburn sees the poem unfolding in three stages: Adam in paradise, drinking divine and spiritual wine; savage man, drinking only water or human blood; and man struggling towards civilization, seeking inspiration or relief, drinking wine in the search for the temple, but sometimes straying into despair, the twin directions that man's fallen choice can make. The 'Heavenly Bacchus' brings spiritual wine or wisdom; the 'Bastard Bacchus' brings actual wine, which in turn has two outcomes, unconscious, creative vivacity on the one hand, and on the other, the Gnome, a figure derived from Paracelsus and made popular by the Rosicrucians,[77] who seems to have allegorical significance here as a shrunken, debased, hard and material form of mind,[78] one way in which drinking manifests itself.

The Bastard Bacchus and the Cave of the Gnome return the myth of Dionysus to the cruel reality of drunkenness in the divided and diminished beings that Coleridge fears. He writes with wisdom in an early essay, 'The whole faculties of man must be exerted in order to [en]noble energies; and he who is not in earnest, self-mutilated, self-paralysed, lives in but half his being.'[79] The two Bacchuses appear in the dialogue of the twentieth-century poem by Dudley Randall, 'Hail, Dionysus', that serves as the epigraph to this chapter: one voice sees the 'frenzy and release', the 'trance and visions'; the other sees the vomit, the stumbling, the stuttering, the all but bestial incontinence. The two aspects of Dionysus, Heavenly and Bastard, compressed in Coleridge's plan, suggest that the narrative poem might have been an amalgamation of 'Kubla Khan' and 'The Pains of Sleep', one segment rapturously spinning outward, then in the next reversing the spin and swirling inward to vacancy, absence, emptiness, and the cave of the Gnome.

How does the acolyte determine the path he will take? Why do some seekers lose themselves on the way to the heavenly Bacchus and stumble into the cave of the Gnome? Questions of how much and when to stimulate pleasure arise here and show that Coleridge, with Wordsworth, is troubled by the fine line between acceptable and unacceptable stimuli, by naturally flowing, or artificially induced, pleasures. Clearly the two men part company early on. Wordsworth struggles to purify Coleridge, both directly and through his substitute figures such as Montagu, Lamb and Burns, to keep him from actively seeking rather than passively receiving pleasure. Meanwhile, Coleridge slips away to reach the Heavenly Bacchus as best he can, even if it means erring into the cave of the Gnome in pursuit of what Wordsworth would call 'gross stimulants' and crying out, like the mad poet Collins, at his divided being. On one level, the divergence between Wordsworth and Coleridge, which can be seen beginning at the very start of their collaboration, is a disagreement about pleasure and prudence, about stimulants of pleasure and denial of them, about preserving oneself and throwing oneself away. The Heavenly Bacchus is the realm of pleasure, of the intellectual, spiritual, energetic pleasure that Coleridge sometimes describes as intoxicating. This is the pleasure that poetry aims for, that Coleridge seeks in heightened moments. Sometimes a breeze will be stimulating enough to arouse it; other times 'a stifled, drowsy, unimpassioned grief' greets the 'peculiar tint of yellow green'. When anxieties and losses weigh it down, even a tempest does not always work to rouse the spirit. The gleam may be gone.[80] The poet can acquiesce in the loss and find mild consolations or can turn to rousing substances that briefly stir the imagination, even if this remedy compromises self or soul.

These are moral, philosophical and temperamental differences. When Hazlitt in his essay on Burns calls Wordsworth a 'Puritan genius', he aligns the prudent against the wild; he recreates a Restoration division of puritans and cavaliers, ants and grasshoppers, those who prudently save and watch and those who drink and sing and take no heed for the morrow. But interpersonal struggles for power also influence the alignment: when his own joy withers, Wordsworth needs to check Coleridge's search for 'passion and joy', for 'a felicity above and beyond Prudence', as a fatal example, and for his own good. And Coleridge needs to throw himself away to show that he is not a thing to be used, that he is free.

5

In the Cave of the Gnome: Hartley Coleridge

The whiskey on your breath
Could make a small boy dizzy;
But I held on like death:
Such waltzing was not easy.
　　　　　　– Theodore Roethke, 'My Papa's Waltz' (1948)

We defy augury.

　　　　　　　　　　　　　　　　– *Hamlet* V, 2, 230

Coleridge's older son David Hartley Coleridge (1796–1849) was a model for how a child becomes a whole person or fails to become one. Born while Coleridge was in the full flush of his interest in Hartleyan associationism, the boy contributes by his own recalcitrance to the overthrow of this philosophy. While Coleridge learned that a good environment does not necessarily turn a child into a stable adult, he did not notice until it was too late that many of his own actions and the atmosphere that those actions created did in fact influence the boy's later failure, and that even more influential in forming his son's nature were the words he uttered about him. The insight of the poet and the foresight of the prophet conspired to predict the boy's future failure, even while the boy, hearing the words, fatalistically watched the failure approaching.

Coleridge's beloved first-born son was an alcoholic of the most abject kind, insisting on his own insignificance, submerging his much praised genius in imitating his elders, wandering drunk around the Lake District for days on end, homeless except for the kindness of strangers. Since the previous chapter established that along with being an opium addict Coleridge senior was also cross-addicted to alcohol, the question of the alcoholic father's influence on this alcoholic son must arise. Recent work on family history, on parent-child psychology, and on the peculiar qualities of the adult child of an alcoholic come to bear on biography and art. This inter-disciplinary material suggests that Hartley Coleridge can be seen as an early 'child of an alcoholic', whose desperation to woo his alcoholic father and keep him near through his own dependency produced the insecurity, low self-esteem, role-playing, irrational loyalty, irresponsibility, self-loathing, and passive susceptibility to the words of others that have recently been shown to characterize such victims.[1] In addition to the sorrow caused by his father's many long absences and outbursts of anger, Hartley's subservience to a prearranged plan for his life, which psychologists call 'a script', is a noteworthy aspect of his alcoholism.[2]

The always complicated relationship of fathers and sons is additionally complicated by the inherited propensity to addiction and by family stresses of housing and hiding an addict, especially an addict who is supposed to play a parental role. The Coleridge father-and-son bond was especially intense because the father began by taking his role seriously, using his fatherhood as an opportunity to experiment with his changing theories of mind. He loved the boy but at the same time recognized in him elements of himself that he disliked. From the boy's point of view the father was glorious, even though he abandoned him at age eight (the age at which Coleridge himself had been abandoned). This chapter's epigraph from Theodore Roethke's 1948 memory of waltzing with his own drunken father, written from the perspective of the child but with adult knowledge of his own alcoholism, recreates the devotion, fear and attraction the son feels for the wild, brilliant father, who hurts him with his belt buckle but also brings a drunken, whirling joy and force into the dour kitchen controlled by the sober and disapproving mother. Some of the interplay of the Roethke family in this poem can be glimpsed in the Coleridge family of Samuel, Sarah and Hartley, who idolized his father but was often hurt by him, knew that his mother and her allies disapproved of his father, yet clung to him loyally. This chapter examines the power of an alcoholic and opium-addicted father to harm his son by example, rage, and, most decisively, prophecy, and to do so 'unawares'.

As a 22-year-old new father, Coleridge adhered to advanced principles of child-rearing and the new ideal of the middle-class companionate marriage as a matrix for humanizing offspring,[3] but he was not always able to act on these principles. On the one hand he advocated Rousseau's plan for the child's freedom; on the other he wished to mould and determine. He believed in 'educing' knowledge rather than inculcating it and fought against any kind of corporal punishment in schools; and yet his verbal punishments were so powerful that his child never forgot their formulations. As a testament to his belief in the power of early impressions, his 1825 *Opus Maximum* pioneered the study of mother–child bonding as essential for the growth of personal identity,[4] and yet he rarely mentioned his wife's role in the upbringing of his first-born son, and in his early plans for Pantisocracy feared that mothers might import petty-bourgeois values of materialism and superstition. Not stuffed with extraneous information by autocratic fathers as were William Pitt the younger, Wolfgang Mozart, the later John Stuart Mill, or other earlier eighteenth-century 'prodigies' mocked by Wordsworth, the new free child would prove that nature never did betray the heart that loved her, that natural impulses guided the malleable infant mind, and that beautiful external impressions formed beautiful minds,[5] and yet this particular child was sad and bounded.

Shaped by the fascination with child development seeded by eighteenth-century philosophers of mind and by the concurrent glorification of the nuclear family, with the first glimmerings of the ideal of the participatory father,[6] David Hartley Coleridge was a prime experiment, often indeed described as an experiment, scrutinized by poets and philosophers at each stage of his development. The childless Charles Lamb writes to Coleridge that David Hartley is 'your little reality', implying that here was the true test of associationist theories of personal development that might eventually prove their overthrow.[7] The little boy's wise words are passed by letter among the Pantisocrats, the Wordsworths, and Thomas Poole, as the subject of wonder. When he looks in a glass and 'struggles to express himself concerning the Difference between the Thing & the Image' or when he piles stones together as 'symbols of the imagination',[8] letters about his brilliance race around England. Expectations for his future as the 'small', 'minute', 'best philosopher' were unrealistically high and loudly proclaimed,[9] difficult to fulfil. Although words, theories and reports predominate, much evidence also exists that Coleridge loved his infant, played with him, touched him and laughed with him. He tells Thelwall, the baby 'makes us weep for very fondness'. He tells Josiah Wade, 'David H. is a very Seraph in Clouts – and laughs, till he makes us cry for very overflowing joy & tenderness.'[10] The boy will remember this joyful love during the father's many long absences, which may have seemed to him to be his own fault. At forty he still longs to 'dive to find my infant self / In the unfathomed ocean of the past; / I can but find a sun-burnt prattling elf,/ A forward urchin of four years at least.'[11]

Even before Coleridge the father set eyes on his prematurely delivered infant, he began to imagine and create him in words. Coleridge's script-writing on the basis of his adult insight and foresight begins with the three sonnets he wrote at his first son's birth. Curiously, he did not commemorate the births of his other three children. In 'Sonnet: On Receiving a Letter Informing me of the Birth of a Son', he frankly and immediately records his own inappropriate feelings: 'When they did greet me father, sudden awe / Weigh'd down my spirit.' Coleridge 'inly felt / No heavenly visitation upwards draw / My feeble mind, nor cheering ray impart'. Unable to pray, feeling a confused mixture of gloom, foreboding, enclosure, and suffocation, he confesses:

> Ah me! before the Eternal Sire I brought
> Th' unquiet silence of confused thought
> And shapeless feelings: my o'erwhelmed heart
> Trembled, and vacant tears stream'd down my face.

He is disappointed by his own failure to feel the rapture and 'engrossment'[12] that he expected to feel when he learns of his son's birth. Indeed, he 'groan[s]' to God 'for future grace',

> That ere my babe youth's perilous maze have trod,
> Thy overshadowing Spirit may descend,
> And he be born again, a child of God.

The ambiguous syntax of this prayer suggests that he wishes that the baby should be taken up to heaven by God before reaching 'the perilous maze' of youth, and be born again, this time not as a mortal child, but as a 'child of God'. The father's 'confused thought', 'shapeless feelings', 'vacant tears', and ambiguously phrased wishes reflect his own fear of inadequacy as a parent but also hint that he fears that the child may be unable to negotiate youth's perilous maze and would do better dying young. Since he has not yet seen the baby, and is only recording his own experience on hearing of the birth, this foreboding of failure is prescriptive rather than descriptive.[13]

The second sonnet, now quickly written as he heads home from Birmingham to see his baby, intensifies the theme of the infant's early death. In this sonnet the ambiguities of wishing, fearing, fore-seeing, dreading and hoping are even more intertwined in the syntax than in sonnet one. He tries to arrange the 'strange fanc[ies]' of past and present that 'roll' through his feelings and 'perplex the soul' with shadowy dreams of pre-existence and reincarnation.[14] He toys with the Platonic notion that souls lived before they took on 'this robe of flesh'. These fancies are concentrated in the last eight lines of the sonnet on the particular premonition the father has of his new baby's death and return to the pre-existing heaven he came from:

> O my sweet baby! when I reach my door,
> If heavy looks should tell me thou art dead,
> (As sometimes through excess of hope, I fear)
> I think that I should struggle to believe
>   Thou wert a spirit to this nether sphere
>   Sentenc'd for some more venial crime to grieve;
> Dids't scream, then spring to meet Heaven's quick reprieve,
>   While we wept idly o'er thy little bier!

As he anticipates the child's death, he reveals in his tortuous par-enthetical aside that in some depth of his consciousness he might even hope for it. He imagines that the infant has committed a crime in a previous life and is sentenced to this bodily existence to pay for it. The child screams at the horror of fleshly life and is pardoned, allowed to return to heaven. He leaves behind him his abandoned corpse – the tiny corporeal remains of a briefly incarcerated and now released spirit – , his bier and his grieving parents. Although in a time of high infant mortality it is not unusual to prepare oneself for a child's death, Coleridge's close analysis of his complex feelings permits him to elaborate this death in detail, experiencing the birth proleptically as a funeral. Clearly, this sonnet has a power-ful influence on Wordsworth's 'Ode: On Intimations of Immortality from Recollections of Early Childhood', particularly on its stanza five on the pre-existent life of the infant soul, coming from else-where and returning thence. The sonnet also influences Hartley Coleridge's many poems on dead babies, with whom he identifies, and his own frequently stated wish that he had died as a baby and spared his parents the shame and failure of the maze of his life. At his father's death he writes to his mother that he grieves 'it was not I; . . that my beloved parents did not close my eyes; that my death should have been the only sorrow I had ever caused them; that when they talked of me, they might weep tears of tender joy, thinking of what I might have been, and no painful thought of what I had been.'[15] He thinks back to this newborn moment recorded by his father when he could have died, and should have.

Overwhelmed by the many confused and perplexed feelings he has written down on the way home, Coleridge now confronts his infant in the flesh, and records his feelings yet again in a third sonnet subtitled 'To a Friend Who Asked, How I Felt When the Nurse First Presented My Infant to Me'. He exclaims to Charles Lloyd that as he looks at his newborn infant son 'my slow heart was only sad, when first / I scann'd that face of feeble infancy'. Having thought on his ride of death, punishment, and reincarnation, he finds the actual face 'feeble'. To this first impression he adds his own sense of his past self, 'For dimly on my thoughtful spirit burst / All I had been, and all my child might be!', memories and forecasts which also oppress. But now, as he watches the intimacy between mother and child, he begins to feel: love grows from seeing the mother's love and the child's need. These sights briefly 'beguil'd' the 'dark remembrance and presageful fear' that looked backward to his own memories of childhood, whatever they might have been (forgotten in the mist of many deaths and rejections[16]), and forward to what he imagines he foresees in the child's future. This 'presageful fear' will dominate many subsequent references to the future of this particular boy, either because all life is precarious, or because some quality in this boy struck observers as fragile.

As the first Romantic father, Coleridge broadcasts his emotions about this new elemental experience in these three sonnets (the second two were repeatedly published), in the conversation poems, and in letters to friends, which also record his feelings of 'annihilation' before this birth. Because of this publicity Hartley must surely have seen these forecasts when he learned to read, and could not have looked happily on these gloomy prophecies of his future: an early death; a previous crime and resulting guilt and punishment; a future that rouses 'presageful fear'. Like the child, the father, too, is an experiment. He was not feeling the way he was supposed to feel (though no manual of fathering existed to guide him), and seems to be trying to justify this vacancy or absence in himself by something in the child's face of 'feeble infancy'. Projecting his own inadequacies onto the newborn, he deeply compromises the freedom of the experiment by providing in advance a vocabulary for failure.

From the beginning the infant lived in and through the father's words of praise and criticism. The formative power of the father's theories is made more powerful by the unpredictable enthusiasms and rages of an alcoholic parent, exacerbated by long absences during vulnerable years (1799–1801; 1804–6; and sporadically thereafter) that further bewildered and unsettled the child.[17] Thus rational plans were undercut by personal insecurities and arrogance. The new 'nuclear family' already contained the germs of the 'dysfunctional family', for heredity and environment – Coleridge's own 'disease or a weakness – the penalty in yourself of sin or want of caution'[18] and the environment that he created because of his own sorrows, disappointments and addictions – could not be reasoned away.[19] Theory did not do away with the old Adam.

The early plans for the child's freedom can be seen to be riddled with contradictions in two well-known conversation poems of 1798, when the baby was a year and a half. In 'The Nightingale' Coleridge pronounces his plans 'To make [the baby] Nature's playmate', promising thus to *make* him what he himself was not. Seeming to criticize the 16-month-old baby's own efforts to express himself –

> My dear babe,
> Who, capable of no articulate sound,
> Mars all things with his imitative lisp,

– and finding his 'sobs' inexplicable, since according to associationist theory 'an infant's dream' could have no source except an exterior one, he hurries the baby outside to be soothed by the moon. He 'hushed at once' in the moonlight and 'laughs most silently'. The father silences his child's autonomous outbursts and decides what his impressions will mean: 'his childhood shall grow up / Familiar with these songs, that with the night / He may associate joy.'

In 'Frost at Midnight', written the same year, the father explicitly plans his son's life in contrast to his own urban upbringing, describing it in a future tense which is part command and part prophetic anticipation:

> But *thou*, my babe! shalt wander like a breeze
> By lakes and sandy shores, beneath the crags

Of ancient mountain, and beneath the clouds,
Which image in their bulk both lakes and shores
And mountain crags, so shalt thou see and hear
The lovely shapes and sounds intelligible
Of that eternal language, which thy God
Utters, who from eternity doth teach
Himself in all, and all things in himself.
Great universal Teacher! he shall mould
Thy spirit, and by giving make it ask.

This prediction of the wild wanderings of the free child of nature gives details of a future adulthood lived out of doors and communing directly with a god of nature, but it is an adulthood distinctly deprived of human companionship. Like Frankenstein's creature, this baby will grow up to roam about the crags; indeed, later observers recall seeing Hartley as a young man flitting along the hills with his arms outstretched, oblivious that guests had arrived.[20] His spirit will be *moulded* by a great universal teacher who speaks the words of his own father.

While these stirring poems to his baby reveal Coleridge's passionate commitment to a revolutionary method of child-rearing, and his attention to the baby whose little finger is raised to the moon, they also hint at a sinister aspect of the philosophy itself and of the father's own personal desire to determine his son's character.

Later references to these poems acknowledge their power to mould and direct the future. Glossing a reference to these lines borrowed in one of his own poems, the adult Hartley tries to minimize the power of these words: 'As far as regards the *habitats* of my childhood, these lines, written at Nether Stowey, were almost prophetic. But poets are not prophets.'[21] Derwent (Coleridge's second son, later a clergyman and editor of Hartley's works) sees them as the words of a prophet: 'Whether these lines be taken as expressing a purpose or a hope, the prediction which they contain was fulfilled in a manner and to an extent which could not at the time have been anticipated.'[22] Coleridge himself learns the hard way that the poem was 'a prophecy – written by me,' and 'fulfilled'.[23]

Coleridge maintained his faith in Rousseau's unstructured ideal of child-rearing after his overthrow in 1801 of other aspects of eighteenth-century theories of the mind's passive formation. In a marginal note from 1803 he laments having to impose Christian superstitions on a 'child of free Nature':

> My sweet Hartley! ... – To day thou art to be christened, being
> more than 7 years of age, o with what reluctance & *distaste* have I
> permitted this silly [crossed out] unchristian, & in its spirit &
> consequences anti-christian, Foolery to be performed upon *thee*,
> Child of free Nature. On thy Brother Derwent, & thy sister Sara,
> somewhat; but chiefly on thee.[24]

Christening, ceremonially naming a child by sprinkling water on
him to wash away his supposed sin, is 'Foolery' for Coleridge
because it assumes that the innocent child has sinned, and because
it has a magical element that names, fixes and thereby limits the
child's possibilities. It might stunt the spontaneity of Hartley's development, turning him from his own open-ended choice of life by
forcing him to adhere to an alien script. Such freedom mattered
more for him as a genius than for his less brilliant siblings, as they
had already (aged three years and three months) been designated.

   If Coleridge were true to this principle, however, the very name
he gave his infant might itself be considered silly, anti-Christian
Foolery. It is a name beset by internal inconsistencies. The
'Christian' name David, the Biblical singer and active leader, was
dropped very early, and the middle name, a synecdoche for the
associationist philosophy that governed the experimental upbringing but was disproved by this very boy's dreams and oddness, pre-
vailed. In letters to Tom Poole and Benjamin Flower at the time of
the boy's birth, Coleridge hopes that 'ere he be a man... his head
will be convinced of, & his heart saturated with, the truths so ably
supported by that great master of Christian Philosophy.'[25]
Coleridge's claim that David Hartley was a Christian philosopher
glosses over a startling disjunction at the heart of this philosopher's
work; for Volume 2 of *The Observations on Man* reverses the
assumptions of Volume 1. Volume 1 ends with the sudden realization that the principles of associationism leave no place for the free
will required for Christian faith, that materialism 'is unfavourable
to the Immateriality of the Soul; and by consequence, to its
Immortality.' Volume 2 corrects this profound loss of personal
autonomy by giving ten arguments for the immortality of the soul.
In Chapter 7 of the *Biographia Literaria* Coleridge explains that he
rejected the associationism of Hartley's Volume 1 because it leaves
no room for free agency; he realized that a theory of externally
imposed impressions, 'mere articulated motions of the air', dis-
counted the creative power of the self.[26] While the realization that

external impressions do not entirely shape the person was gradual, it occurred in his first son's early childhood. For the boy's 'nature' belied the theory denoted by his name.

Hartley, the boy, thus bears through life the name of a discarded philosophy that his own being helped to undermine, of a philosophy that was itself split into contradictory halves in its two volumes. When Lamb writes Coleridge to 'give little *David Hartley* – God bless its little heart – *a Kiss for me* – bring him up to know the meaning of his Christian name, & what that name (imposed upon him) will demand of him', he points to the parental imposition of an allegorical burden.[27] Nor was Coleridge indifferent to the prophetic and formative power of names; in a sonnet of 1797 on the christening of his friend Anna Cruikshank's eponymous daughter, he calls the name 'a potent spell', and urges the baby to 'deserve thy name!'

The naming of David Hartley Coleridge is a confusing hodge-podge of different feelings and philosophies, theories of freedom strangely mixed with theories of fatality. The last name, the patronymic, further confuses the language surrounding the child's inner being. For 'Coleridge' has its own significances; it is a sound always fascinating to the father, because its sliding syllables, stresses, elisions and diphthongs seemed to him to express the weaknesses of his character and the indecision of his face.[28] (Hartley late in his life can mock the uncertain vowels of 'My Surname Collridge.'[29]) Hartley the boy may have within him already at birth aspects of the 'Coleridge' nature. As Anna Cruikshank resembles her mother Anna – 'the rude green bud / Alike in Shape, place, name, / Had bloom'd where bloom'd its parent stud, / Another and the same!'[30] – so between Coleridge and his son there is a 'fond deceit' in sameness. Coleridge early notes that the babe is the very miniature of me; later he says 'his talka-tiveness is mine'; later yet Dorothy Wordsworth tells Lady Beaumont that Hartley resembles his father particularly in 'the weak points of his character',[31] such as procrastination, fear of pain, indolence, hypochondria. She does not mention a tendency to addiction. This very resemblance will be a source of anger and frustration on both sides.

But it is the power rather than the weakness of the Coleridge name that haunts the son in many self-abasing poems. If people pay any attention to his words, it is because of the glow of his great father's name:

Full well I know – my Friends – ye look on me
A living spectre of my Father dead –
Had I not borne his name, had I not fed
On him, as one leaf trembling on a tree,
A woeful waste had been my minstrelsy –

(*New Poems*, p. 69)

Even more cravenly, he sighs,

Because I bear my Father's name
I am not quite despised,
My little legacy of fame
I've not yet realized.

And yet if you should praise myself
I'll tell you, I had rather
You'd give your love to me, poor elf,
Your praise to my great father.

(*New Poems*, p. 93)

In his father's shadow he perceives himself as a spectre, a parasitical mistletoe or ivy (an image derived from 'Christabel'), a might-have-been, and, often, since he was not five feet tall, an elf, small, half-human, marginal. The famous name, when applied to himself, is 'too oft pronounced / With sighs, despondent sorrow, and reproach'.[32]

The contradiction at the heart of 'making' a 'free child of nature' and of naming and thus fixing him turns on the problem of guidance or criticism. Disregarding his own formative words in 'The Nightingale' and 'Frost at Midnight', Coleridge is aware of the dangers of intervention as it might skew the experiment. He counsels in opposition to the philosopher David Hartley, who is already shown to be violating his own principles, 'an *urgent* Dissuasive from teaching Virtue to Children by Inducements or Examples', for Coleridge assumes that virtue will arise naturally with human feelings and that 'inducements' belie the freedom of the original theory.[33] Advice, guidance, rewards, and moral stories impose an alien adult experience on the child's inchoate, susceptible and still radiant consciousness.

Coleridge knows that these adult scripts cut off future options. Writing in 1805 when his son was nine, Coleridge disapproves of Maria Edgeworth's moral tales and 'all similar attempts to cure faults by *detailed* Forewarnings – which leave on the similarly faulty an impression of *Fatality*, that extinguishes *Hope*.'[34] Coleridge's understanding of the dangers of prophecies anticipates the work of the contemporary psychologist Claude Steiner describing the power of parental injunctions on alcoholics. Steiner writes, 'the Injunction, or in fairy-tale language, "the curse," is always a prohibition, or an inhibition of the free behavior of the child. It is always the negation of an activity. The injunction reflects the fears, wishes, anger, and desires of the Child in the parent.'[35] Coleridge's warning against 'Forewarnings' becomes a fateful example of the maxim, 'Do as I say, not as I do.'

Even a child of nature might develop imperfectly, however; he or she might be lazy, wilful, weak-willed, or forgetful, despite the breezes and the vistas. Hartley Coleridge was all of these. Along with being oddly brilliant, excellent in Greek, an informed and voluble talker, and a fluent if rambling writer, he fails in uncountable ways: he is sad, lonely, strange; as a boy he lives in his fantasy world of Eujuxria; he learns to read late and never learns mathematics; he eats messily; he has 'paroxysms of rage' that anger his father; he has no friends and no capacity for interactive play; he yields easily to slight temptations, 'as if swayed by a mechanical impulse apart from his own volition';[36] after a brief success at Merton College that gains him a probationary fellowship at Oriel College, Oxford, he loses that fellowship in a cataclysmic failure on the charge of 'sottishness'; he continues his intemperance in London, escaping for long periods from Basil Montagu's house where he is being sheltered; he fails as a schoolmaster when the big boys bully him and call him by his first name; he abandons his brother during a dangerous fever to go on a binge; he fails to say goodbye to his mother when she leaves Rydal for good; he is shunned by his father for twelve years; yearning for female companionship, he feels himself too odd to marry and pass on the oddness. As he writes his mother, he is 'bare, barren, and blasted, ill-omened and unsightly'.[37] He watches himself fail, mourning the pain he causes his family, and fails yet again. Sitting over a glass of John Barleycorn whisky at the Red Lion Inn in Grasmere, pitied and cared for by the dalesmen, his many writings maudlin and derivative, he is fascinated by his failure.

Such an outcome might suggest either that the experiment was improperly performed or that the theory behind the experiment was wrong. If the scrupulously scientific parent notices a problem, how is he or she to correct this obliquity before it tilts into full-blown failure or vice, without running the risk of curing faults by detailed forewarnings and thus extinguishing hope or free choice in the child? Should the parent warn, but in warning outline and direct and perhaps cause? Or should the parent watch silently while the seemingly inevitable fate unfolds?

Thus, slowly deviating from the theory, the parent might return to some old notion of an essential self, insusceptible to outside impressions, a 'Nature – for by what other word can I express a quality or character prominent from earliest childhood? the germ of which disclosed itself even in earliest Infancy', as Coleridge learns when his son's sottishness has been revealed.[38] This inborn self will be what it will be, in another kind of fatality, that the father notices ruefully late in life: 'There is in every human countenance either a history or a prophecy, which must sadden, or at least soften, every reflecting observer.'[39]

Coleridge's deliberate effort to avoid scripting his son's life by detailed forewarnings that become self-fulfilling prophecies lies in startling contrast to his actual practice. That his son heard these forewarnings, absorbed them, and allowed them to become the story of his life can be observed in Hartley's poems, letters, essays, marginalia, and in Derwent's Memoirs of his brother, which echo his father's words about him. The words 'prophecy', 'fatality', and 'destiny' appear almost as often as the awed references to his father, the poet and prophet who both created and foreknew: 'a semi-divine "blessed one," *ho makarites*', as Hartley celebrates him.[40] The fatalism that led him to destroy himself because he knew destruction was coming no matter what he did had originally been seeded by his father's words about him, which Wordsworth elaborated and thereby ratified.

Coleridge the father creates the life script for his child, even while he believes that he is merely observing. His observations and worries about a newborn infant make us wonder what prophecies are, what fate is, and how these two terms come to coincide. Coleridge notes in the margins of John Davison, *Discourses on Prophecy* (1825) that the subject of prophecy is 'a Mine, the richest Veins of which still remain to be opened'.[41] Only in myth does the prophetic truth of any utterance mean that God has given the words detailing future events to the prophet, which he then relays as the given truth to the people. Outside the context of myth, it means that either the prophet has discovered some seed of being that he foresees will grow in one direction, or that the prophet names the direction and thus gives a push to the direction of growth. In the second sense he is as much a magician, who calls something into being with words, as a prophet, who foresees what will happen in spite of what he or anyone else does to forestall it. In the first sense the prophet shows insight into 'an essential nature' of the 'agent'; in the second, he provides the vocabulary which determines the fate of the 'agent', crowding out words that might arise to create other options. In either case, the 'agent' is not free.

The power of the dire prophecies in the three sonnets bursts forth full-grown in Wordsworth's poem to this same child, 'To H. C.: Six Years Old' (1802). The vocabulary that Coleridge established in the sonnets now takes the form of precise predictions. This is another poem that provides Hartley as a youth and a man with ways of summarizing his nature and life, a self that he sees as invariably feeble, ephemeral, fragile and impotent. With his mother reinforcing the image by referring to him as 'Poor Fellow' and 'Poor Hartley', he seems to have no power to ward off these alien words imposed by his elders.

Although many readers see 'To H. C.: Six Years Old' as a paean to innocence and imagination, its pessimistic predictions reverberate gloomily when read in conjunction with Coleridge's three precursory sonnets on the same theme. An unhappy note is struck in the first reference to Hartley's words as a 'mock apparel'. This phrase suggests that language is borrowed and derivative for Hartley, that his language is not his own or is not 'natural'. The phrase seems to echo Coleridge's criticism of the boy's language in 'The Nightingale'. The boy's words, discordant or inappropriate in the father's poem, have now become derivative and superficial, perhaps symptomatic of Hartley's later reliance on cadences borrowed from adults. Both poets, first Coleridge, then Wordsworth, suggest that Hartley's use of words is flawed rather than merely tentative.

The worry about the boy begins in earnest at the end of Wordsworth's first verse paragraph, and gathers force through the second. Because of the boy's wildness (a result of the father's theory) Wordsworth thinks of his friend's child 'with many fears/ For what may be thy lot in future years.' This couplet closes the first verse paragraph, but launches the spectres of the future that fill the second verse paragraph with allegorical figures of Pain and Grief, and with images of early death or stunted growth. Pain will be the Lord of his house, Grief will cling to him. But such imaginings are vain, for Nature will either 'end thee quite' or keep him child-like, with 'a young lamb's heart among the full-grown flocks'. 'Ill-fitted to sustain unkindly shocks', the child will evaporate like a dew-drop; 'at the touch of wrong', unable to adapt to stress or to overcome adversity with inward patience and steadiness, the child will 'slip[] in a moment out of life'. Wordsworth predicts weakness in the 'faery voyager' suspended in the air; 'so exquisitely wild', he is not made for this world. In connection with Coleridge's sonnet on the escape of the screaming spirit who leaves behind him his little bier, 'To H. C.: Six Years Old' embellishes the script of an odd and failed life. Wordsworth's 'faery voyager' 'so exquisitely wild' is transmuted from Coleridge's 1801 conclusion to part II of 'Christabel'. The lines directly about Hartley –

> A little child, a limber elf,
> Singing, dancing to itself,
> A fairy thing with red round cheeks,
> That always finds, and never seeks –

further reinforce the otherworldliness, isolation, involution and passivity of the child.

Disastrously, the word 'elf' rhymes with 'self'. The two words, introduced in 'Christabel', recur in Hartley's own later verses almost as a mantra as he pursues his father's words in his own disgusted introspection. An example of a painful concatenation of self-abnegating themes occurs in a notebook from January 1827, when Hartley was 31. Referring to the notebook, he writes, 'like a candle lighted at both ends, my book is exhausted at the centre. ... Its conclusion finds me a beggar, bankrupt in estate, in love, in friendship, and, worst of all, in self-esteem.' Poem XLIV follows, with this ominous first stanza:

> A woeful thing it is to find
> No trust secure in weak mankind;
> But ten-fold woe betide the elf
> Who knows not how to trust himself.

(New Poems, p. 48)

Empty at the centre, bankrupt, and enduring what is now a buzzword for the constant sorrow of an alcoholic – 'lack of self-esteem' –, he curses the 'elf' that he has programmed himself to be with an archaic prophecy: 'tenfold woe betide the elf. ...' As so often in his own view and in those of others, his empty centre is overtaken, invaded, occupied by a subhuman sprite or fairy. 'Elf' is uncomfortably close to 'Gnome'.

The empty self, like the split self noted in the chapter on Lamb, is a condition frequent in alcoholics, though not exclusive to them. The sociologist Norman K. Denzin reveals that 'every alcoholic I observed drank to escape an inner emptiness of self.'[42] Samuel Johnson lamented 'the vacuity of life' that made drinkers drink; Charles Lamb confessed to Charles Lloyd that he 'kn[e]w the painfulness of vacuity, all its achings & inexplicable longings';[43] Coleridge calls Hartley's later 'sottishness' 'the *Habit* charged on him – woeful, and ruinous, and all-hollow-making and *future*-dizzying as *that* is!'[44] Alcoholic 'vacancies' were to be the subject of the dark half of Coleridge's proposed poem on the two Bacchuses, the interspersed vacancies in the Cave of the Gnome, described in the previous chapter.

The script of Wordsworth's 'To H. C.' with its many phrases adapted from earlier phrases in Coleridge's three sonnets and two conversation poems about child-rearing, seems inexorable, not only to Hartley who uses its phrases to describe himself and 'without a strife' accommodates the plan, but also for numerous commentators who refer to this poem as 'prophetic'. Hartley calls himself a 'waif of nature', a dew-drop, a prodigal, a wanderer, a failure. He laments, 'Long time a child, and still a child, when years / Had painted manhood on my cheek, was I.'[45] Infantilized in his relations to his elders, he has not grown to manhood. He is a 'nothing', dragging 'wasted years'.

As Hartley conforms to his described fate, so others see with wonder how truly his life was foreknown. Southey prophesies an early death, calling his presentiments a 'forefeeling': 'I am perfectly astonished at him, and his father has the same forefeeling that it is a prodigious and unnatural intellect – and that he will not live to be a man.'[46] Southey, Coleridge recalls, 'burst into audible weeping' at the fulfilment of the prophecy in Wordsworth's 'To H. C.'.[47] Coleridge writes toward the end of his life, 'I can never read Wordsworth's delightful lines "To H. C. at six years old" without a feeling of awe, blended with tenderer emotions – so prophetic were they!'[48] If they are prophetic, one wonders, how can the lines seem 'delightful'? Derwent in his memoirs mentions prophesy and fate many times: in reference to Wordsworth's 'To H. C.' he praises the wise poet's 'insight, of which foresight is but the developed form.'[49]

Hartley's persistent dread that he is fated, that he has no choice, appears with overwhelming frequency in asides and in long self-analyses. Even his father's death (following twelve years of estrangement and guilt) came to him not as a natural end but as 'the fulfillment of an unbelieved prophecy'.[50] He cannot shake free of his elders' words of prediction, and speaks of them as 'fulfilled'. His poem 'Presentiment' describes his foreknown life – 'Something evil does this load / Most assuredly forebode'[51] – and in a later note to 'Presentiment' he describes the poem itself as a prophecy, prophecies thus piling on prophecies and ratifying each other in fatal circles. Lines from his poem, 'On an Infant's Hand' – 'The branchy lines where Gipsy eld / Had all the course of life beheld' – suggest that all fates are inscribed at birth and can be read by soothsayers. For Hartley dread forecasts lie everywhere he looks. Chauncey Hare Townsend reports that during his first summer vacation Hartley intoned the fourth stanza of Wordsworth's 'Resolution and Independence' as if it had meaning for himself: 'And fears and fancies thick upon me came; / Dim sadness – and blind thoughts, I knew not, nor could name.' Even though this poem was not written for him, he identified with the wastrel addicts Chatterton and Burns, who could not reverse the courses into which they plunged. Hartley confessed that the lines, 'The fear that kills; / And hope that is unwilling to be fed,' have come to him in 'a voice, yes, not like a creation of the fancy, but an audible and sensuous voice foreboding evil to me.'[52] He lacks the will to fend off the foreboding voice.

Hartley is interested in superstition and magic, perhaps influenced by his father's study of Obeah witchcraft and the development of its themes in the family romances, 'The Three Graves' and 'Christabel'. As both of these narratives depict the transfer of energy from one being to another and the sapping or depleting of selfhood, they both inform Hartley's sense of being emptied out or substituted at the centre by some larger being, who may be his father. Revealing a curious blindness to the parental rejection of a child in 'Christabel', Hartley writes a poem to his brother Derwent's infant daughter, whom Derwent, with equal blindness, named 'Christabel Rose Coleridge'. Telling the baby girl that he himself is childless because of 'the doom severe/ Of my own faults', Hartley turns at poem's end to bless her, forgetting perhaps that the original 'Christabel' of his father's poem ends up silenced, hissing like a snake, and rejected by her father, having been taken over by Geraldine's magical power: 'May'st thou for aye in love and fancy dwell / Like thy good grandsire's lovely Christabell!'[53] Neither son could bear to read the poem to its often revised end. Hartley's interest in superstition and witchcraft emerges less personally in his charming essay, 'On Cats', and in random observations such as the following, to his brother, about their mother's 'funny things': 'The words, indeed, may be handed down from generation to generation, like relic bones and sacred nail-parings of the saints.'[54]

Such superstitious passivity before a prearranged script may trouble many 'adult children' who submissively follow the prophecies in parental injunctions. But when the psychologist Claude Steiner describes these fatal curses, he applies them specifically to alcoholics, suggesting that alcoholics suffer more from such predictions than others. He argues that 'parental injunctions, like curses, are often introduced into a person's life at the day of birth. ... Characteristically, the grown person believes that his state is fated rather than produced by the parental prediction. The effect a prediction of this sort may have has been amply explored in the concept of the self-fulfilling prophecy. In general, expected behavior is likely to occur simply because it is expected.' Steiner observes that in real life family tragedies, as in *Oedipus Rex*, the 'spectator' 'learns, or should learn, that human beings are deeply affected by and submissive to the will of the specific divinities of their household – their parents – and that they feel essentially impotent against their injunctions.'[55] Psychologists John Zinner and Roger Shapiro note that disturbed adolescents, whether alcoholic or not, 'walk a fine line between fulfillment of their own strivings for an autonomous identity and conformity with a parental delineation serving parental defense.' They ask, 'How do we account for the extent to which adolescents may collude in this activity, with the result that parental defensive delineations become a self-fulfilling prophecy?'[56] Steiner, Zinner and Shapiro discern an impotence and a collusion of the troubled child in his parent's naming of his fate. Judith S. Seixas and Geraldine Youcha see the chaos of the alcoholic family as the cause of the impotence: 'some of the sadness that envelops adult children [of alcoholics] like a cloud is related to a sense of having little grasp or control over their own destiny. Since they are often helpless, they feel hopeless or out of control.'[57] This compliance is as powerful as any genetic susceptibility to alcoholism, which is another form of fatality. Raymond Carver, in a poem to his daughter written 'too late to put a curse on you', warns her of her alcoholic inheritance and predicts that it will kill her if she does not stop:

> Clean up your act, I'm asking you.
> Okay, telling you. Sure, our family was made
> to squander, not collect. But turn this around now.
> You simply must – that's all!
> Daughter, you can't drink.
> It will kill you. Like it did your mother, and me.

The alcoholic parent sees the dangers, warns against them, predicts what will happen. In this case the predictions are based on family biology and patterns of behaviour.

Fatalism is indeed Hartley's fatal flaw, and it arises from genetics, his father's example, his father's unpredictable absences, the chaos of his family, and his father's, mother's, and Wordsworth's injunctions that become self-fulfilling prophecies. His father knows it, and Hartley describes its early onset. Looking back on his son's failures and describing their self-circling inevitability, Coleridge writes to Dawes, the Ambleside schoolmaster, hoping that he will hire Hartley: 'But for self-condemnation Hartley would never have tampered with Fatalism; and but for Fatalism he would never have had such cause to condemn himself.'[58] The father does not recognize his own role in these predictions. Hartley describes the sources of his own fatalism: 'it was not the mere loss of the prize, but the feeling or phantasy of an adverse destiny. I was as one who discovered that his familiar, to whom he had sold himself, is a deceiver. I foresaw that all my aims and hopes would prove frustrative and abortive, and from that time I date my downward declension, my impotence of will, and melancholy recklessness.'[59] He saw himself as a Faust with a devilish pact, as an empty centre inhabited by a 'familiar' spirit.

Sadly, Coleridge does not limit his prophecies to poetry, but directs them, often in rage, to the boy himself. In an April 1807 letter from London, Coleridge specifies the 11-year-old boy's faults:

> you are likewise gifted with a very active & self-gratifying fancy and such a high tide & flood of pleasurable feelings, that all unpleasant and painful Thoughts and Events are hurried away upon it, and neither remain on the surface of your memory, or sink to the bottom into your Heart. So far all seems right, and

matter of thanksgiving to your maker – and so all really *is* so, & will be so, if you exert your reason and free-will. But on the other [hand] the very same disposition makes you less impressible both to the censure of your anxious friends, and to the whispers of your conscience – nothing that gives you pain, dwells long enough upon your mind to do you any good. ... In like manner this power, which you possess, of shoving aside all disagreeable reflections, or losing them in a labyrinth of day-dreams, which saves you from some present pain, has on the other hand interwoven into your nature habits of procrastination, which unless you correct them in time ... must lead you into lasting Unhappiness.

After numerous specific strictures, Coleridge adds, 'I have not spoken about your mad passions, and frantic Looks & pout-mouthing: because, I trust, that is all over.'[60] The harsh detail in this letter seems to fix the boy with its brilliant and persuasive formulations and its elegant antitheses offering unalterable choices, probing deeply into the 'essential' nature to shape or to capture it in language. Coleridge ends the letter predicting 'lasting Unhappiness', terrible words that will ring in the youth's ears as he cultivates sorrow or submits to it.

This letter hints at what he might have said in angry face-to-face confrontations, and gives some credence to Coleridge's regret in the conclusion to part two of 'Christabel' about his words of anger:

And pleasures flow in so thick and fast
Upon his heart, that he at last
Must needs express his love's excess
With words of unmeant bitterness.

(ll. 662–6)

He cannot take back these written and spoken words that have been lodged in the timid consciousness as a formative magic. Hartley tells Derwent, 'I have forgot myself too often, but I never forgot my father ... wherever the final bolt of judgment may drive me, it will not be into the frozen regions of sons that loved not their fathers.'[61] As every opinion and phrase of his father's, written or spoken, pervades Hartley's essays and poems like a tissue of quotations because of his 'astonishing verbal memory', so must these enraged formulations have been burned on his image of himself.[62] His mother's words also echoed in his thoughts. Hartley's late letters to her explore his life-long fear of her criticism: 'I despair of ever becoming exactly the son you would choose';[63] 'even your commendations seem'd like reproaches set out at interest'.[64] Although her words may have had lasting impact in undermining his sense of his own free possibilities, especially as recalled by an alcoholic memory, they did not seem as significant to him as his father's at the time.

The anger of parents at children who resemble them too much has been examined by psychologists Melanie Klein, Julia Kristeva and Alice Miller, who see how a parent can feel suffocated by the re-emergence in the child of his or her own weaknesses.[65] Writing about Marguerite Duras and her fictional depictions of mother–daughter and mother–son relations, Kristeva speaks of the intimacy of this '(Re)duplication' as 'a blocked repetition': 'The double is the unconscious depth of the same, that which threatens it, can engulf it.'[66] Alice Miller shows how a narcissistic parent requires a child who will fulfil the parent's fantasies and thereby chokes off the child's own autonomous development as a separate being.[67] All three of these interpretations enrich our understanding of Coleridge's actions in regard to his son and to his feelings of frustration at not being able to control his son's failures any better than he could control his own; in addition, losing his own position as youngest child and centre of attention may have lead Coleridge the father to jealous contempt for the inferior copy of himself.

A useful twentieth-century father-son parallel appears in Eugene O'Neill's interpretation of Tyrone and his first son Jamie in *Long Day's Journey into Night*, O'Neill's effort to lay to rest the ghosts of his family. Tyrone sees in Jamie his own looks, talents and drunkenness in a degraded form; he belittles him by predicting his failure and ascribing his small successes to his own intervention in getting him parts. Tyrone and Jamie the eldest are clones; their resemblances sicken the more powerful father. He despises the qualities in the son that are like his own. Tyrone is able to treat his second son (actually third, since 'Eugene' died by Tyrone's neglect) as an Other, not like him except in his admirable freedom to throw himself into art. This separateness may apply to Coleridge in regard to his second son Derwent, who is also actually the third son, since the second son Berkeley died in infancy. The suffocation of cloning is unlikely with this more independent and jolly 'cube of fat', and so the rage need not be as intense and personal. Although little has been written about fathers and sons in the Romantic era, other such pairs whose intensities were accentuated by drinking are the doting Patrick Brontë and his drunken son Branwell (Branwell having paid at least one visit to Hartley from Yorkshire to Grasmere[68]), and William Hazlitt and his son William, whom he admonished in a detailed letter for faults resembling his own.[69] Wordsworth had worried, as we saw, about the potentially inherited weaknesses of the sons of Burns.

The predictions of lasting unhappiness, grief, and pain come true in 1820. Hartley, aged 24, is expelled from his provisionary fellowship at Oriel College on charges of 'sottishness'. He may or may not have been found dead drunk in the road, after consorting with a young woman of low estate. He admits to twice having been too drunk to carry his candle after a wine party, as was reported by a servant. He denies that late night intemperance kept him from morning chapel. He may or may not have spoken disrespectfully of the august and puritanical fellows of the college, whom E. L. Griggs has described as setting the tone for the Oxford Movement of mid-century;[70] he does seem to have held forth loudly at wine parties, behaviour which would have been acceptable, if not actually expected, at most other colleges, certainly when his own father was enjoying the bacchanalia at Jesus College, Cambridge, twenty-five years earlier.

The disaster paralysed Hartley and made him want to drink more to forget it; it struck his father like a blow. As Derwent remembers, 'I was with him at the time, and have never seen any human being, before or since, so deeply afflicted: not as he said, by the temporal consequences of his son's misfortunes, heavy as these were, but for the moral offence which it involved.'[71] Coleridge did not believe that his many predictions could be so horrifically and publicly fulfilled, or that Hartley would so passively follow the script for lasting Unhappiness, even to the point of confessing and begging for mercy. In asking for a statement of facts from Hartley and using it to negotiate with Dr Edward Coppleston, the Provost of Oriel College, the father hopes to instil assertiveness in the son, to restore the lacking self, but instead he inserts his own will in the empty core.

Coleridge *père* is whirled into action by the event, while the son whimpers in the background. The father moves in once more to control the 24-year-old man's life, to name it in some other way, encouraging the son's passivity, composing in many frantic versions the letters of confession that the remorseful young man is to sign. The letter to Coppleston and to the fellows disputes the charges of 'sottishness', the frequency of intemperate acts, and the habitual or occasional nature of them. Coleridge tries to substitute for the dread word 'sottishness' (a term 'too mortifying for me to transcribe'[72]) a less damaging one, such as 'fondness for wine', or 'occasional intemperance'; he argues that there are various kinds of drunkenness and some of them are benign. Words, again, are key.

But drafts of the letters try to depict Hartley's 'nature' since childhood as something the boy could not help. Writing these letters to strangers in high positions, the father reveals that his son lacked a self, snatched at food and drink without thinking, much like his friend Charles Lamb, was forgetful and impulsive. He quotes his own 'Frost at Midnight', which he calls 'the prophecy, written by me', to depict how his son wandered alone along the crags, and Wordsworth's 'To H. C.' for its prophecies of pain and unhappiness.[73] In these frenzied revelations he tells secrets that should have been private and that would not be likely to enhance the young man's chances of being reinstated. He not only directs the life but lives it for him, as if it were his own, as in some ways it is a re-enactment of his own failures such as his 'Army-freak' but on a far more public and damaging level. In explaining Hartley's pathetic personality, he paints it sharply, but then blames it on his own heredity, especially his own father's 'filling his wine-glass too often' in eager conversation;[74] again Hartley is deprived of personal responsibility for his deeds.

As so often, Hartley is depicted as an empty shell, filled with the will and words of another. In one of the drafts to Dr Coppleston Coleridge writes, 'From his earliest childhood he had an absence of any contra-distinguishing Self, any conscious "I"'; he had a 'more than usually prolonged habit of speaking in the third person, of himself & others indifferently'; his 'seemingly constitutional insensibility to the immediate impressions on the senses ... made him appear deficient in affection & almost unimpressible.' Ingratiating himself with Coppleston, Coleridge betrays his son as a near imbecile, with no self, deficient in a sense of reality or affection. How would such a defence help the young man? But Coleridge goes on in an increasingly chatty and literary vein, speaking to a grown up as if over his son's head: '– and never can I read De la Motte Fouqué's beautiful Faery Tale, founded on a tradition recorded in Luther's Table-Talk, of Undina, the Water-Fay, before she had a Soul, beloved by all whether they would or no, & as indifferent to all, herself included, as a blossom whirling in a May-gale, without having Hartley recalled to me, as he appeared from infancy to his boyhood.'[75] He sees Hartley as a Water Fay, indifferent and soulless, as elsewhere he saw him as an elf or sprite; he depicts his son as empty within, hollow, and susceptible to invasions of subhuman or supernatural images. 'He used to sink at once from a state of whirling activity into – it is painful to me even to recollect him – for he looked like a little statue of Ideotcy.'[76] Coleridge's impassioned pleas were touching to Dr Coppleston, but not calculated to make him and the fellows reverse their decision.

When all of these pleas and other interventions from uncles and from Southey fail, Hartley tries to live on his writing in London (placed with the teetotaling Montagus ironically by his father, who ten years earlier had been ejected from their home for drinking) but sinks more deeply into 'sottishness'. A familiar alcoholic circularity ensues, as his brother elegantly euphemizes: 'As too often happens, the ruin of his fortunes served but to increase the weakness which had caused their overthrow.'[77] Two years of binge drinking in London are beyond Coleridge's endurance; Hartley's very name makes him 'shrink, like a burnt Quill'; he would 'fain confine his name to my Prayers.'[78] In terms familiar from the letters to Coppleston, Coleridge begs Hartley's old school master Mr Dawes to employ Hartley in his school in Grasmere, far out of sight. Again, Hartley's lack of self is discussed as a job recommendation:

> alas! it is the absence of a Self, it is the want or torpor of Will, that is the moral Sickness of Hartley's Being, and has been, for good & for evil, his character – his moral Idiocy – from earliest Childhood. ... He has neither the resentment, the ambition, nor the Self-love of a man – and for this very reason he is too often as selfish as a Beast – and as unwitting of his own selfishness. With this is connected his want of a salient point, a self-acting principle of Volition – and from this, again, arise his shrinking from, his *shurking*, whatever requires and demands the exertion of this inward power, his cowardice as to mental pain, and the procrastination consequent on these.[79]

This lack of centre, this failure of will and self-hood, 'this moral Idiocy – from earliest Childhood', was fearful to the father, who again saw the distorted image of what he had struggled against in bringing into oneness his own scattered fragments of will, volition, reason, understanding. Hartley moves north into exile, challenging by his shabby misbehaviour the respectability of the Southeys and Wordsworths; once again he fails, even bringing the school down with him.

When Hartley agonizes about his own dividedness and lack of will, he sounds very much like his father. As his father wrote about his dividedness to J. J. Morgan (noted in Chapter 4), so Hartley writes to his father as to a fellow-sufferer: 'You must be aware that the pain arising from the contemplation of a life mis-spent is often the cause of continuance in misdoing, even after the temptations which first misled have lost their power, and when the sophisms which have long deluded appear in their true deformity.'[80] Writing to his father from the Ambleside school where his students were tormenting him, Hartley confesses that he was 'afflicted with a sense of incapability – a dread of looking at my own cure. The more my faults became obvious to those interested in me, the more I was possessed with that helpless consciousness of them, which conduces to anything rather than amendment.' He admits that he was 'in a state of mind and body truly pitiable', but now has improved: 'with the recovery of health I have recovered free-will and hope.' Free will and hope might have lifted him out of his fated course; but as Derwent says, 'the worm was within. ... As hope declined, his habits became less regular, and, after a struggle of four or five years, the undertaking was abandoned.'[81] His 'irregular' habits, to use one of the euphemisms of the day that had also been applied to Burns and to Coleridge, were easier to yield to than to fight.

Hartley examines his own circling impotence, but unlike his father his introspection does not dart outward to other topics but spirals inward. He is a good example of the adage, 'the alcoholic is an egomaniac with an inferiority complex.' As in the last pages of Lamb's 'Confessions of a Drunkard' when the alcoholic narrator called himself, oxymoronically, 'a poor nameless egotist', Hartley is obsessed with himself, with a self viewed as a nobody, a nothing, a little 'ignoramus', an 'uprooted weed', not content to be merely a weed. He positions himself on the underside of greatness. He is Wordsworth's violet by a mossy stone, he is the lesser celandine, while above him, looking down on him, are the giants, Coleridge, Wordsworth, Southey, who are pleased to grace his insignificance with their gaze. An example of Hartley's self-obsession is his revamping of his father's sonnet 'Human Life: On the Denial of Immortality' in his own sonnet IV. Coleridge's sonnet is a tortured inquiry into the consequences for life on earth of the loss of immortality:

O Man! thou vessel purposeless, unmeant,
Yet drone-hive strange of phantom purposes!
Surplus of Nature's dread activity,
[...]
Blank accident! nothing's anomaly!
[...]
Why waste thy sighs, and thy lamenting voices,
Image of Image, Ghost of Ghostly Elf,
That such a thing as thou feel'st warm or cold?[82]

Hartley's sonnet brushes past the terrifying proto-Darwinian religious and existential queries in his father's sonnet to concentrate on the lack of value of his own time on earth as a nobody:

Let me not deem that I was made in vain,
Or that my being was an accident,
Which Fate, in working its sublime intent,
Not wish'd to be, to hinder would not deign.[83]

In Hartley's feeble imitation, vanity and emptiness contract around the small empty centre of a single troubled 'Ghostly Elf'.

Sometimes, rarely, Hartley rebels. He writes secret poems mocking Wordsworth's 'Peter Bell' and 'White Doe of Rylestone';[84] he even dares, given his bad reputation, to write one drinking-song, modelled on Horace, that skilfully suspends the drinking until the end of his undulating periodic sentence:

Nay, nay, my boy – 'tis not for me,
This studious pomp of eastern luxury:
Give me no various garlands – fine
            With linden twine,
Nor seek, where latest lingering blows
            The solitary rose.
Earnest I beg – add not, with toilsome pain,
One far-sought blossom to the myrtle plain,
For sure, the fragrant myrtle bough
            Looks seemliest on thy brow;
Nor me mis-seems, while, underneath the vine,
Close interweaved, I quaff the rosy wine.[85]

The flowers of death fade in importance to the poet hidden beneath the dark vine drinking; Hartley may be echoing Keats's 'Ode to a Nightingale', where the beaded bubbles contrast with the dark, sepulchral flowers. He admired the dead Keats, almost his own age (whose hand his father had clasped on Hampstead Heath), and wrote a poem to him, 'I have written my name on water: the Proposed Inscription on the Tomb of John Keats', finding an affinity with this heroic poet's ephemeral impulse.[86] Like Keats, too, Hartley in an essay on 'The Poetical Use of the Heathen Mythology' reveals the lure of Dionysus. Alluding to Wordsworth's *Excursion* and to his father's lectures, he is tempted by the Greek myths that infuse holiness into existence: 'the riotous joy of the vine-yards, the tumultuous pleasure that blazes itself to darkness, the enthusiasm which makes a man a trifle to himself, the intoxication of wine and of glory, these "were no feats of mortal agency;" and who might blame the madness which a God inspired?' Quaffing wine under the closely woven leaves, he would be imaginative, free of guilty responsibility, a 'trifle' whirled around in drunken enthusiasm in a culture where 'no dark misgivings' and 'no remorse' shadow a god-filled joy,[87] as innocent as the grape-gathering children in Plate 6.

Hartley's many essays and poems explore terrain already travelled by his father, Wordsworth, and Southey, though he sometimes seems to nail down points more firmly than did his speculative elders. He writes about the sixteenth- and seventeenth-century poets and prose writers whom his father rediscovered, such as Drayton and Daniel. He expands the extended footnote of his father's *Biographia Literaria* and *Aids to Reflection* to marvellous proportions; page after page of tiny print dangles at the feet of his fifty-page introduction to *The Dramatic Works of Massinger and Ford*, where the note form allows him to jump nervously and frenetically from topic to topic. For he follows his father in cultivating the improvisation based on a scrap of text, the marginal lecture of several hours, but increases his own posture as a parasitical and marginal being. As his father quips to him, 'A blessing, I say, on the inventor of Notes!'[88]

His *Hamlet* essay was in his view his best, on a subject dear to his heart, the exoneration of a wronged father, who has become a ghost, a haunting presence, meeting him in every corner. He justifies Hamlet's harsh words to Ophelia by quoting lines from his father's 'Christabel': 'For to be wroth with one we love, / Doth work like madness in the brain' (ll. 412–13). As he sympathizes with Hamlet's rage, as with the rage of fathers against children in 'Christabel', he also finds common ground with a Hamlet like himself, whose 'active powers' 'are paralysed', whose few 'deeds are like startlings out of slumber, thrustings on of his destiny'.[89]

Seeing, as his father also did, a Hamlet passive to his destiny, Hartley does not notice how Hamlet comes to active manhood in the course of the play, for he could never have the strength of identity and self-determination to say, with royal power, 'We defy augury', the second epigraph to this chapter. Although he hopes 'poets are not prophets' in a note to a poem alluding to his father's 'Frost at Midnight', he lives his life passively, following the script designed by the sometimes cruel man he adored.

As Hartley's centre is empty, replaced by 'the evil spirit that has taken possession of my eldest born',[90] Coleridge imagines that Hartley has taken possession of his own centre during the twelve years of silence between them. 'What Queen Mary said, on the loss of our last Stronghold in France – that if her Heart were opened, Calais would be found written at the core – I might say of my poor dear Hartley.'[91] In fact, however, his 'Hopeless Heart-gnawing' about the son's failure, which he calls one of the 'four griping and grasping Sorrows' of his life,[92] does not prevent the father from developing his philosophy, from writing the kaleidoscopic *Aids to Reflection*, from formulating his plans for a clerisy and balance of powers in *On the Constitution of Church and State*, from dictating to Joseph Green his mature philosophy of persons, souls and spirits in the *Opus Maximum* manuscript, with its important (and, in regard to his first-born child, ironic) section on rearing strong children, and from commenting on the books of the Bible in his late notebooks, even while entertaining friends and admirers on Thursday evenings at Highgate and carrying on his habitual round of jolly London dinners. Indeed, he seems to experience a resurgence of power after 1820, the year of Hartley's Oriel failure, enacting the eerie phrase from 'Christabel' – 'A star hath set, a star hath risen.'[93]

While Hartley's vagrant life in the hills around Grasmere is haunted by his father's words, disapproval and predictions, and by guilt and shame at his own nothingness, his father thrives. In the last year of his life Coleridge annotates his son's *Worthies of Yorkshire and Lancashire* (1832–3), and raucously mocks his style. 'It is this petulant ipse dixi smartness & dogmatism ... a sudden *jerkiness* in the *mood*, and *unexpectedness* of Phrase, something between Wit and Oddity, but with the latter predominant ... [that] he has *caught* [from] Southey ... that annoy & mortify me in Hartley's writing.' He notices his son's 'unsteadinesses, tutites, hums and has, orange-suckings', his 'sneeringness', his 'petulant crudities of indigested thoughts'. He coins the word 'interpocular' to describe the drunken intonations in his son's chatterings that 'vex my Spirit'.

Heavy mockery continues: 'What can H. mean by this fling?' 'Neat, my dearest Hartley! more *clumsy*, involved common place I have seldom seen.' 'O, dearest H! but this is sadly vulgar!'[94] Where the father blames the rival influence of Southey as well as the son's oddness for the 'mortify[ing]' and 'vex[ing]' failures of this book, the son dedicates his book of poems to 'Father, and Bard revered! to whom I owe, / Whate'er it be, my little art of numbers / ... If good therein there be,/ That good, my sire, I dedicate to thee.'[95] But even his 'little art of numbers' is not his own.

Coleridge's experiment with a free child of nature, who became the fated child of paternal and avuncular language, also contributed to Coleridge's inquiries on the difference between persons and things that are scattered through his writings in the last two decades of his life. Here, once again, Hartley is an experiment, an example of a non-person, lacking volition, will, and the clarity of self to face his failures and struggle against them. When he repeatedly says that Hartley is not a self, but is nevertheless selfish,[96] he believes that he lacks the ability to say 'I', and to accept responsibility for his deeds. When he writes to Coppleston that Hartley was very late in ceasing to refer to himself in the third person, this observation becomes part of his work in the *Opus Maximum* on how children develop a strong sense of their own autonomy after they have first learned to find themselves in the mother's touch. He writes,

> the child now learns its own alterity, & sooner or later, as if some sudden crisis had taken place in its nature, it forgets hence forward to speak of itself by imitation, that is by the name which it had caught from without. It becomes a person, it is and speaks of itself as I, and from that moment it has acquired what in the following states it may quarrel with, what it may loosen and deform, but can never eradicate, – a sense of an alterity in itself which no eye can see, neither his own nor other.[97]

Coleridge locates this moment of crisis when the child shifts from third person to first person in referring to him or her self. He knows that this crisis occurred very late for Hartley, who lived surrounded by voices talking about 'Hartley' and predicting what Hartley would do. These other voices may account for Hartley's failure to acquire a self-driving identity.

Hartley is thus an example of how not to be a person because he lacks a will;[98] as a sot, he becomes a 'Beast', to use Coleridge's words for him in the letter to Dawes, or as he defines the drunk in his late notebooks, a 'thing'. In either case he does not occupy his own centre, having given it up to his father, to the fetish John Barleycorn, to nothingness, or to evil spirits or supernatural sprites, fays, elves or gnomes.

Although Coleridge is usually disgusted with himself and his own failures of will and volition, he believes that he differs from his son by struggling to bring his person into coherence and free agency, rather than collapsing in fatalism and allowing the long expected destiny to happen. Whether the son's refusal to fight is his '*Nature* ... the germ of which disclosed itself even in earliest infancy', perceived by the prophetic father, or whether the father's words, further magnified by Wordsworth's, scripted this collapse is a question deep in the mysterious sources of alcoholism.

Hartley is unusually passive to fate, but at the same time Coleridge is unusually vocal about creating his child, moulding him, and defining him. The father is trying to succeed this time, as he did not for himself. But, on the one hand, he directs too minutely, and on the other hand, he leaves home for years, abandoning his creation in mid-stream (as another creative experimenter, Dr Frankenstein, also abandoned his experiment). The child, unable to direct his own life, never expresses hostility at his father's abandonment and failure to raise money for his university studies. Coleridge had said truly that they both suffered from an absence of will. They were 'will-maniacs', as they both believed that Hamlet was.

By planning, predicting, foretelling his life, and taking over his free agency in crises, Coleridge takes away his son's responsibility for his life. He takes away his capacity to hope and by hope to effect the future. Coleridge knew this danger when he said that 'detailed Forewarnings' took away 'Hope'. Weaving his son in a web of words, he creates a creature of his own language, a text without substance, a text circling around an empty centre. Hartley hears foreboding on all sides, and knows how his life will turn out; what use is it to go on living it? It has all been foretold. Taking away hope takes away the power of imagining a new way to be. In Raymond Carver's short story 'Chef's House', the alcoholic ex-husband expects defeat and is powerless to ward it off. His wife, hoping that he can imagine and therefore choose a different ending, says, 'Suppose, just suppose, nothing had ever happened. Suppose this was for the first time. Just suppose.' But the husband is fixed in failure: 'Then I suppose we'd have to be somebody else if that was the case. Somebody we're not. I don't have that kind of supposing left in me. We were born who we are.'[99] He shuts the curtains on the view of the sea. He feels fated to succumb and cannot imagine not doing so. Hope needs options, and options arise out of imagining alternatives.

As Coleridge served as the weak alter ego in Wordsworth's *Prelude* and Richard Savage enacted the image of hitting bottom for Samuel Johnson, so Hartley plays his father's self as it might have been, had he not fought life-long for free agency, had he not roamed, imagined and supposed. Of the two aspects of Bacchus that Samuel Taylor Coleridge proposed to explore in his unwritten long poem, Hartley is the Bastard Bacchus, the Gnome, twisted and incomplete, fixed in his foreknown life by a script spoken by his father; the father, although sometimes huddled in his cave of the Gnome, more often bursts free in Dionysian power uttering prophetic words, potent to create or maim.

6

'Joy's Grape': Keats, *Comus*, and *Paradise Lost* IX

Dionysius is the guardian of life because of generation, but of death because wine produces an enthusiastic energy: and we become more enthusiastic at the period of dissolution.

– Thomas Taylor, 'On the Mysteries of Bacchus' (1790)

The riot of the tipsy Bacchanals,
Tearing the Thracian singer in their rage.

– *A Midsummer Night's Dream* V, 1, 48–9

Keats's early familiarity with disease and death, his grim work as a dresser at Guy's Hospital, and his ease with the facts of pharmacy and medicine gave him a constant awareness of the precariousness of human lives and of mental stability.[1] He knew in others and in himself the desire to escape pain and to submerge consciousness as well as to intensify it and expand the brief sensations of life. Real experience insistently drove him to this double awareness of intense sorrow pulsing at the centre of intense joy. But real experience was also filtered through the language of previous poetry, particularly Milton's *Paradise Lost*, Book IX, where Milton conveys the moment of death-in-life and life-in-death, which is for him the Fall.

Milton gives Keats a language for conveying this double intensity. One aspect of Milton's language is his creation of simultaneous sequence, time caught in stasis even as it starts to move. For Milton, this is the moment when death, decay, fermentation and rot begin through the created world. Keats is inspired by this intense moment when people and other parts of nature, including fruit and grapes, begin to rot. He learns from Milton to see this organic and spiritual shift as an intoxication.

I. *PARADISE LOST* IX, 1008–10013 AND 'ODE ON
MELANCHOLY', 3

Paradise Lost, Book IX, is the seed of Keatsian transgressions, the moment when innocence is forever transformed into experience, the beginning of sorrow, of solitude, of the frisson of pain and pleasure. Keats absorbs the consciousness and intensity of this Miltonic moment and fills his poems, particularly the 'Ode on Melancholy' and 'Ode to a Nightingale', with the double awareness peculiar to this necessary, if not fortunate, fall.

The moment when fragmentation occurs is depicted in *Paradise Lost* Book IX as a double, or syncopated moment: Eve's eating, and Adam's knowingly following her into doom. The moment of transgression will change forever these first parents themselves, us, their progeny, the natural world and all its denizens. Though the character weaknesses (jealousy, pride, rebelliousness and uxoriousness) that led to this moment lurk in Eve and Adam from the start, Milton splices this continuity with the sudden change of the moment that marks the enactment of these previously suppressed doubts. Amorphous, shadowy, potential feelings take shape in deeds, and can never be returned to their Pandora's box of unconscious and unrealized possibilities. This moment Milton describes as a transformation, using allusions to Circe, and as an intoxication, using another vocabulary of transformation – the fermentation and decay that produce wine.

Possibilities lie in wait in the instant, poised to start disintegrating, their fall compressed in the very words describing them. As the Satanic serpent, or serpentine Satan, approaches Eve in oblique folds and sidelong tacks, she hears him but 'minded not, as used / To such disport before her through the field / From every beast, more duteous at her call / Than at Circean call the herd disguised' (IX, 519–22). The comparison of Eve's power over the animals with Circe's power is an ominous forecast of what will happen after the Fall, especially since Eve's 'call' is said to be more powerful than Circe's. Like Circe, Eve will summon the men (her husband and all her later progeny) whom she has transformed into beasts, and this potentiality is revealed in cryptic shorthand in this mythical allusion before she actually performs her Circean magic. As the allusion predicts, she will transform her husband into a mortal animal, and he will come when she calls. Alastair Fowler explains: 'Circe was in Milton's time regarded allegorically as a Type of the Excess that leads to the imbruting of man', luring men from the temperate rational path between animals and divinities. Circe debases men as Eve will (though since Eve is the first woman she actually antici- pates Circe, who is said to anticipate her here), but only when their own weaknesses acquiesce in the temptation.[2] Milton's allusion to a particular moment in the *Odyssey* when Odysseus' men behave like swine, swill, drink, lose control, with the drunken Antenor dying from a fall from the roof, while waiting for their subsequent visit to the underworld, summons to this reading the multiple losses that the coming moment of enchantment will bring.

Goaded by pride, gluttony, envy, malice (qualities already latently hers), Eve yields to the beast's eloquent temptations, himself a fallen angel willingly taking a beast's form in a Circean reversal, urging her to hear that the prohibited fruit 'gave elocution to the mute', humanizing the brute, as humans will by analogy be divinized, in a falsely imagined upward-moving metamorphosis. The moment of eating encompasses all the sins (gluttony, murder, pride, arrogance, unbelief, ingratitude, disobedience, theft, suicide) and the eating of death *intoxicates*. Milton says that Eve is 'height- ened as with wine' (IX, 793), mentioning wine for the first time, but in anticipation since it can occur only when rot and fermentation have begun, processes that start in the approaching moment. Milton had described her innocently crushing grapes in Book V, 345, but the juice is only 'inoffensive must' (V, 347), 'the unfer- mented juice of the grape'. Now she is intoxicated by the already fermenting fruit at the moment when she herself begins to decay. Fowler notes (note to IX, 793) that 'At least since the time of St. Bernard, drunkenness has always been a convenient symbol of the loss of rationality resulting from the Fall', and because it results from fermentation, a symbol, too, of the delicious agony of love in death. In her intoxicated state, the errant nature within Eve is released. She idolizes the tree; she raises herself above God; she plots to dethrone Adam; she fears the future rivalry of another woman; she dissimulates; she feels the 'agony of love, till now / Not felt'. Fragmentation of desire, futility, falsehood, ambition, begin; harmonies of being and of community end.

As Adam listens to her false and desperate chattering, his garland drops from his hand, the roses 'faded'. Fowler believes that this is 'the first instance of decay in Paradise', not counting the mention of wine at Eve's transgression because it is anticipatory of a condition that cannot yet exist as an 'instance'. He suggests that this dropping garland 'may be an allusion to Statius' *Thebais* (7, 149 ff.) when Bacchus, frightened by the impending destruction of Thebes, drops his thrysus and 'unimpaired grapes fall from his head'. Keats seems to draw on Adam's fading garland in 'Lamia' –

> the loud revelry
> Grew hush; the stately music no more breathes;
> The myrtle sicken'd in a thousand wreaths

> (2, ll. 262–4)

– when the exaltation collapses into reality, and the spell of love (however false and artificially stimulated) is broken.

Fowler adds that Adam has earlier been cast as Bacchus (*PL* IV, 279) in a list of other unsuspecting frail strangers in mythological gardens who will be snatched by Death, ripped to pieces, or transformed from their original shapes. In casting Adam momentarily as Bacchus, Milton singles out Bacchus's miraculous birth, his ease in nature, his power over the animals, and his victimization at the hands of women as described by analogy with Orpheus in the later accreted myths. Milton may wish to minimize less noble elements of Bacchus – his riotous, irrational, mesmerizing, transfiguring and cruel nature – but these elements inevitably surround the mention of this ambiguous figure, and by contagion darken the figure of Adam.

When Adam, fully realizing the loss, freely chooses 'the bond of nature' (*PL* IX, 956), the two first parents eat their fill and earth trembles. The effect is again intoxication:

> As with new wine intoxicated both,
> They swim in mirth, and fancy that they feel
> Divinity within the breeding wings
> Wherewith to scorn the Earth: but that false fruit
> Far other operations first displayed,
> Carnal desire inflaming ...

> (IX, 1008–13)

Milton chooses to call the effect of the two transgressions *intoxication* because the eaters are artificially and falsely lifted above their natures and filled with delusory images of their own powers; at the same time, they poison themselves, cloud their perceptions, and prepare a plunge into disillusion. The wine, from the now suddenly decaying fruit, is poised at the moment before vinegar sets in, and by a parallel with their own new mortality, putrescence.[3] This poised moment is the one that Keats captures in 'The Ode on a Grecian Urn', just before time enters, which can be held only in the frozen pastoral of art. In life, the process, once in train, 'leaves a heart high-sorrowful and cloy'd,/ A burning forehead, and a parching tongue', for Adam and Eve, as for Keats's ardent, panting human lovers.[4] Once Adam and Eve satisfy their hunger and thirst, they break out of the artful pastoral stasis, begin the process of tragic descent, and enter the human world. As the drunken exaltation dissipates, the disordered consciousness breeds lust, recrimination, cruelty and spite in the fallen human beings, and in nature, climactic change, seasons, tempests, draughts, floods, famines, pestilence; in both, death. 'Have, get, before it cloy', writes Hopkins of this moment of 'juice' and 'joy', borrowing Keats's word for the excess of deliciousness tipping into nausea – *cloy*.

The moment of the Fall brings consciousness as we know it in the world of experience – sorrow, uncertainty, exile, strife, exploitation, submission, vanity, 'here where men sit and hear each other groan.' Innocence is gone forever, and experience shifts erratically from ecstatic and false illusions of grandeur to irrational, vain and fierce hostility and paranoia. Such swings of our fallen and irrational life are described by Milton as intoxication, among other images for disordered consciousness, for the intoxicated person has lost his centre, his clear vision of reality. Intoxication is one of the most evident ways in which the human being (at least initially) chooses to harm himself (to the amazement of the King of Brobdignag in *Gulliver's Travels*, Book 2) in the expectation of briefly raising himself up. Intoxication is an image for the shortsighted deeds a person does, knowing that the result will eventually be painful, risking disgrace, illness, madness and death, for an instant of *Erhebung*. In *Paradise Lost* XI, 472–537, Milton's Michael warns of this 'inabstinence', 'intemperance', and 'ungovern'd vice' and the foul diseases that result.

In his deliberate consideration of drunkenness as a contingent effect of the Fall, Milton draws on the complex and contradictory attitudes toward drink in the Renaissance, represented by Erasmus's Folly, nursed by Drunkenness; by Falstaff, with his energy, freedom and moral ambiguity; by Pantagruel's quest for drink as spirit and community; and by the Anacreontics of the Sons of Ben. These literary memories flow into Milton's image in positive and negative form. Eve's being heightened as with wine by the serpent's temptations may also allude to the corruption of Caliban. Eve's 'civilized' self is as shaky as the innocent 'savage', both seduced by gaudy surfaces. In *The Tempest*, Shakespeare's natural man, savage man, in a state of innocence, is seduced by Stephano's wine; like Eve, Caliban turns to idolize false gods, to imagine false omniscience, and to crave more of the irrationality that corrupted him in the first place – 'the celestial liquor' brought by the 'brave god' (*Tempest* II, 2, 121) who is really 'a poor drunkard' himself (II, 2, 170). The arguments for drunken rapture are also parodied, as we will see, in the speeches of that charming satanist Comus, countered by the Lady voicing Milton's own arguments for temperance.

Milton sharpens the connection of intoxication with the Fall in *On Christian Doctrine*, in a chapter significantly also numbered 'nine'. He defines the virtue of Temperance as 'the virtue which prescribes bounds to the desire of bodily gratification. ... Under temperance are comprehended sobriety and chastity, modesty and decency.' He specifically defines 'sobriety' as 'abstinence from immoderate eating and drinking', and cites supporting evidence from scriptures.[5] 'The opposites of this virtue are drunkenness and gluttony', he states, amassing scriptural passages about Noah, Lot and other drunken biblical heroes, that warn of the dangers of drunkenness, and do indeed seem to correspond to the excess, dishonesty, woe, sorrow and contentiousness that overwhelm Adam and Eve in their 'intoxicated' state: 'Drunkenness, revellings, and such like ... shall not inherit the kingdom of God.'[6]

I have been suggesting that intemperance as an aspect of willed disorder is a serious concern for Milton, that the several references to intoxication in *Paradise Lost*, Book IX, in conjunction with the references to Adam as Bacchus encapsulate the unregulated highs and lows of the human condition after the Fall and are chosen with the same deliberate precision as the rest of Milton's diction.

Hand in hand with these observations about Milton, I want to suggest that Keats as an avid student of Milton adapts Milton's language of intoxication for his own uses, which subvert Milton's puritanism and metamorphose into celebrations of the brief joys of life, but which also rejoin with Milton in ultimately rejecting wine in favour of some higher mental or spiritual pursuit.

Though Keats's volume of *Paradise Lost* reveals only a double line along the margin of the wreath-dropping passage and no written marginalia near the intoxicated moments,[7] his frequent descriptions of intoxicated states as images of the transience of human pleasure suggest that he read Milton's passages closely. But Keats is not as sure as Wordsworth was about Milton's own temperance, and seems to suspect that a poet so luxurious must have known the inspiration and pleasure of drunkenness. On the title page of his copy of *Paradise Lost*, around 1818, Keats records a curiously Blakean understanding of Milton's struggle. He recognizes in Milton's genius 'an exquisite passion for what is properly in the sense of ease and pleasure, poetical Luxury', but feels that Milton cannot indulge it and still keep his 'self-respect and feel of duty perform'd'. Keats sees a Milton, torn between his Apollonian and Dionysian selves, who 'devoted himself rather to the Ardours than the pleasures of Song, solacing himself at intervals with cups of old wine – and those are with some exceptions the finest parts of the Poem.' Keats imagines, perhaps jokingly, that Milton was drinking cups of wine while he composed the luxurious parts of the poem, parts about pleasure, song, and the 'spirit of mounting and adventure'.[8] As Blake had welcomed Milton among fellow rebels for being 'of the Devils party without knowing it', so Keats delights in his Puritan hero's secret 'Maenadism'.[9]

This pleasure in Milton's suppressed luxuriance intensifies Keats's affinity for the sickening sensuality of Milton's syncopated moment of desire, suffocation, fury and distaste.[10] But where Milton sees this moment as an enactment of latent potential evil, Keats purges the moment of falling of its guilt, and sees it as a description of the sorrows of consciousness. It is human experience with its inevitable loss of innocence, its sweet and sour passion of decay, its 'grosser sleep, / Bred of unkindly fumes' (*PL* IX, 1049–50), its sense of estrangement and dis-ease, the 'weariness, the fever, and the fret' of mortal reality. Milton's one free act of gluttonous disobedience, purged of guilt, is Keats's flux and growth. Keats reproduces these moments of rapturous pain and intense and wincing pleasure, when the stasis of incorruptibility suddenly and inexorably switches to corruption: 'Ripe was the drowsy hour.'[11] Ripeness is organic; it comes of its own; it is nobody's fault.

When Keats, steeped in his reading of Milton, lingers at these moments of ecstatic decay, poised between magnificence and rot, he often uses the Miltonic oxymoron, as in his cry, 'O the sweetness of the pain' in 'Welcome Joy and Welcome Sorrow', itself an adaptation of Milton's 'L'Allegro' and 'Il Penseroso' that opts for both possible human experiences rather than asking us to choose one as superior to the other, or much later and far more painfully the cry, 'O the sweetness of the pain!' (*KCP*, p. 494). He relishes the too-much-ness of the body on the crest of corruption.

The 'aching Pleasure' of Book IX provides a context for understanding the last stanza of 'Ode on Melancholy', where the allegorical figure of Melancholy is found to dwell not with morbidity and depression, as one might suppose, but rather with the intense experience of Beauty's fragility, with 'Joy, whose hand is ever at his lips / Bidding adieu'. When read in the context of Milton's oxymoronic condition of loving a life that is dying in one's grasp, this stanza, usually ignored as strange and 'embarrassing',[12] begins to make sense. The ode's hero reaches the exquisite core of Melancholy by forcing his tongue into the recesses of delight:

> Ay, in the very temple of Delight
> Veil'd Melancholy has her sovran shrine,
>   Though seen of none save him whose strenuous tongue
> Can burst Joy's grape against his palate fine.

> (ll. 25–8; *KCP*, p. 375)

'The Knight of the Strenuous Tongue' dares to burst the grape, but how heroic is it to raid the 'sovran shrine' of a grape?[13] This sexual tongue, weapon of taste, lust and language, 'muscular', to use Sperry's word,[14] breaks open against the arching palate the grape of joy, its fleshy violence releasing the sadness within the heart of the grape. When read in connection with *Paradise Lost* IX, 1008–13, the stanza participates in the double moment of tasting delight and losing it. Joy and Melancholy are not surface and depth but simultaneously exultant at their most intense points.

Helen Vendler describes the quest for intensity in the 'Ode on Melancholy' in the language of chemical distillation, tincture and metabolism. She captures the moment of pleasure turning to poison: 'there is no distillable sweet tincture of pure Pleasure; all pleasure is metabolized to poison not after, but during, the moment of the ingestion of that pleasure.' Although Vendler denies the grape's connection to wine and admonishes the reader 'that the grape here yields only its own juice, not wine' and that 'Keats's intoxication will never again, after the repudiation of wine in Nightingale, be that of any earthly drink',[15] her image of the metabolism of pleasure to poison applies to fermentation as well. The Miltonic model of the moment poised before fermentation provides a context for this explosive taste, suggesting that every burst grape is on the verge of wine, if only a millisecond before it begins.

The burst grape scatters its purples, crimsons, reds and roses through the ruby grape, rosary, yew-berries, morning rose and globed peonies of the other stanzas of the ode, showing that Keats's delectation of wine's many reds is as intense as his connoisseurship of the varying crimsons of arterial and venous bloods – 'deep dying scarlet', as he learns to call drinking.[16] The poet of this ode rejects in the first stanza Lethe's 'poisonous wine', because it is a passive way to oblivion. He chooses instead a liquid he makes himself by crushing the grape in the act of daring to taste it, a destruction necessary to the delight, as Milton's freely chosen fall, too, had been necessary for releasing a new, complex intensity of experience.

The heroic questing poet reaches the inner sanctum of joy and discovers that its core is melancholy; face to face with this withering truth, he is captured as one of 'her cloudy trophies hung', perhaps on the walls of the inner sanctum, like other human heroes who have flown too close to the sun, or impiously viewed naked god or goddess. The Keatsian hero of the 'Ode on Melancholy', like the cousins Actaeon and Semele, is changed by tasting the forbidden fruit and then seeing the duality of life and death in its split centre. Where a mortal is imprisoned at the moment of intense experience, a god can endure the new knowledge. In *Hyperion* Book III the young Apollo is filled like Eve with new knowledge of good and evil, 'creations and destroyings', and, like her, feels divinized by the sudden explosion. He cries out at this change, which, like Eve, he likens to intoxication:

Names, deeds, gray legends, dire events, rebellions,
Majesties, sovran voices, agonies,
Creations and destroyings, all at once
Pour into the wide hollows of my brain,
And deify me, as if some blithe wine
Or bright elixir peerless I had drunk,
And so become immortal.

(ll. 114–20; *KCP*, pp. 355–6)

The agitation and fullness of knowledge pours into him like wine, turns him into a god, and then, seen from outside, he is suddenly shaken by 'wild commotions', turns 'flush', 'convulses' with the pangs of birth or death. As the poem thrashes to an end in a starburst of asterisks, it, too, echoes with the drunken moments of Milton's Book IX, the moment of tasting and dying.

II: *COMUS* AND *ENDYMION* IV, 135–325

In addition to the experience of intoxication as ecstatic death, dying
into our life in time, of *Paradise Lost* Book IX, Milton provides in
Comus another source for meditations on intoxication. Milton's
invention of Comus's genealogy, fathered by Bacchus, mothered by
Circe (influencing Shelley's genealogy of the Witch of Atlas) brings
together the magic, vitality and delusive power of both these
entrancing Greek immortals. Comus's father Bacchus 'first from out
the purple grape/ Crushed the sweet poison of misused wine'
(*Comus*, 46–7), and his mother Circe also offered a 'charmed cup /
Whoever tasted, lost his upright shape / And downward fell into a
grovelling swine' (*Comus*, 51–3). Comus follows the family tradition, offers a transforming cup of orient liquor, and walks surrounded by a 'herd'. Milton releases this wild son Comus with his
transformed followers, bodies and minds still human, but heads
brutal, into a Celtic forest of romance, where the Lady and her
brothers err in the dark wood; she is 'woo'd' by Comus, as his
victims are 'wood', or 'mad'. In these confusing woods, or uses of
'woo'ds', the chaste Lady must listen to conflicting lures in varying
voices and find her way. She hears the 'wanton dance' (176), the
'rudeness and swilled insolence/ Of such late wassaillers' (178–9);
she wanders in 'blind mazes' (181); she hears 'the tumult of loud
mirth' (202) and protects herself by singing a song about Echo, 'that
liv'st unseen' (230), 'in the violet embroidered vale/ Where the
love-lorn nightingale / Nightly to thee her sad song mourneth well'
(233–5). The attendant Spirit, worried that the Lady will be seduced
by Comus and 'his monstrous rout' (533), hears her song in the
darkness:

> Amazed I stood, harrowed with grief and fear,
> And 'O poor hapless nightingale,' thought I,
> 'How sweet thou singest, how near the deadly snare!'

> (*Comus*, 565–7)

In these 'faery lands forlorn' ('Ode to a Nightingale', l. 70), these
dark woods of romance, the Lady rejects the 'cordial julep' (672),
cries 'Hence with thy brewed enchantments, foul deceiver' (696),
and chooses 'a well-governed and wise appetite' (705). Many of
these phrases will echo through the lines of Keats's 'Ode to a
Nightingale'.

Comus tries to convince the Lady to drink his enchanting potion by his *carpe diem* argument, to use her beautiful body while she still can, not 'strangled with her waste fertility' (728), the argument of Milton's cavalier contemporaries who seduced coy virgins with images of nature's flowing energy, often imaged as wine, and the transitory joys to be grasped before the grave. Anticipating *Paradise Lost* Book IX, here, too, Comus argues for excess that promises freedom but in reality brings imbrutement. The Lady rejects these luxurious arguments, teaching Romantic women writers of the next century strength in self-sufficiency.[17]

In addition to the rich echoes from 'Il Penseroso', 'Lycidas', *Samson Agonistes*, *Paradise Lost*, and Shakespeare's *Measure for Measure* and *Hamlet* that have been noted by other readers,[18] a startling number of words and themes from *Comus* feed into Keats's 'Ode to a Nightingale' – the dark woods, the songs heard in the gloom, the nightingale at the centre of the Lady's song and her own voice perceived by the attendant spirit as a nightingale's, the enamelled flowers and verdurous glooms, the rejection of Comus and his monstrous rout like the rejection of Bacchus and his pards, with the command 'Hence with thy brewed enchantments, foul deceiver', like the 'Away, away' of the Ode, and the choice of a more noble means of flight than drink.

But Keats also re-evaluates *Comus*. When he writes about Milton and especially *Comus* to John Hamilton Reynolds, 3 May 1818, he does not agree with Milton that these rousing intoxications are to be rejected by the well-governed appetite. He argues that Milton's belief that they are immoral is historically conditioned, subject to his seventeenth-century Puritanism: 'who could gainsay his ideas on virtue, vice, and Chastity in Comus, just at the time of the dismissal of Cod-pieces and a hundred other disgraces?' (*KL*, 1, 281–2). 'Surely the mind of man is closely bound / In some black spell,' he writes in the 'Sonnet written in Disgust of Vulgar Superstition' (*KCP*, p. 88). Keats would be much more likely to agree with Comus's own argument to use the body before it is too late, since he would not deprive 'this mortal body of a hundred days' of any briefly grasped sensation. Perhaps this is why he subversively envisions Milton drinking cups of old wine while he intones.

Several of Keats's love songs do indeed argue in the *carpe diem* mode of Milton's cavalier opponents, borrowing Anacreontic verse forms and sentiments from Robert Herrick, Abraham Cowley and Lord Rochester, what Keats calls 'a glorious folio of Anacreon'

(*KCP*, p. 287). Keats ravages Comus's long speech for orotund words for fullness: 'bounties', 'spawn', 'sate', 'plenty', 'ore', 'riches', 'surcharged with her own weight', 'cumbered', 'o'erfraught', 'swell', 'hoarded', and 'mutual and partaken bliss', which he will adapt to fill the 'o'erbrim[med] cells' of the 'Ode to Autumn', loading its 'every rift with ore'. The deliciousness of the body is for Keats not a temptation but a triumph, and he nowhere shows his paganism more decidedly than in embracing Comus's tempting luxuries, preferring Comus's lush and fertile profligacy to the Lady's 'lean and sallow Abstinence' (*Comus*, 709). In 'O blush not so! O blush not so,' examining the ambiguous meanings of women's blushes and sighs, the poet delights in suspecting that his imagined woman has already experienced sexual pleasure, for her sigh 'sounds of Eve's sweet pippin' (l. 10). He urges her to throw herself into experience, rejecting the coyness of Eve's slow choosing:

> There's a sigh for yes, and a sigh for no,
>   And a sigh for I can't bear it!
> O what can be done? Shall we stay or run?
>   O cut the sweet apple and share it!

> (*KCP*, p. 226)

So Comus had urged the Lady to share the wealth, or nature would choke in its own abundance. A new, enthusiastic (not resigned and melancholy) Adam welcomes a share of the sweet apple (like the later burst grape) and the joys and sorrows that will come in its trajectory.

Keats speaks out boldly against Milton's superstitions, particularly as they repress the life-spirit in *Comus*. By way of rejecting Milton's temperance arguments, Keats absorbs the language of Comus's luxuriance, and its cavalier parallels, transposing Comus's arguments from temptingly satanic to rhapsodically celebratory. *Comus* is a hidden subtext of many of Keats's poems, absorbed in reverse of its intended doctrine, and suffusing its deliciousnesses in despite of Milton's will, in a lifelong battle with Milton and the parsons on the subject of sensations and pleasure. Where Wordsworth, still smarting from the guilt of getting drunk in Milton's rooms, had faulted his predecessor Burns for indulging too freely, Keats faults Milton for denying himself pleasure, like a male Sabrina.

Keats's fascination with the figures of Bacchus and Circe,[19] with Ovidian embrutements, with Spenserian indolence and impotence,[20] with a nostalgia for the old Renaissance England of merry taverns and convivial geniuses, with his general hunger for 'the wine of love ... and the bread of friendship' (quoted Ward, 180), and with the actual material or physical sequences of drinking – taste, heady exaltation, and oblivion – courses through short songs early and late, through the Indian Maid's song in *Endymion* Book IV, through 'Lamia' Book II, to culminate in the 'Ode to a Nightingale' and the 'Ode to Melancholy'. Even when he rejects Bacchus and drunkenness, he cherishes wine's transitory power to glow more brightly in the moment of dissolution.

The glowing Bacchic moment irradiates *Endymion* Book IV. The Indian Maid's roundelay might be read as a recasting of *Comus*, where, instead of resisting, she joins the rout. The positive and gleeful representation of Bacchus may be learned from Lemprière's *Classical Dictionary*, for Bacchanalia, Bacchante and Bacchus all appear there in detailed delight, purged of cruelty.[21] The Indian Maid's song is a transitory suspension of sorrow that is effective and real notwithstanding its brevity.

The roundelay begins with invocations to the doubleness of sorrow, describes the arrival of Bacchus and his crew and her adventures following him, and then admits her preference for sorrow and her return to it. The Bacchic triumph is thus surrounded by sorrow; it rears up in exultation and joy for 76 lines and then subsides back into the reality of pain. Weeping beneath her palm trees, the Indian Maid is visited by 'a noise of revellers':

> the rills
> Into the wide stream came of purple hue –
> 'Twas Bacchus and his crew!

Music, merriment, flushed faces, and dancing bodies are represented as a purple stream or 'a moving vintage'. Suddenly abandoning her melancholy, the maid 'rush'd into the folly' (l. 203). Young Bacchus with his thrysus laughs and drips crimson wine in rills; Silenus is near, 'tipsily quaffing'. Merry Damsels dance along in wild minstrelsy, following Bacchus; they have left behind their melancholy, and also, like the later celebrants around the priest and heifer in the 'Ode on a Grecian Urn', they have left behind their 'bowers desolate', their little towns and 'gentler fate'. Jolly Satyrs have left their 'nuts in oak-tree cleft',

> 'For wine, for wine we left our kernel tree;
> For wine we left our heath, and yellow brooms,

                    And cold mushrooms;
        For wine we follow Bacchus through the earth;
        Great God of breathless cups and chirping mirth! –
        Come hither, lady fair, and joined be
        To our mad minstrelsy!' (ll. 231–8)

The maid recalls the Asian travels of the young god, which the
choral Bacchante recount also in Euripides's *The Bacchae*; she delights in the exotic animals associated with Bacchus in his iconography, panthers, leopards and dolphins; she recounts the god's
mythical triumph over 'Osirian Egypt' and 'parch'd Abyssinia';

        "I saw the whelming vintage hotly pierce
            Old Tartary the fierce!
        The kings of Inde their jewel-sceptres vail,
        And from their treasures scatter pearled hail;
        Great Brahma from his mystic heaven groans,
            And all his priesthood moans;
        Before young Bacchus' eye-wink turning pale. –

                                              (ll. 261–7)

Bacchus conquers other gods by pleasure and wine, a triumph
shown in the engraving after Giulio Romano in Plate 7.

    Despite admiration for this song as one of the high points of
Endymion, influenced, Robert Gittings believes, by the free and wild
rhythms of Coleridge,[22] most readers have concentrated on the
song's welcome to sorrow, ignoring the section on Bacchic revelry
that interrupts it.[23] Although the Bacchic section is seventeen lines
longer than the sorrow section and occupies the centre of the song,
little has been written about its celebration of energy, allure and
adventure, nor about its parallels with other Bacchic moments in
other poems by Keats. That a radiant moment fades or vanishes
does not make it less radiant, but more. That the wine inspiring this
radiance, whether in perception, passion or intellect, is finally
rejected does not mean that the wine did not do its work when it
did. And that it is rejected because of some view (heroic, creative,
logical or puritanical) that reality must be faced and endured with a
sober eye does not cancel the real pleasure of the illusion.

    In *Endymion* the Indian Maid leaves the procession of Bacchante
suddenly, and for contradictory reasons. As the conquest of the god
Bacchus is sudden, and the maid's infatuation the work of a

moment, so, too, her renunciation of the god is abrupt, a 'whim' (l. 269), and the return to melancholy only haltingly explained. It is uncertain whether she is imagined to have 'motives', and if so whether they are moral, realistic, or solipsistic. She tells Endymion:

> 'Young stranger!
> I've been a ranger
> In search of pleasure throughout every clime:
>   Alas, 'tis not for me!
>   Bewitch'd I sure must be,
> To lose in grieving all my maiden prime.
>
> 'Come then, Sorrow!
> Sweetest Sorrow!
> Like an own babe I nurse thee on my breast:
>   I thought to leave thee
>   And deceive thee,
> But now of all the world I love thee best.

(ll. 273–84)

The Indian Maid rejects the search for pleasure as 'not for me', but recognizes in a contrary swerve that she is grieving away her prime, for sorrow is her child, mother, brother, wooer and comfort. Lacking pleasure or fellowship, she must be loyal to sorrow in an obsessive melancholy, even if the sorrow is another sort of bewitchment.

Surely her devotion to sorrow is no more realistic or healthy than her participation in the Bacchanalian rout. In a letter to Benjamin Bailey of 22 November 1817, two weeks after copying out for him the song of the Indian Maid, Keats exults that 'all our Passions as of Love they are all in their sublime, creative of essential Beauty.' He cries, 'O for a Life of Sensations rather than of Thoughts!'; he calls the after-life a continuation and refinement of earthly happiness, and thinks 'such a fate can only befall those who delight in sensation rather than hunger as you do after Truth.' He tells Bailey 'it is necessary to your eternal Happiness that you not only drink this old Wine of Heaven which I shall call the redigestion of our most ethereal Musings on Earth; but also increase in knowledge and know all things' (*KL*, 1, 184–6). Pleasure, enjoyment, the here and now, are foremost in Keats's mind as he writes this Bacchic section of *Endymion*. Although the return to 'a world of Pains and troubles' may two years later seem 'necessary ... to school an Intelligence and make it a soul', as Keats writes to George and Georgiana Keats (21 April 1819, *KL*, 2, 102), the 'redigestion' of 'this old Wine of Heaven' creates 'essential Beauty' and allows us 'to enjoy ourselves hereafter'.

The positioning of this Bacchic interlude resembles the positioning of Bacchic interludes in the 'Ode to a Nightingale' and in 'Lamia'. In all three poems raucous, vinous celebrations interrupt sadness, relieve it temporarily, seem preferable to its obsessive and tedious reiterations, but are ultimately rejected in favour of a return to sorrow, on the assumption that sorrow is more true than these exultant and giddy illusions.

III: LIFE OF SENSATIONS AND HERITAGE OF DRINK

Some of Keats's fascination with Bacchus's riotous lore, with drinking songs, and with drinking imagery stems from Keats's real relish of wine. He takes pleasure in recording the nuances of drunkenness as a dizzying peak of multiplying sensations, feelings, impressions and thoughts. He is not a habitual drunkard, but he delights in watching himself getting drunk as part of his self-conscious and even medical attention to the intensity of his own sensations. Literary sources alone do not inspire his language; so do the lived intensities of a life that he always knew would be so short that he would need to live it kaleidoscopically.[24]

In his description of claret-drinking to his brother and sister-in-law 19 February 1819, two months before the great May of the Odes, Keats weaves together Bacchus, Aladdin's enchanted palaces, Silenus, Hermes, the palate and the heated brain, as these assorted impressions dart excitedly up and down the 'pleasure thermometer':

> now I like Claret whenever I can have Claret I must drink it. – 'tis the only palate affair that I am at all sensual in – Would it not be a good Speck to send you some vine roots – could I[t] be done? I'll enquire – If you could make some wine like Claret to d[r]ink on summer evenings in an arbour! For really 't is so fine – it fills the mouth one's mouth with a gushing freshness – then goes down cool and feverless – then you do not feel it quarelling with your liver – no it is rather a Peace maker and lies as quiet as it did in the grape – then it is as fragrant as the Queen Bee; and the

more ethereal Part of it mounts into the brain, not assaulting the cerebral apartments like a bully in a bad-house looking for his trul and hurrying from door to door bouncing against the waist-coat: but rather walks like Aladin about his own enchanted palace so gently that you do not feel his step. Other wines of a heavy and spirituous nature transform a Man to a Silenus; this makes him a Hermes – and gives a Woman the soul and immortality of Ariadne for whom Bacchus always kept a good cellar of claret – and even of that he could never persuade her to take above two cups – I said this same Claret is the only palate-passion I have I forgot game … . (*KL*, 2, 64).

Keats's rapture spins through a range of associations: the practical demands of vineculture in Kentucky; the grateful and receptive bodily organs washed by wine; the reality of street life; myths and legends of drunkards and exotics. He recreates the wine's vigorous movement in the velocity of his own sentences. Keats's sense of pleasure is

> as brisk
> As a bottle of whisk
> Ey and as nimble
> As a milliner's thimble,

as he quips in an early song (*KCP*, p. 46); his imagination is heated as he speeds from image to image, freed from the sober constraints of punctuation.

Whether or not he is exaggerating, or darkening his memories as he himself contemplates suicide, Benjamin Haydon tells the story of Keats's excesses of feeling and sensation. Just after hearing the news of Keats's death, Haydon describes the poet's intensity:

his eyes glistened! his cheek flushed! his mouth positively quivered & clentched! … fiery, impetuous, & ungovernable, … having no decision of character & not strength enough to buckle himself like a porcupine, & present nothing but his prickles to his enemies, he began to despond, flew to dissipation as a relief, which from a temporary elevation of spirits, plunged him into deeper & more inextricable despondency than ever. For six weeks he was scarcely sober, & once to shew what a Man of Genius does, to gratify his appetites, when once they get the better of him, he covered his tongue & throat as far as he could reach with Cayenne pepper, in order as he said to have the 'delicious coolness of claret in all its glory!' This was his own expression, as he told me the fact. Ah Keats, how soon art thou passed!

Haydon reveals that he and Keats quarrelled over Keats's drinking: 'Latterly he grew angry because I shook my head at his irregularity, and told him he was destroying himself.' Three years later Haydon rereads *Endymion*, regrets not finishing his portrait of Keats, and recalls, 'He got dissipated & used never to come near me for weeks latterly.'[25] Although his judgements of Keats's weak character are faulty, Haydon's story of cayenne and claret corresponds to Keats's delight in amassing sensation until his head, heart and senses reel. If the story is not true, it might as well be.

Some of this delight in sensation may be in the blood, that is, inherited from both sides of his family, plumping his genes. Gittings believes that Keats's silence about his parents seals 'shattering knowledge', but he does not specify what it might be.[26] Evidence that Keats's parents were drunkards comes from John Taylor's interview with Keats's guardian, Mr Abbey, after Keats's death. Taylor, Keats's publisher, was seeking biographical information but was sickened by the 'gross' details he found and hoped to hush them up. Mr Abbey's reminiscences have been doubted because of his bias against the wilful grandchildren of his friend Mrs Jennings, whose wild daughter abandoned them to her care. But given his friendship for Mrs Jennings, his loyalties and his judgements might be well placed. Mr Abbey's memories are all we have, and revulsion against such gross realities is no reason to ignore the 'raw' material that Keats distills or refines in his own life and art of sensation.

From Abbey, who as the friend of Keats's mother's mother saw Frances Jennings Keats and her impulsive choice of husband from a disapprovingly avuncular angle, Taylor learned that Keats's father died in a grisly riding accident after 'a carouse, probably very much in Liquor'; that Keats's mother's father was a 'compleat gourmand' whose womanfolk spent days preparing each of his dinners; and that Keats's mysterious mother, whose 'ardent' 'passions' were sensual as well as sensuous, after the death of her first husband 'became addicted to drinking and in the love of the Brandy Bottle found a temporary Gratification to those inordinate Appetites which seem to have been in one stage or other constantly soliciting her.' Keats's mother was a high-spirited woman of intense appetites, whose lustfulness seemed to verge on nymphomania;

drinking brandy substituted perhaps for lusts she could not, as a woman, properly satisfy. Taylor tut-tuts to Woodhouse about Keats's mother: 'The Growth of this degrading Propensity to liquor may account perhaps for the strange Irregularities – or rather Immorality of her after-Life – I should imagine that her children seldom saw her, and would hope that they knew not all her conduct.' Taylor's records and Abbey's reminiscences may explain Keats's mother's long absence and her return, sick with consumption and other unspoken afflictions, to be nursed day and night by her fiercely loyal, eldest son, then thirteen, who is said to have resembled her in looks (but not stature), high spirits, intelligence, ardent passions, restlessness, and sometimes even 'Irregularities' – the euphemism, used also of Burns and Coleridge, which Haydon applied to Keats in his Diary, provoking Charles Cowden Clark's defence.[27] Old grandfather Jennings seems to have passed on to his daughter and then his grandson his sensuality, which ramified from food to drink to sex to sensation to the intensity of all life's brief experience. Specifically connecting orality and language, Keats's mother's high spirits and notably 'wide mouth' seem almost allegorically transposed in Keats's heightened essences and his vowels that seem to have been deliberately chosen to sound as if they have been rolling around in oral cavities, vibrating in sinuses and fricating on teeth, what M. H. Abrams has called 'the oral palpability of his material signifiers'.[28] The feel of the mouth as it makes sounds by moving, salivating and slurping is one of Keats's craftsmanlike sensualities.

Taylor closed his letter to Woodhouse suggesting that he not 'communicate to the world' these 'Materials for a life of our poor Friend' – 'they are too wretched ... How strange it seems that such a Creature of the Element as he should spring from such gross Realities – But how he refined upon the Sensualities of his Parents!'[29] Refinement and distillation were processes built into Keats's own personal self-building as an orphan sorting out the strands of his lost family inheritance.

There is some dispute among his biographers about how heavy Keats's actual drinking was. Walter Jackson Bate describes Keats's active social life in January 1818; he frequently drinks heavily, at Redhall's dance, at card-playing clubs, and at nightly and very late dinners.[30] Gittings finds him in the same period giggling at Haydon's, imitating the sounds of instruments in hilarity, pursuing the etymology of bawdy words in masculine raucousness; and generally 'racketting'.[31] A year later, in a deep depression, this drinking had become excessive, but Bate believes his 'dissipation', described by Benjamin Haydon, was exaggerated: 'The grain of truth in Haydon's story' – that 'for six weeks he was scarcely sober' – 'may be only that Keats occasionally drank a half bottle or more of claret; and this can seem something of an excess to Keats, however amusing the notion might seem to men of the Regency who could take five or six bottles of port in an evening.'[32] Aileen Ward sees more cause for concern, writing that 'Keats now began drinking fairly heavily for the first time in his life. His rhapsody on claret, his attempt to ration himself to two or three glasses a meal, his getting tipsy at a claret feast for Dilke in March – all support Haydon's statement that Keats, in his depression after Tom's death, "flew to dissipation as a relief."'[33]

A pattern of release through drink, followed by oblivion and despair, occurs even in the early poems. In the August 1814 poem, 'Fill for me the brimming bowl', wine heats and inspires, and also provides oblivion from the cruelty of life, in this case the indifference of a mysterious lady in the Vauxhall gardens:

Fill for me a brimming bowl,
  And let me in it drown my soul:
And put therein some drug design'd
To banish Woman from my mind.
For I want not the stream inspiring,
That heats the sense with lewd desiring;
But I want as deep a draught
As e'er from Lethe's waves were quaft
From my despairing breast to charm
The image of the fairest form
That e'er my rev'ling eyes beheld,
That e'er my wandering fancy spell'd!

(ll. 1–12; *KCP*, p. 30)

The wine alone in the brimming bowl would heat up his sense with lewd desiring; the added drug would make him forget and would free him from the woman's spell. In rudimentary form this lyric in the Renaissance and cavalier tradition proposes some of the connections developed later in the 'Ode to a Nightingale': the drowning soul, the intensifying drug added to the wine, the heated sense, the drinking from Lethean waves, the despairing poet, the magical charm, the revelling eye and the wandering fancy. In this early poem the brimming bowl is 'vain', and the haunting woman who causes his sorrow cannot be banished. In the 'Ode to a Nightingale', stanza 2, by contrast, the draught of vintage does succeed in briefly obliterating the poet's despair.

IV: DISTILLING, INTENSITY AND SONGS

Not only literary plots and images fill Keats's coffers but also images from chemistry, especially the word *distil*, with its many meanings. Stuart Sperry has shown that the words 'abstract', 'sublime', 'essence', 'intensity', and 'distil' all have precise chemical applications in Keats's time that allow the words to work on 'ethereal' as well as empirically observable levels.[34] For Keats, as for Coleridge, who was also deeply interested in science, science is not sharply separated from spirituality, but rises toward it on a continuum. The overlap occurs in occultism for some thinkers, as for instance Newton's simultaneous investigations into science and occultism. The vocabulary of alchemy still lurks in chemistry.[35] Keats the medical scientist uses the word distil with its full meaning, still current: 'to vaporize a substance by means of heat, and then condense the vapour by exposing it to cold, so as to obtain the substance or one of its constituents in a state of concentration or purity.' Where Milton uses *distil*, but only of dewy liquids, not with its implication of alcoholic transformative power, Keats's interest in extracting the quintessence, in condensing, concentrating and vaporizing as aspects of drinking bears similarities to Abraham Cowley's fluid poem 'Drinking', which uses the scientific processes of evaporation and condensation in rain, ocean and sun to encourage human participation in the cycle of global drinking, condensing and volatilizing:

> The thirsty *Earth* soaks up the *Rain*,
> And drinks, and gapes for drink again.
> The *Plants* suck in the *Earth*, and are
> With constant drinking fresh and fair.
> The *Sea* it self, which one would think
> Would have but little need of *Drink*,
> Drinks ten thousand *Rivers* up,
> So fill'd that they o'erflow the *Cup*.

Though no reference to Cowley appears in Keats's letters, Keats attended Hazlitt's 1818 lectures on the English poets; Hazlitt praised

Cowley, speaking warmly in particular of Cowley's drinking-songs, saying that the *Anacreontiques* reach 'the perfection of that sort of gay, unpremeditated lyrical effusion. They breathe the very spirit of love and wine.'[36] Cowley's poem seems to be an influence on concatenating science, drunkenness, healths, and the pleasures of life.

More immediate than Cowley as an influence was Robert Herrick. Herrick's *Select Poems*, reissued in Bristol in 1810, were in Keats's library, and their praise of simple joys can be glimpsed in Keats's *carpe diem* songs.[37] Herrick's poems connect drinking wine, enjoying life, creating songs and participating with revelry and imagination in the vitality and artistry of great poets of the past, as in 'To live merrily, and to trust to Good Verses' and 'When I would have my Verses Read'. Herrick's love of the good things of life – wine, women and song – is sharpened by his sense, as least in the early pagan poems, that even poets end as little piles of ashes, while 'onely Numbers sweet,/ With endless life are crown'd'.

The scientific concern with volatile and condensing states, distilling and intensifying, intensifies the study of the state of intoxication; as we saw, John Wesley was interested in the new word 'dissipation', David Hartley in dissolution as applied to fluctuating personality under the influence of wine, and the late eighteenth-century doctors in the newly intense state of drunkenness as physiological transformation. Science thus multiplies the possibilities for opening out philosophical study of personality and poetic analysis of the explosive instances of feeling.

When Sperry points to Keats's chemical interest in distilling as a form of intensifying, he does not extend this scientific precision to the pervasive reference to alcohol itself as a heightening, glowing intensification of perceiving and living.[38] Such references occur in short unnoticed songs and at climactic moments of *Endymion* and 'Lamia'. Alcohol performs quickly evaporating flights in an increasingly horrifying world of fierce destruction. It is for Keats still exhilarating, since he does not get old enough for it to cease to produce the 'glow'. As an apothecary, Keats knows how volatility works, and he uses the vocabulary of chemistry, including distilling, which he applies largely to many forms of the process, refinement and volatility, condensation, concentration and essentializing. Ricks, whose seminal work on Keats's sensations informs this study, shows that Keats's lusciousness and fullness swell every word, though Ricks does not in fact mention that luscious and full fact of claret.[39]

Keats's refinement of the gross sensualities he inherited rises upward from them rather than kicking them away. His own love of tastes, liquids, bodies, pleasure, overflow and excess is as physical as Ben Jonson's, whose rowdy, sometimes violent, drinking bouts at the Mermaid Tavern Keats wished he could have joined (*KCP,* pp. 230–1). Where his friends call these realities gross, Keats himself seems to make no moral or prudish differentiations between levels of sensations; even brutal or brutish sensations he savours, such as the instinctiveness of hawks (*KL,* 2, 79) or the energies released in a quarrel in the street, however wounding. His own desires, lusts, and suffocating and choking jealousies, which can be summarized in the sentence 'I should have had her when I was in health, and I should have remained well',[40] are as insistent as his mother's, who lifted her skirts in the muddy street to show her 'uncommonly handsome' legs and whose desires were too 'inordinate' for a man to sit comfortably in the same room with her, though this may say more about Mr Abbey's fantasies than about her actual behaviour.[41]

The word *refinement,* originally applied to physical rather than moral processes, as metals purified of dross, but then attracting meanings of elegance, cultivation, polish, and freedom from vulgarity or coarseness, is perhaps better replaced by *distillation,* with its morally neutral chemical accuracy depicting vapours. Even in its physical origin the word *distil* does not denigrate the goodness of the liquid before distillation occurs, whereas refining casts out the dross as 'corruption', lending moral meanings to the word early on. These sensualities are distilled into their essence by being heated and cooled in the retort of language, feelings vaporized into syllables. The words are air, volatile essence of senses. Lamb also used this metaphor of distillation continuing upward into words; he is cited in OED: 'draughts of ... wine distilled into airy breath to tickle vain auditors.' The senses are essentialized not abstracted; they are made more intensely themselves by concentration.

Keats's delight in claret (*KL,* 2, 64), his three glasses of claret a day after renouncing spirits and water (*KL,* 2, 64), his joy in a claret feast (*KL,* 2, 90), his tasting of whisky toddy in Scotland, as we saw in Chapter 1, even, at a desperate time, the gift of bottles of his favourite Château Margaux are physical realities. He cannot conceive of Brown's rejecting such pleasures, as his mocking stanzas suggest:

Ne cared he for wine, or half and half
Ne cared he for fish or flesh or fowl

And sauces held he worthless as the chaff
He 'sdeign'd the swine herd at the wassail bowl
[...]
He sipp'd no olden Tom or ruin blue
Or nantz, or cheery brandy drank full meek
By many a Damsel hoarse and rouge of cheek.

(KL, 2, 89–90)

Seeing Brown as too stuffy to drink what rouged women dare, or the 'blue ruin' consumed in buckets by Coleridge's chimney-sweeps, Keats repeats the machismo taunting that other male critics applied in reverse to his own effeminate lusciousness.[42]

Perhaps with some empathetic act of living into his mother's mysterious activities during the two years when she abandoned him and her other children, Keats is more interested than his contemporaries in drunken women. These rouged women have an analogue in the drunken 'Mrs C' in 'Upon my life, Sir Nevis, I am piqu'd' (*KCP*, pp. 279–81), another poem from the Scottish trip associated with whisky, like those on Burns noted in Chapter 2. Mrs C. wishes to be swept away by the sublime mountain, but thinks of pickles and preserves and putting more whisky to her lips; she dashes her whisky to the ground in terror of the mountain's roar. Also acknowledging that women can be wild and tippling, if incapable of the sublime, a letter to Georgiana imagines her drinking to pass the long boring days in an uncivilized outpost:

> Do you get any Spirits – now you might easily distill some whiskey – and going into the woods set up a whiskey [shop] for the Monkeys. Do you and the miss Birkbecks get groggy on any thing – a little so so ish so as to be obliged to be seen home with a Lantern. ... Then you may saunter into the nearest coffeehouse and after taking a dram and a look at the chronicle, go and frighten the wild boars upon the strength ... put a hedgehog into George's hat – pour a little water into his rifle ... . (16 April 1819, *KL*, 2, 92–3)

Georgiana, for some reason, elicits comments and jokes about drinking. A year before, Keats had sent her an acrostic on their shared last name that also plays on wine-drinking:

> Kind Sister! aye this third name says you are
> Enhanced has it been the Lord knows where.

Ah! may it taste to you like good old wine –
Take you to real happiness and give
Sons daughters and a Home like honied hive.

(28 June 1818, *KL*, 1, 304)

In his chapter 'Taste and Distaste', Ricks focuses on honey and
treacle, but says that this verse 'insists upon the importance of
tasting and of wine, and upon the climactic importance of the
"honied hive," in its associations with the fecundity of future sons
and daughters.'[43] In addition, Keats seems to suggest that 'good old
wine' could take Georgiana to 'real happiness', and that it is wine
that will loosen the pair and make them fertile.

In joking with Georgiana about sex, pleasure and getting a
little 'so so ish', and in mocking Brown's rejection of pleasures,
Keats continues his Comus-like rebellion against Milton. Moral
censorship is for parsons, festering within from self-denial (*KL*, 2,
63), though priests are more mysterious, some of them being
secret 'topers' (*KCP*, pp. 282–4). Condemning 'pious frauds of
Religion' (*KL*, 2, 80), he takes on Comus's deliciously seductive
role: live; eat; be fat (a skinny woman inspires a riff of compar-
isons to cribbage pins, lynch-pin, staff, walking-stick, fishing-rod,
tooth-pick, hat-stick, flag-pole [*KL*, 2, 68–9]); enjoy; drink; get
'warm' (slang for having sex[44]); use the body; for tomorrow we
die. 'Give me women, wine, and snuff / Untill I cry out "hold,
enough!,"' calls the young dandy Keats, trying out a cavalier
mode (*KCP*, p. 47).

Liquor, especially wine, is physical and immediate; it is a multi-
fariously changing taste, a fume, an odour, a perfume, a scintilla-
tion, some oenologists say (needing a synaesthetic vocabulary)
even an oceanic or cloudy sound. More than that, its effects
heighten, suffuse with a glow, quicken, exalt and multiply the
facets of each moment of experience. It is loved in itself and for
what it does. It heats up the 'pleasure thermometer', from sun and
earth, to vine, to grape, to wine, to inspiration, to words, to voice, to
the listening ear, to the spirits of reader or auditor, as Francis Place,
too, recalls when he describes the warmth suffusing body and
mind, heart and eye (a glow that all alcoholics keep hoping to
recapture). Even Keats's late nervous poem 'The Jealousies' sports a
distraught emperor whose brandy is cooled with a little wine, who
drinks the 'ripest claret' from a 'Flemish glass', and who fills his
bumper so as not to weep (*KCP*, p. 520).

Hazlitt's admiration for Keats resembles his admiration for Burns, and arises from the same earthy physicality, gusto, immediacy and 'ferment' of energy. Although before he looked closely at the 1820 volume he charged Keats with 'a deficiency in masculine energy of style' and found in *Endymion* 'nothing tangible in it, nothing marked or palpable',[45] he finds later just that palpability and heft that had seemed lacking. What Hazlitt says about Burns (defending him against the abstemious Wordsworth, as we saw in Chapter 2), may apply also to his defence of Keats: 'He had a real heart of flesh and blood beating in his bosom – you can almost hear it throb. Some one said, that if you had shaken hands with him, his hand would have burnt yours.'[46] (Coleridge did shake Keats's hand on Hampstead Heath, but too late for burning; he thought he felt death in it.) For Keats, as for Burns, heaven is here on earth and so is hell. In heaven Keats 'would, with his maid Marian, / Sup and bowse from horn and can.' He would take pleasure in

> Sipping beverage divine,
> And pledging with contented smack
> The Mermaid in the zodiac.

> (*KCP*, pp. 230–1)

Comparing the work of the imagination with drinking, he sees how

> [Fancy] will mix these pleasures up
> Like three fit wines in a cup,
> And thou shalt quaff it.

> (*KCP*, p. 291)

He loves spicy ale and merriment (*KCP*, p. 229). Hell is the lonely wait in Rome to bid it all adieu.

Keats's intensity is not an ordinary hedonism, for his pleasures become so exquisite that they ache, and his pains so powerful that the are felt as explosions of energy. His pleasure, with its stiletto probe, is not always pleasant. He writes, 'if I am not in action mind or Body I am in pain – and from that I suffer greatly by going into parties where from the rules of society and a natural pride I am obliged to smother my Spirit and look like an Idiot – because I feel my impulses given way to would too much amaze them – I live under an everlasting restraint – never relieved except when I am composing – ' (*KL*, 2, 12). His overswelling of power and spirit, held in, suffocates him, makes him clench his mouth, makes his eyes glisten, as Haydon noted.[47] The highest point of intensest pleasure may teeter over into pain: 'know there is richest juice in poison flowers' (*KCP*, p. 249). The multiplicity of passions burst kaleidoscopically in the song 'Spirit Here that Reigneth', the first stanza to the spirit of pain, the second to the spirit of laughter and quaffing:

> Spirit here that reignest!
> Spirit here that painest!
> Spirit here that burnest!
> Spirit here that mourneth!
>   Spirit! I bow
>   My forehead low,
> Enshaded with thy pinions!

Having acquiesced to this spirit of pain, he turns to the allegro spirit, who laughs, quaffs, dances, and prances. The song concludes rousingly with the poet flushed, experiencing these contradictory feelings in the wake of his eager participation (no 'Hence! Away!' of Milton's Lady for him) in Comus's luscious offerings:

> Spirit, I flush
> With a Bacchanal blush,
> Just fresh from the banquet of Comus!

> (*KCP*, p. 295)

Flushed in the moment, the poet still knows that many of his joys are imaginary; like the exaltation of bowsing, they collapse the morning after. They vanish, like the wedding fare and decor at the end of 'Lamia', inspired by excesses of wine. Could these rich illusions, beneficial for a while despite their falseness, inspire Lamb's vision of Captain Jackson in the last essays of Elia (written after Keats's death), whose rich table and empty glasses are replenished by compensatory imagining?[48]

V: 'ODE TO A NIGHTINGALE' STANZA 2 AND 'LAMIA' 2, 173–276

Many of the elements of stanza 2 of the 'Ode to a Nightingale' have been adumbrated not only in Milton's *Comus* as noted above, but also in Keats's earlier poems and letters about the pleasures of wine, the brief release wine offers to suffering mortals, and even the rejection of wine's joys in favour of realism, duty and work. One of the several drinking-songs of his earlier days demonstrates this pattern of sadness, release through wine, and rejection of wine:

> Hence burgundy, claret, and port,
> 	Away with old hock and madeira!
> Too earthly ye are for my sport;
> 	There's a beverage brighter and clearer!
> Instead of a pitiful rummer,
> My wine overbrims a whole summer;
> 		My bowl is the sky,
> 		And I drink at my eye,
> 		Till I feel in the brain
> 		A Delphian pain –

> 					(*KCP*, p. 227)

The brewed enchantments come out of the 'deep-delved earth', and are indeed bright and clear, but he bids them adieu in Comus's Lady's word 'Hence' and in the Nightingale Ode's 'Away', when he realizes that he can drink the 'golden sunshine' and fill the brain with the 'glory and grace' of Apollo. Drinking is replaced by inspired writing that may feel like overbrimming wine but is 'Not charioted by Bacchus and his pards'. Keeping in mind this song and the many others previously mentioned, we can see that Bacchus offers an earthly joy that an epicurean can clasp, a taste, a scent, a gurgling, a bubbling, a giddiness, a dizziness, a heightened wit and racing pulse, that are real, as far as they go. But the pleasures of drink must be banished for they impede art.

As in the Indian Maid's song, stanza 2 of the 'Ode to a Nightingale' follows a complicated depression, leads out of it, and then, after a brief spurt of sensuality and pleasure, returns to it. The stanza is surrounded by sorrow, as is the Indian Maid's song; it is crowded around by suicidal depression in the poet himself in stanza 1 and by sickness and groans in other people he cares about or does not know in stanza 3. The stanza bursts up like a Bacchante's shouted 'Evoe!' offering momentary delight:

> O, for a draught of vintage! that hath been
> 	Cool'd a long age in the deep-delved earth,

Tasting of Flora and the country green,
    Dance, and Provencal song, and sunburnt mirth!
O for a beaker full of the warm South,
    Full of the true, the blushful Hippocrene,
        With beaded bubbles winking at the brim,
            And purple-stained mouth;
That I might drink, and leave the world unseen,
    And with thee fade away into the forest dim:

(ll. 11–20; *KCP*, pp. 369–70)

The vintage rises out of earth; it retains its organic origin in vines, its communal origins in the country pleasures of its pickers and stompers, and its chemical origins of sunlight and soil; it recalls its warm and bright Mediterranean littoral – Greek in Hippocrene, French in Provencal; it retains its immediate physicality in the bubbles prickling the lips, their dance at the rim of the glass, the stain on the mouth.[49] These physical sensations immediately transmogrify into spiritual ones: wine allows the drinker to leave the world, himself 'unseen', and also not seeing the world with its disease and misery; to fade away both from the world and into his own unconsciousness, so that even if the evils persist, he will not perceive them. So effective is the wine that this is the only one of the stanzas of the 'Ode to a Nightingale' that does not mention death, and that successfully obliterates its pain. This stanza is not a joke, as Bromwich suggests,[50] but participates in a career-long pattern of offering wine-drinking as a real if temporary consolation.

Far less satisfactory than drink is the escape through imagination. Though it is instantaneous and magical, it does not bring the poet into a warm, sunlit, living world, but into a cold, damp, dark and dead one. Though poesy is 'viewless', in that it is self-enclosed and need not see or represent the palsy and suffering of real human beings, it nevertheless recreates the morbidity of that reality in its own symbols, drawing on a literary tradition of funereal flowers like Ophelia's litany of disappointment and betrayal cryptically revealed in the flowers she names. These unseen flowers are not the 'poetry of earth' but flowers like those the mourner names in 'Lycidas', in a tradition of embalming. However much poesy was meant to soar above suffering, it still reproduces it in its oblique notations, as if the ground of pain must be rendered somehow, and human words can only grow out of that pain. Wine, on the other hand, resurrects the dead and revitalizes the living, if only temporarily, physically, and hence unheroically.

In passing beyond the dark embalmed fields of symbolic flowers into the recreated worlds where the unchanging nightingale has passed, the imagination still is unable to escape sorrow, but transmutes the ground of suffering from emperors and slaves, to Ruth's exile, to the faery lands forlorn that 'La Belle Dame Sans Merci' had shown to be cruel and blasting. The imagination can create only more and various versions of our pain, as it covers or averts the underlying desire for non-existence with its verbal images.

The poet's inescapable sense of being forlorn, abandoned, solitary, without culture, in a world of isolated individuals each dying his own death within earshot of the groans of others, is not overcome by any work of the imagination. The 'fancy cannot cheat so well, as she is said to do', whatever Wordsworth or Coleridge might claim. For pain, death, fragmentation, isolation and lostness continue to rise up in the myths, stories and images of art, transmuting but not evading the reality that only drunkenness can briefly assuage. Waking or sleeping is all one, for even our dreams reveal the obsessions of mortal consciousness.

While art is inevitably tied, sometimes by submerged references, to the dying reality, intoxication provides a temporary but for that moment complete release from it. The stanza on wine is in fact the only one that does not mention death in any way at all – no Lethe, no dying, no embalming, no requiem, no sod, no richness of death, no ceasing without pain, no hungry generations, no forlorn solitude, no plaintive anthems, no vanishing song. Instead, it presents life as it used to be lived in another time and place of joy, brought back in its glowing reality, and recreating that vitality in the present, a life of sensations, not of thoughts, of exquisite and heightened pleasure and communal forgetfulness at the moment when taste lifts into knowledge, and body and spirit are one.

While the poet rejects wine-drinking as a means to fly to the Nightingale's insouciant and invisible song –

> Away! away! for I will fly to thee,
>   Not charioted by Bacchus and his pards,
> But on the viewless wings of Poesy

(ll. 31–3)

– he tires similarly of art, bidding it adieu as he returns to his own unalterably mortal self: 'Adieu! the fancy cannot cheat so well / As she is fam'd to do, deceiving elf' (ll. 73–4). Thus, although numerous commentators speak of the wine stanza as a false and deluded escape and praise the brave choice of art, both of these choices are temporary. Of the two art takes its subject matter and rhymes from 'easeful Death', drink from ebullient life.

A similar pattern of drinking and its rejection occurs in the second part of 'Lamia'. When Lycius in 'mad pompousness' (2, l. 114) forces his affair with Lamia into public recognition, Lamia creates a festival to enchant the Corinthians. In a magically induced paradise of architecture, sensation and glittering appearance, she loads the tables, and includes 'huge vessels, wine / Come from the gloomy tun with merry shine' (*KCP*, p. 471). Music, oil, robes and incense soften up the guests, who are inspired by wine into flushed enthusiasm. Keats describes precisely how wine works to energize a party:

> Soft went the music the soft air along,
> While fluent Greek a vowel'd undersong
> Kept up among the guests, discoursing low
> At first, for scarcely was the wine at flow;
> But when the happy vintage touch'd their brains,
> Louder they talk, and louder come the strains
> Of powerful instruments.

> (2, 199–205)

So lubricated are the guests – 'freed' 'from human trammels' – that they welcome the strange hostess:

> Beautiful slaves, and Lamia's self, appear,
> Now when the wine has done its rosy deed,
> And every soul from human trammels freed,
> No more so strange; for merry wine, sweet wine,
> Will make Elysian shades not too fair, too divine.

> (2, 208–12)

Throughout this passage wine is 'the happy vintage'. Its 'rosy deed' frees the soul 'from human trammels'. It is sweet and divine. It causes vivacity, tolerance, warmth, affection and pleasure. At the party's peak, before Appollonius's icy sceptical look destroys the hostess, her lover, and the whole illusion, wine has created a joyful community: 'Soon was God Bacchus at meridian height; / Flush'd were their cheeks, and bright eyes double bright' (2, 213–14). Wine creates illusion, but so, this narrative seems to say, does love. Realistic philosophy that looks askance at such illusions withers, blights and kills, leaving nothing in the place of the vanished illusion. In her fine analysis of ambivalence in 'Lamia', Tillotama Rajan writes: 'That Lamia is projected from two radically inconsistent points of view, alternately humanized and demonized, reflects Keats's continuing uncertainty about the value of illusion in life.' The artifice of the palace, the illusions of love, the drunkenness that fosters it and lets others share it, bathing them in the luxurious colours, textures, flow of desire and physicality, are shattered by the cold eye of logic, and vanish like magic. Rajan asks us to see Lamia as both illusion and reality, but wonders if Keats himself has a language for these wrenching demands.[51] In Lamia's wedding feast magical illusion is created for the eyes of the public by gorging them on wine, wine that creates the pleasure dome of luxuriance. Why discard these pleasing illusions if they foster harmony?

Rajan's question about the value of illusion in Keats is central to the purpose of alcohol for him and for his contemporaries. It engages the problem of false pleasures that Wordsworth decries and the blurred line between artificial and natural pleasures, between wine and breezes, that Coleridge worries about when he rejects Islam's outlawing of alcohol on the grounds that everything we sense and feel is a stimulus. Wine is a false pleasure to the extent that it has been heightened, but fermentation occurs in nature, as decay and death are part of the process. Wine is false because it lifts away pain and worry, because it rouses wit and garrulity, because it makes people tolerant and welcoming, because it activates sensation and intellect; it is false only because it cannot sustain the transformations that it causes. Is there anywhere a pure and true happiness that is not heightened? If even the young Apollo in *Hyperion* III (ll. 116–20) describes his deification as a drunkenness – 'creations and destroyings, all at once/ Pour into the wide hollows of my brain,/ And deify me, as if some blithe wine / or bright elixir peerless I had drunk, and so became immortal' – how false can intoxication be? Even a god knows that this metaphor conveys the fullness, intensity and explosiveness of essential moments.

Wine as one escape from human treachery is still being proposed
and then rejected in a poem found among Keats's papers in Rome,
'What can I do to drive away'. Trying to forget the memory of
Fanny Brawne's lost touch and his obsession with her imagined
infidelity, the poet asks,

> How shall I do
> To get anew
> Those moulted feathers, and so mount once more
> Above, above
> The reach of fluttering Love,
> And make him cower lowly while I soar?
> Shall I gulp wine? No, that is vulgarism,
> A heresy and schism,
> Foisted into the canon law of love; –
> No, – wine is only sweet to happy men;
> More dismal cares
> Seize on me unawares, –
> Where shall I learn to get my peace again?

> (*KCP*, p. 493)

Keats's pain in exile from Fanny, friends, health and the vitality of
London, is so intense that it becomes unspeakable. This late
outcry, recognizing that to stay drunk now to escape the dying
would be vulgar, that even this simple consolation works only for
happy men, reminds us, if we need reminding, that Keats's five
months with Severn offered no consolation until the last day,
quietly listening to Severn read Jeremy Taylor's Art of Dying.[52] He
looked deep into the abyss that he had always known was
waiting.[53]

The presence of Bacchus, wine and varieties of inebriate lunacy
in the whole of Keats's writings is far more insistent than critics
have suspected. When Keats's many references to wine, the gods of
wine, and the effects of wine are brought together as they are in
this chapter for the first time, the sheer number of them indicates
Keats's concern with the sensations and state of drunkenness;
moreover, the fairly consistent use of this ancient solace to
heighten, intensify, purify, sharpen, and speed up the process and
techniques of creativity turn it into a serious option, if ultimately
unsatisfactory by contrast with the seeming permanence of art.

Alcohol as a stimulant to sensation and thought, and as an exalted heady state, forms part of a pattern of offering the experience of intoxication as a real possibility, an interlude, which is finally, usually sadly, rejected, in favour of rejoining the world and its miseries. Intoxication works in *Endymion*, 'Lamia', the 'Ode to a Nightingale', and in the many shorter poems mentioned earlier, if only briefly; it is an artificial heightening, an illusion and an escape, but more power to it if it brings solace and sharpens the experience of being in a world without afterlife.

7

Bacchus contra Venus:
Alcoholic Husbands and
their Wives

'But think how hard I try and how seldom I dare. Think – and have
a bit of pity. That is, if you ever think, you apes, which I doubt.'
— Jean Rhys, *Good Morning, Midnight* (1974)

'He stalls above me like an elephant'
— Robert Lowell, "To Speak of Woe That Is in Marriage" (1959)

Drunkenness has long been a criterion of manliness: men keep their
excesses secret from women; they describe their escape into a jovial
male world in a coded language of euphemism and humour designed to shelter men's pleasures and to keep women at bay.
During the Romantic period a number of women novelists ceased
to regard this secret world as a boyish indulgence, and spoke out
against the damage that drunkenness caused in marriages and
estates. Thus men and women developed very different approaches
and tones of voice when speaking of men's drunkenness, while the
reality of drunkenness among women themselves was still almost
unspoken, and the wry bitterness, the residue of years of defeat,
such as that of Jean Rhys in the first epigraph to this chapter, was
just beginning.[1]

Profound differences in perception according to gender created a
war between Bacchus and Venus that took, and to some extent still
takes, covert forms. It is a war between club and home, London and
the country, riot and domesticity, male group solidarity and isolated female discontent, euphemism and outspoken advocacy of
temperance, pleasure and duty. The ancient incompatibility of
Bacchus and Venus is wagered by Lord Rochester a century earlier
in a letter of 22 June 1674 to Henry Savile:

of the three buisnisses of this Age, Woemen, Pollitics & drinking,
the last is the only exercise att wch. you & I have nott prouv'd our
selves Errant fumblers, if you have the vanity to thinke otherwise,
when wee meete next lett us appeale to freinds of both sexes & as
they shall determine, live & dye sheere drunkards, or intire lovers;
for as we mingle the matter, it is hard to say wch. is the most tire-
some creature, the loving drunkard or the drunken lover.[2]

The drunkard in love cannot concentrate on his drinking; the
drunken lover is an 'errant fumbler'; 'mingling the matter' spoils
both activities. The difficulty of 'mingling the matter' rises not only
from the lack of time to do both, or shift in attitude required, but
also from the dread of drunken impotence, engulfing females and
censorious mothers. These fears may lie at the base of the larger incompatibility of the safe shelter of men in groups with the dangerous obligations of 'love'. On top of physiological facts rises a
complicated structure of responses to male drinking based on
gender, economic dependency, and the differentiation of public
and private spheres.

Although we have seen in previous chapters that euphemisms
prevail in mentions of drunkenness, even in recent discussions
about twentieth-century authors, euphemism forms a closely
woven veil behind which men protect each other's riotous group
behaviour. While the word 'irregularities' has served manfully, a
more extensive language of formality muffles male high-jinks.
Samuel Johnson, for example, summarized the drunken career of
his fascinating friend Savage in sentences so dignified that they
elevate the profligate into a tragic model for failure: 'an irregular
and dissipated manner of life had made him the slave of every
passion that happened to be excited by the presence of its object,
and that slavery to his passions reciprocally produced a life irregular and dissipated. He was not master of his own motions, nor
could promise anything for the next day.' A man whose irrational
resentment had alienated his most patient protectors becomes an
image of tragic humanity, ruined by a cruel mother and twists of
the law, a lesson to others 'that negligence and irregularity, long
continued, will make knowledge useless, wit ridiculous, and genius
contemptible.'[3]

The depiction of the famous drunkard Richard Brinsley Sheridan
(1751–1816) exemplifies the protective euphemisms spun by his
fellow drinkers. In this case we can see both the raw material of

drunken anecdotes in letters from one drinking companion to another, and then the bowdlerized life presented to the public in painstaking denial by one of these companions. In 'Detached Thoughts' jotted down between 15 October 1821 and 18 May 1822, Byron recalls Sheridan's behaviour in the years 1812–15 when Byron frolicked with him in London. Praising Sheridan's wit and eloquence, Byron adds, 'Poor fellow! he got drunk very thoroughly and very soon. – It occasionally fell to my lot to convey him home – no sinecure – for he was so tipsy that I was obliged to put on his cock'd hat for him – to be sure it tumbled off again and I was not myself so sober as to be able to pick it up again.'[4] Byron recalls that Sheridan 'told me that on the night of the grand success of his S[chool] for S[candal] – he was knocked down and put into the watch house for making a row in the street & being found intoxicated by the watchmen. – Latterly when found drunk one night in the kennel and asked his *Name* by the Watchman he answered – 'Wilberforce' –. ... I met him in all places and parties ... and always found him very convivial & delightful' (*BLJ*, 9, 15–16). Byron praises his sentimentality, his charm, his sense of justice, but always returns to Sheridan as a drinker:

> I have got very drunk with [both George Colman and Sheridan] – but if I had to *choose* – and could not have both at a time – I should say – 'let me begin the evening with Sheridan and finish it with Colman.' – Sheridan for dinner – Colman for Supper – Sheridan for Claret or port – but Colman for every thing – from the Madeira & Champaigne – at dinner – the Claret with a *layer* of *port* between the Glasses – up to the Punch of the Night – and down to the Grog – or Gin and water of day-break – all these I have threaded with both the same – Sheridan was a Grenadier Company of Life-Guards – But Colman a whole regiment of *light Infantry* to be sure – but still a regiment. (*BLJ*, 9, 48)

The amount and variety of drinks, and the long continuance of the drinking, allow a glimpse into masculine sociability of the period, with Byron keeping up stalwartly.

In a correspondence studded with nostalgia for past and remedies for present drunkenness, Byron repeatedly urges Thomas Moore (1779–1852) to write Sheridan's biography. On 31 October 1815 he tells Moore the story of how, after a drunken party, Kinnaird and he helped Sheridan down a corkscrew staircase, 'which had certainly been constructed before the discovery of fermented liquors, and to which no legs, however crooked, could possibly accommodate themselves... Both [Sheridan] and Colman were, as usual, very good; but I carried away much wine, and the wine had previously carried away my memory; so that all was hiccup and happiness for the last hour or so, and I am not impregnated with any of the conversation' (*BLJ*, 4, 326–7). Byron urges Moore to excuse Sheridan's behaviour by placing it in the context of men's excesses in that age. In one letter he asks Moore, 'Did Fox ⁕⁕⁕ pay *his* debts? – or did Sheridan take a subscription? Was the Duke of Norfolk's drunkenness more excusable than his? Were his intrigues more notorious than those of all his contemporaries?' (*BLJ*, 6, 47). In another he similarly directs Moore's judgements by comparing Sheridan with other wild men: 'In writing the Life of Sheridan, never mind the angry lies of the humbug whigs. Recollect that he was an Irishman and a clever fellow, and that *we* had some very pleasant days with him. Don't forget that he was at school at Harrow, where in my time, we used to show his name – R. B. Sheridan, 1765, – as an honour to the walls. Remember ⁕⁕⁕⁕⁕' (and here Moore cleans up an extended anecdote); 'Depend upon it that there were worse folks going, of that gang, than ever Sheridan was' (*BLJ*, 6, 68).

Preoccupied with how to judge an 'irregular' genius like Sheridan, analogous to Wordsworth's efforts to judge the irregular genius of Burns, Byron writes his publisher John Murray contrasting Sheridan's behaviour with that of the even drunker Richard Porson, the legendary classical scholar. In a long analysis of the differences between the two drunks, Porson is 'drunk and brutal', takes a poker to a student, uses 'language as blackguard as his action', insults the students' ignorance 'with the most vulgar terms of reprobation', is gross and bestial. 'I have seen Sheridan drunk too with all the world, but his intoxication was that of Bacchus – & Porson's that of Silenus – of all the disgusting brutes – sulky, abusive – and intolerable – Porson was the most bestial' (*BLJ*, 6, 12).

Eager that Moore write 'poor dear Sherry's' biography, Byron feeds him material. Sherry, though older than Byron and Moore, serves a function in his personal mythology similar to Savage's for the older Johnson: he is the rioter who goes all the way, risks all, loses all (in Sheridan's case in the fire that destroyed the Drury Lane theatre, his assets and his hopes). Byron himself makes the parallel decisively when he tells Moore, 'I do not know any good model for a life of Sheridan but that of *Savage*' (*BLJ*, 6, 47). Byron and Johnson can control themselves when necessary, for as Byron writes to Hobhouse, 'my head aches considerably from a Symposium of yesterday ... But in general I am temperate – taking only a pint of light Clary wines at my *one* meal' (*BLJ*, 6, 125). (In answer to Moore's complaints about being drunk [5, 164], he urges abstinence as the only cure, as Johnson did before him when counselling Boswell.) Their subjects do not have such will-power. Sheridan, unlike Savage, however, exercises his genius on the stage and in parliament; he transforms his love of drinking into exonerating the prodigal hero of *The School for Scandal*, Charles Surface, whose drinking-song names women as excuses for more drinks; Sheridan is a star somewhat tarnished, whereas Savage blames the world for his failure.

When Moore finally writes Sheridan's biography in 1825, with help from Samuel Rogers, the protective language thickens with distance, as well as in conformity to a more prudish social climate.[5] A few scattered references in the two volumes to Sheridan's appearance – 'It was, indeed, in the upper part of his face that the Spirit of the man chiefly reigned; – the dominion of the World and the Senses being rather strongly marked out in the lower' – or to his use of wine for inspiration – 'Wine, too, was one of his favorite helps to inspiration; – "If the thought, (he would say,) is slow to come, a glass of good wine encourages it, and when it *does* come, a glass of good wine rewards it"'[6] – culminate in this paragraph, a dazzling obfuscation of Sheridan's drunkenness:

> We have seen the romantic fondness which he preserved toward the first Mrs. Sheridan, even while doing his utmost, and in vain, to extinguish the same feeling in her. With the second wife, a course, nearly similar was run; – the same "scatterings and eclipses" of affection, from the irregularities and vanities, in which he continued to indulge, but the same hold kept of each other's hearts to the last. ... To claim an exemption for frailties and irregularities on the score of genius, while there are such names as Milton and Newton on record, were to be blind to the example which these and other great men have left, of the grandest intellectual powers combined with the most virtuous lives. (2, 329)

Given Sheridan's careless early life, the temptations of London and the stage, the treacherous uncertainty of income, and the 'intoxication of draughts of fame', it is not surprising that his career takes the shape of 'one long paroxysm of excitement – no pause for thought – no inducements to prudence, the attractions all drawing the wrong way and a Voice, like that which Bossuet describes, crying inexorably behind him "On, on!"'

> Instead of wondering at the wreck that followed all this, our only surprise should be, that so much remained uninjured through the trial, – that his natural feelings should have struggled to the last with his habits, and his sense of all that was right in conduct so long survived his ability to practice it. (2, 330–1)

No incidents in the biography document how he worked to alienate his beautiful, patient wife Elizabeth Linley, for whose hand at age 19 he had fought a duel with an old Captain Mathews and with whom he had eloped to France. There is no word of what neglect, infidelity and even violence she may have suffered, no hint of what the country-bound, child-caring wife of a drunken actor, play-wright, producer and legendary party-goer endured, similar perhaps to Mary Tyrone's isolation from her drunken actor husband in Eugene O'Neill's *Long Day's Journey into Night*. The words 'irregularities', 'habits', 'frailties', 'scatterings and eclipses', muffle the man's behaviour: his companions close the circle to hide his 'weakness'.

Thus the example of Sheridan shows the process at work: men watch the drunkard debase himself; they are entertained, shocked, and dazzled; but they hide their risky hero's dual nature from the outside world in a public, decorous, coded language. When women write about this same behaviour, however, they cut through the euphemisms and describe a bestiality which they believe is the reality. Women see men as wild men come in from the woods, crashing around their own drawing-rooms.

For Byron, intoxication epitomizes the engagement with life. It is the 'sap' coursing through men's energies, imaginations, creations, even failures. Getting drunk, whatever the aftermath, reveals courage and vitality; like Werther, cited in Chapter 1, Byron in *Don Juan* scorns those who fear to pursue this thirst for action:

> Man, being reasonable, must get drunk;
>   The best of Life is but intoxication:
> Glory, the Grape, Love, Gold, in these are sunk
>   The hopes of all men, and of every nation;
> Without their sap, how branchless were the trunk

> Of Life's strange tree, so fruitful on occasion!
> But to return, – Get very drunk, and when
> You wake with headache – you shall see what then!⁷

Among masculine activities love takes a place in the list as one accomplishment, to be laughed off between drinks: 'Let us have Wine and Woman, Mirth and Laughter, / Sermons and soda-water the day after' (2, CLXXVIII) and regretted the next morning.

The delight that men take in regaling each other with their drunken escapades is a repeated theme in Byron's letters and journals. He riots with Scrope and Hobhouse, and recalls Scrope literally dripping with wine and blood (*BLJ*. 9, 38–9). The year 1814 glows as the year of revelry. He is proud of the tribute from the fox-hunter Chester, nicknamed Cheeks: 'Chester ... and I sweated the Claret – being the only two who did so – Cheeks who loves his bottle – and had no notion of meeting with a "bon vivant" in a scribbler – in making my eulogy to somebody one evening summed it up in – "by G–d he *drinks like a Man*!" ... . However we carried our liquor discreetly – like "the Baron of Bradwardine"' (*BLJ*, 9, 44–5). Drinking is manly, and manliness (as Byron's criticisms of Keats's piss-a-bed poetry and masturbatory boyishness suggest) is commendable. Dandies, though they accept Byron in their exclusive clubs, are too fastidious to drink, and thus are somewhat feminine. Recalling his own 'loose life about town – before I was of age', Byron contrasts a delicate dandy with a real man:

> A *beau* (dandies were not then christened) came into the P[rince] of W[ales] and exclaimed – 'Waiter bring me a glass of Madeira Negus with a Jelly – and rub my plate with a Chalotte' This in a very soft tone of voice. – A Lieutenant of the Navy who sate in the next box immediately roared out the following rough parody – 'Waiter – bring me a glass of d—d stiff Grog – and rub my a–e with a brick-bat.' (*BLJ*, 9, 29)

In delighting in the manliness of real men who would rather have their asses wiped with brick bats than their china with shallots, Byron anticipates the later opponents of dandyism, as Ellen Moers has described them; these sturdy manly English gentlemen drink quantities of wine and whisky, for it was the 'proud badge of their trade to be always drinking and often drunk'.⁸

In this search for a fine line between manly and feminine behaviour, demarcated here by drinking and elsewhere by the cut of a jacket, Byron veers into the range of beasts, the 'apes' and 'elephant' of the epigraphs to this chapter. In his preference for the beastly over the foppish or feminine, he agrees with his brother under the skin, Samuel Taylor Coleridge. For even as Coleridge feared the brutishness that excessive drinking induced and signalled, he also feared the vain emptiness of the fop. As Byron reacts against a new feminization of the male, the male as fop, delicate in dress, abstemious in appetites that might mess up the lean look and the white cravat, so, too, Coleridge saw this domestication coming. Berating his second son Derwent in 1822 for trifling his time away on dress, 'dissipating' himself at 'a Concert or a Lady Party', he asserts 'I cannot retract my assertion – that Dangling and Dandyism threaten a schirrhus of the Heart, where this precious Dyad finds any heart to work on.' Central to 'Dandyism' is 'Time-Murder in *Narcissism'*. Coleridge the father warns Derwent (warnings in a different key from his earlier warnings and predictions to his older son Hartley) that he will become 'a gay youth, likely to outshine Tom Moore as a poet & pleasant fellow', implying that Moore, the prince of *ton*, is the vapid essence of dandyism, at its hollow centre.[9] Coleridge knew from his own experience that drink transformed the human being into a beast or a thing, but dandyism transformed the male human being into something worse, an empty shell, a costumed surface.

Is such a feminized man worse than the honest male animal frolicking wildly in his spontaneous, unpredictable, often naughty freedom? Hazlitt is fascinated by the feminized dandy, whose jests 'hover on the very brink of vacancy' and who is separated from the dunce by 'the thinnest of all intellectual partitions'. In 'Brummelliana' (1828) Hazlitt recounts how Brummel, laid up with a lame foot, tells a visitor, '"I am sorry for it too ... particularly as it's *my favourite leg*!"' Hazlitt marvels at the man of fashion who has 'nothing else to do than to sit and think of which of his legs he liked best. ... there is an Horatian ease and elegance about it – a slippered negligence, a cushioned effeminacy.'[10] Where Hazlitt views the dandy as languid and feminine, Ellen Moers suggests that the dandy's self-involvement makes him 'a-sexual' and cold.[11] Perhaps the sexuality of the languid dandy is directed toward himself.

Between the Dandy and the Drinking Gentleman, which is more hostile to Venus? Real men, as Eve Kosofsky Sedgwick has shown for Restoration comedy and nineteenth-century gothic, route their bonding with each other through compulsory heterosexual relationships. Even cuckolding a friend brings men closer together, as it further commodifies the wife. Sedgwick cites the punningly named seducer, Horner, in Wycherley's *The Country Wife* as saying, 'Come, for my part I will have only those glorious, manly pleasures of being very drunk and very slovenly.'[12] Both 'manliness' and 'dandyism' reject Venus.[13] Women disrupt or cement the male groups, and drink both corrects the disruption and celebrates the cohesion.[14]

That the non-dandy, randy, brandy male verges on the animal even Byron notes when he speaks of Porson as a brutish Silenus to Sheridan's Bacchus. When wives await their husbands they often await such animals, raging, predatory and irrational, returning after having spent the wives' portions to gratify their own appetites. The husband returns 'to stall above me like an elephant', to recall the epigraph to this chapter, Robert Lowell's sonnet imagining a wife's anxiety about her 'hopped up' husband 'cruising' the avenues and 'whiskey-blind, swaggering home at five'.

In the male drinking-group tales of love are most amusing when shaped into sagas to entertain drinking friends, the women usually ridiculed for their irrationality, stupidity and rapacity. Byron's letters tell of riot and prowess, women who scream and sneak disguised into his private quarters, women who, no matter how sick, still, with pathetic self-abnegation, desire him over and over, flattering his manliness. Of one Venetian woman he crows, after counting the times he has had her, 'she is the prettiest Bacchante in the world – & a piece to perish *in*. ... I have a world of other harlotry ... so that my hands are full – whatever my Seminal vessels may be '[15] Despite recent efforts to protect Byron from charges of sexism,[16] his escapades with these female 'animal[s]', as he calls one of his Venetian dalliances in a letter to Moore,[17] along with quarrels in the streets, pistols, legacies, and money matters, are the stuff of his letters, intended to entertain his friends in his absence as if he were present lifting healths and toasting conquests. Mockery, ridicule and diminution of women in tavern or club settings provide the topic of jokes, but sometimes spur the men to return in a mood of violence. Here is where the wives meet them.

Moore's own journals speak lovingly of his wife Bessie, but record absences in town of months at a time, ostensibly on business, making connections, seeing plays, meeting friends at the best clubs such as White's or Almack's (whose mysterious invitations to membership were based not on wealth or rank but, as Ellen Moers

says, on the ineffable quality: *ton*).[18] Byron refers to Moore's 'duet-
ting, coquetting, and claretting with your Hibernians of both sexes'
(*BLJ*, 9, 183). Once or twice Moore mentions in passing Bessie's
loneliness and disappointment at his continued absence, and he
sobs violently at the death in 1829 of their daughter Anastasia.[19]
While he does have intense domestic feelings, his real life is lived in
male social groups. Many of his writings reveal his pleasure in
drink, for instance *The Epicurean: A Tale* and *Odes of Anacreon*,
significantly dedicated to the Prince of Wales who set the standard
of regency drinking and who ordered *Henry IV Part I* performed on
his accession to the throne to signal his own princely rejection of his
Falstaffian youth.

Moore's participation in male drinking-groups shines radiantly
in *Irish Melodies*. One of several drinking-songs, 'Wreathe the Bowl'
voices the ancient incompatibility of Bacchus and Venus:

> Wreathe the bowl
> With flowers of soul,
> The brightest Wit can find us;
> We'll take a flight
> Tow'rds heaven to-night,
> And leave dull earth behind us.
> Should Love amid
> The wreaths be hid,
> That Joy, th'enchanter, brings us,
> No danger fear,
> While wine is near
> We'll drown him if he stings us. ...[20]

Drinking together leads to outbursts of wit and soul and lifts the
companions towards heaven. The 'dull earth' that they leave
behind consists of home, children, wives, and their quotidian main-
tenance. Love is imagined as a serpent hiding in the wreaths
around the bowl, capable of stinging and poisoning the happy
males and ejecting them from paradise. Moore reassures his friends
that if their witty and companionable bliss is threatened by this
hidden Love, the wine is plentiful enough to drown it, and keep
the witty fellows soaring in 'a flight / Tow'rds heaven tonight'.
Love – the serpent in the garden, the poisonous enchantment of
women – is associated with the fall out of the garden of Eden or
Heaven and with 'dull earth'. Wine can drown Love; men in

groups wish it to. Plate 8 dramatizes the risk and exuberance of masculine frolic.

Also revealing the war between Bacchus and Venus is Moore's Irish Melody 'Drink of this Cup'.

> Drink of this cup; you'll find there's a spell in
>> Its every drop 'gainst the ills of mortality;
> Talk of the cordial that sparkled for Helen!
>> Her cup was a fiction, but this is reality.

Where Helen's cup of famously irresistible love is a fiction, the cup of wine is reality; it also leads to oblivion of 'the dark world we are in'; if drained to the bottom, it lifts the drinkers 'above earth', turning them into 'immortals themselves'. In the competition between the rival potions of love filter and wine, wine wins:

> Never was philter form'd with such power
>> To charm and bewilder as this we are quaffing;
> [...]
> This wonderful juice from its core was distill'd
>> To enliven such hearts as are here brought together.[21]

Men in groups are wild and free because they are not being supervised by women as mothers, sisters, wives or managers. Their freedom is the antipathy of domestic life, stigmatized as earthly. In 'Fill the Bumper Fair' 'wit's electric flame' 'shoots from brimming glasses'. The 'sages' 'grasp the lightning':

> So, we, Sages, sit,
>> And, 'mid bumpers bright'ning,
> From the heaven of Wit
>> Draw down all its lightning.

The cronies explain the source of 'this ennobling thirst/ For wine's celestial spirit' by a revision of the Prometheus myth. Prometheus, stealing living fires, forgot a cup or urn to carry them in, but joyfully found one of Bacchus's bowls lying 'among the stars'.

> Some drops were in that bowl,
>> Remains of last night's pleasure,
> With which the Sparks of Soul
>> Mix'd their burning treasure.

Hence the goblet's shower
  Hath such spells to win us;
Hence its mighty power
  O'er that flame within us.[22]

These songs, newly charged with electric witticisms, keep alive the long tradition of drinking-songs. Though line lengths and conceits vary, the diction would be familiar to Jonson, to Herrick and to Rochester, for drinking men in groups join over the centuries with their fellow singers. Such bonding is more important than love even for the happily married Moore.

On a lower social level, the form of the drinking-song continues to shape itself almost automatically, as in John Clare's 'Drinking Song':

Push round the glass fill it up to the top
& wash away trouble & pain
& when the old tankard has draind its last drop
We'll go the same over again
[...]
But when evil woman wi man play'd the deuce
& Nick did her maidens head borrow
Then nature for's comfort squeze out the grape guice
So drink boy & stifle y'r Sorrow[23]

Once again men drink because 'evil' women lure them to fall; the serpent, old Nick, the devil, are Eve's henchmen. John Clare's drinking is, however, more friendly to sex and women, suggesting as do Burns's drinking-songs, the freer mingling of men and women among the lower classes. Clare himself emphasizes the differences between lower- and upper-class drinkers when he satirizes Dandy Flint Esqu[ire] in 'The Parish',

A sot who spouts short morals oer his gin
& when most drunk rails most against the sin
A dirty hog that on the puddles brink
Stirs up the mud & quarrels with the stink
Abusing others in his cants deciet[24]

Where the upper-class drinker is a dirty hog, the lower-class poet is a jovial labourer. In his journals Clare recalls his early drunkenness with his fellow labourers on the gardening crew 'when I had taken too much of Sir John Barleycorn & coud get no further', his 'irregular habbits ... at "The Hole in the Wall" famous for strong ale & midnight merriment', and his increasing reliance on drink to solace his despair over land enclosure. Very early in life he 'wrote a long poem in praise of his ale in the favourite scotch metre of Ramsay & Burns'. He describes the patterns of male drinking, and reminisces about Saturday nights, 'what they calld randy nights which was all meeting together at the public house to drink & sing ... in midnight revels.' Drunk, he goes 'gypsying' with 'Lassies'. Although he admits that 'I had no tongue to brag with till I was inspired with ale', he resents the charges of drunkenness made against him by people who never helped him.[25] His drinking-songs, omitted from collections of his poems by the editor Eliza Emmerson and unpublished until 1908, include the vivacious 'Toper's Rant':

Come come my old crones & gay fellows
That loves to drink ale in a horn
We'll sing racey songs now we're mellow
Which topers sung ere we were born
[...]
Away with your proud thimble glasses
Of wine foreign nations supply
We topers neer drink to the lassies
Over draughts scarce enough for a flye [.][26]

'The Toper's Rant' celebrates a labouring class and Burnsian mingling of drink and sex, a 'mingling of the matter' unusual among the higher ranks.

With lower-class exceptions such as Clare and Burns, drinking excuses the indifference to sex and the refusal of sex, halving the options of Dionysus' domain. Drinking is pleasure; sex is duty. Some early psychological and fictional studies of alcoholism took for granted the theory that the retreat from sex into drink revealed latent homosexuality, as did Charles Jackson's *Lost Weekend* (where the exposure of Burnum's crush on a fraternity brother is a recurring nightmare). Other studies saw it as an infantile oral regression, as an infantile revenge reaction, or as fetishism around the bottle, or 'mother's milk'.[27] It may more simply serve as relief from pressure to charm the half of the human race that men trained in the company of men were not used to enjoying. In some cases heavy drinking covers a profound hostility to women, though not necessarily a sexual attraction to men.

When women describe male drunkenness, the euphemisms and the elegant references to heaven, soul and wit vanish. This difference in language is true even of William and Dorothy Wordsworth. William's references to drunkards are euphemistic, as when in a letter to Wilson he mentions Burns's 'irregularity of conduct', or in a letter to Montagu he mentions Hartley Coleridge's 'disappearance, ...arising from a cause which is one [we] can guess at – ,'[28] or in 'Home at Grasmere', acknowledges the occasional 'debased' shout caused by 'some abused Festivity'.[29] Dorothy, by contrast, writes frankly in her journal that 'the Queen of Patterdale ... had been brought to drinking by her husband's unkindness and avarice', 'out all night with other women'.[30] In a letter to Catherine Clarkson, she says that Coleridge 'drank no spirits', 'has seldom had any kind of spirits except in water gruel, which he was always fond of taking when he had a pain in his Bowels.'[31] While this difference in the use of euphemism may arise from many causes such as audience and occasion, in general women do not conform to the male code of euphemism when they write about the drunken deportment that disrupts their carefully balanced family settings.

In a rare instance of a woman poet adapting the form and substance of the drinking-song, Anne Finch, Countess of Winchilsea (1631–79) joins in the drinking festivity of her brother and imagines women's reactions to drunken lovers and husbands.[32] The three poems about drinking sustain a telling sequence. The first, 'A Song, for my Br. Les: Finch. Upon a Punch Bowl', calls Lester 'From the Park, and the Play, / And Whitehall come away,/ To the Punchbowl, by far more inviting'. She agrees with her brother that the bowl holds the world, but ends with a reference to Alexander's drunken rage at Clytus:

'Twas a World, like to this,
   The hott Graecian did misse,
Of whom History's keep such a pother,
   To the bottom he sunk,
   And when one he had drunk
Grew maudlin, and wept for another.[33]

Subtly, this ancient alcohol-induced murder reminds her brother of the dangers of consuming this 'world' in a bowl.

Finch's second song about drinking illuminates the mutually exclusive demands of men and women, what Finch calls 'the ancient quarrell' between Bacchus and Cupid. Finch cleverly gives the voice of love to Cupid rather than to Venus, so that as males the figures can drink to each other, complain about the emotional demands made by tearful women, and promise to be each other's refuge. Cupid (voicing the female point of view) first drinks to Bacchus, 'that turn'st the brain',

> to drown the ancient quarrell;
> And mortalls shall no more dispute
> Which of us two, is absolute.

Bacchus (voicing the male point of view) next 'pledge[s]' the archer, acknowledges Cupid's pre-eminence over the heart, but mocks his watery drink – 'tears thou drink'st, drawn from low courage, / And cool'd with sighs.' Love in Bacchus's view is weak, sentimental and feminine. In the final stanza Cupid responds with a compromise:

> I am content, so we may joyn,
> To mix my waters, with thy wine;
> Then henceforth farwell all defying,
> And thus, we'll still be found complying,
> He, that's in love, shall fly to thee,
> And he thats drunk, shall reel to mee.[34]

The lover will drink, the drunkard will fall in love; the watered wine will allow them to do both in a way Rochester thought impossible. Significantly, it is Cupid, voicing the woman's point of view, who works out the compromise where men can go on with their companionate drinking (with a little watery modification, weakening the wine with water but not with maudlin tears) but also return to the demands of love-making. Both men and women can get what they want.

Finch's third poem about drinking is a comic narrative told in the voice of a wife who tries in vain to scare her drunken husband into paying attention to her (sex identified quite openly with duty, rather than pleasure). The wife rigs a mausoleum scene so the drunkard will awake to find himself dead, an image that inverts the male topos that drinking is heaven. 'Convey'd ... from noisie Tavern ... to dreary Cavern', the husband wakes to bad smells 'Of Bodies kill'd with Cordial Waters, / Stronger than other Scents and quicker, / As urg'd by more spirituous Liquor'. But the wife's trick fails: since the man is dead already, he might as well drink more. He immediately rises up 'on his Crupper':

> Thou Guardian of these lower Regions,
> Thou Providor for countless Legions,
> Thou dark, but charitable Crony,
> [...]
> If thou hast Care too of our Drinking,
> A *Bumper* fetch.

The wife despairs of breaking 'this Habit thou'st been getting,/ To keep thy Throat in constant wetting.'[35] Finch acknowledges the difficulty of managing a drunken husband but plays the game coquettishly.[36]

A century later, wives who write poems or novels take the epidemic of male drinking more seriously. Biographical information reveals that many women writers of the period 1780–1830 turned to writing to support families abandoned by husbands whose behaviour is called variously 'profligate', 'dissipated', and 'dissolute'.[37] These terms used by anthologists and biographers cover a number of vices, such as infidelity, gambling, unemployment and excessive drinking. Rarely is the vice specified, even as the husband lounges around the debtors' prison waiting for his scribbling wife to come with his sustenance. Chances are, however, that drinking accompanies and spurs the other vices.

A remarkably early recognition of the dangers of male drunkenness especially among the labouring classes appears in two poems by Hannah More (1745–1833). Her temperance writing, preceding what is commonly called 'the temperance movement' by thirty years, is part of her multifarious engagement with social injustices such as slavery. Boldly impersonating the voices of men, she chooses to imagine men who stand alone in refusing to drink and who suffer the jeers of their companions. She sets these beleaguered men in a newly industrialized England that requires sobriety to survive the dangers of the new mines and mechanisms,[38] and she gives them a self-righteous, school-marmish tone, quite alien to the male voices of Moore and Byron. In 'Patient Joe, or the Newcastle Collier' (1795), Joe is a Candide figure who 'was certain that all worked together for good', giving praise for war, peace, famine, plenty, the birth of a child and the loss of a child, finding meaning in disasters according to the principles of Dr Pangloss. Joe's fellow miners mock his faith that all is for the best, but their belief in luck and chance destroys them:

> Among his companions who worked in the pit,
> And made him the butt of their profligate wit,
> Was idle Tim Jenkins, who drank and who gamed,
> Who mocked at his Bible, and was not ashamed.

(ll. 41–4)

When a dog steals Joe's lunch, he runs after it, a mischance that providentially saves him when the mine collapses, killing the idle drinker:

> 'The pit is fallen in, and Tim Jenkins is dead!'
> How sincere was the gratitude Joseph expressed!
> How warm the compassion which glowed in his breast!
> Thus events great and small, if aright understood,
> Will be found to be working together for good.

(ll. 64–8)[39]

Joe's glee at being proved correct by his fellow miner's death, a punishment for scepticism, breaks the code of male solidarity. The author of the temperance tract, 'The Gin-shop; or a Peep into a Prison',[40] does not seem to share Voltaire's irony about the absurdities of 'philosophical optimism'.

Similarly in 'The Hackney Coach-man: Or the Way to Get a Good Fare' (1802), Hannah More feminizes and domesticates a man's voice; the tone seems ironic even though the irony is probably unintentional. The driver gloats about the drunkenness of his rich customers and pats himself on the back for being sober, foreseeing the profit that will come from his brave refusal to join the group:

> I never get drunk, and I waste not a shilling.

> And while at a tavern my gentleman tarries,
> The coachman grows richer than he whom he carries;
> And I'd rather (said I), since it saves me from sin,
> Be the driver without, than the toper within.

> Yet though dram-shops I hate, and the dram-drinking friend,
> I'm not quite so good but I wish I may mend;
> I repent of my sins, since we all are depraved,
> For a coachman, I hold, has a soul to be saved.

When a riotous multitude fills up a street,
And the greater part know not, boys, wherefore they meet;
If I see there is mischief, I never go there,
Let others get tipsy so I get my fare.

(ll. 9–20)

Like the 1795 collier, this 1802 coachman is pleased to be sober so that he can profit from the carelessness of the drunken competition and the ignorance of the mob protesting social conditions, which he is too utilitarian to notice. Even if they felt such a secret triumph, few 'real men' would admit it.

Hannah More thus insinuates into her male voices a female or domestic hostility to drunkenness and a delight in the downfall of drunkards that will pervade the temperance songs of the 1830s, 1840s and 1850s and the melodramatic narratives of working-class failure such as those illustrated in 1847 by George Cruikshank.[41] This new breed of non-drinking man, partly invented by women, is mocked by other men for not being manly. Hazlitt berates the abstemious pragmatic goody-goody, Lamb contemns the 'washy fellows', and the aristocrats in Charlotte Smith's *Old Manor House* ridicule Orlando as a 'milk-sop'.[42]

Even Felicia Hemans, who usually sets her verse romances in exotic terrains in Wales, Scotland or the Americas, exhibits a brief delight in punishing male hedonists who eat, drink and are merry without thinking of tomorrow. In 'The Sceptic; A Poem' (1820) she derides at length 'the cold Sceptic, in his pride elate, / [who] Rejects the promise of a brighter state' and she warns against the *carpe diem* philosophy:

Votary of doubt! then join the festal throng,
Bask in the sunbeam, listen to the song,
Spread the rich board, and fill the wine-cup high,
And bind the wreath ere yet the roses die!
'Tis well, thine eye is yet undimm'd by time,
And thy heart bounds, exulting in its prime;
Smile then unmov'd at Wisdom's warning voice,
And, in the glory of thy strength, rejoice![43]

Those pleasure-seekers who, like the contemporaneous Keats, 'spread the rich board, and fill the wine-cup high', even while the roses in their wreaths are fading, exulting in the here and now, will be denied the bliss of immortality in the afterlife.

Anne K. Mellor's astute discovery that there are two Romanticisms, male and female, opposed to one another, and that women's romanticism reacts against the dangers of men's romanticism – the adventurism, risk, wildness, individualism, and being swept away – because these are the qualities that harm women when men exercise them, is supported by the depiction of drinking by women writers. The issue of male drunkenness corroborates Mellor's larger assertions that what looks like freedom for men (but may in fact even for them be fixity and caricature) is bondage for women. Women's writings about men drinking are a subset of women's campaign against male wildness and in favour of an 'ethic of care' imagined to be found in communities of women.[44]

When they come to record the sufferings of wives at the hands of those males who conform to the idle profligacy of the age, women writers seem to be restrained and generalized in poetry, but outspoken and particular in prose. Where women's poems lament sadness in general terms, women's prose often specifies the cause, and very often it is drunkenness. Charlotte Smith's poems, for example, lament her despair and her victimization at the hands of an evil system of justice, as in the 'Ode to Despair' or the long narrative *The Emigrants*,[45] but the root cause of her poverty and desperation – her 'dissipated' husband's waste of his father's money, his loss of the inheritance, his indebtedness, his temper 'so capricious and often so cruel that my life was not safe', his escape to Italy with his mistress leaving her to support their twelve children[46] – is not mentioned in the poems, perhaps because the poems are elevated, transcendent and formal.

In a novel such as *The Old Manor House* (1793), however, male drunkenness is specified in detail sometimes horrific, sometimes ridiculous. The Somerive family losses begin to roll with the drinking and gaming of the older son, Philip, who loses the family fortune, forcing his passive father to 'sell' his two elder daughters to rich old men and to send Orlando, younger son and hero, to the American wars. Philip's 'dissipation', 'debauchery', 'disappearances', and 'dissolute folly' (p. 418) cause his father's illness and death, and contribute to the alienation of rich Aunt Rayland and thence the power over the inheritance attained by oily churchmen and scheming servants.

Philip's life is a Rake's Progress. When he invades Mrs Rayland's feast he is a loose canon, attacking chamber maids, raging through the halls, disgracing the Somerive family and jeopardizing hope of getting Mrs Rayland's money. He is 'so drunk' that he is 'fit only to go to bed'; but in the 'stupid obstinacy of intoxication' he continues to endanger the family (pp. 207–9) and so 'extremely riotous that he had got into a quarrel with one of the young farmers; that he had stripped to box; and that every interposition of theirs only served to enrage him more' (216). Smith seems to have closely observed the irrational behaviour of drunkards, as they snooze and rise up more furious than before. She describes Philip's irrationality, as Orlando finds that Philip, 'awakened from the stupor of drunkenness into its most extragavant phrensy, had taken some offence at a young man of the company, and was now withheld only by the united strength of three stout farmers from fighting. The fury of Philip only changed its object, and was directed against him.' He is put to bed, guarded by a servant to keep him from attacking the servant girls. After causing such havoc in his family and later selling their house to Lord Stockton, Philip dies in sordid circumstances 'in an illness which seemed to be the last stage of a rapid decline, brought on by debauchery and excess' (p. 513).

Philip Somerive is the central drunkard for wasting the patrimony, but most of the males in the novel are also brutish and predatory drunkards. Philip's drinking friends Stockton and Belgrave both try to ravage the delicate and weeping Monimia, Orlando's orphan intended, drunkenly grabbing her on several occasions: 'Evidently in a state of intoxication', Sir John Belgrave with three drunken officers forces her into a back room (p. 481). Like Philip Somerive, Stockton also dies of dissipation, 'the victim of that intemperance which exorbitant wealth and very little understanding had led him into' (p. 531).

The older generation of males does not set a better example. Uncle Woodford 'loves to sit long over his wine, to tell what he thinks good stories, and call for toasts and songs, suffering nobody to quit the room as long as they can distinguish the glass from the candle'(p. 68). Later Woodford's 'liberal potations lead [ ] to improper toasts' to his own niece as he enjoys a 'licentious and vulgar mirth which [he] chose to call conviviality' (294–5). Other drunks in the novel span classes, such as old Fitz-Owen and Jonas the smuggler. Smith recreates the rowdy language and careless friendships of dissolute gentlemen, who prey on young women with fortunes as potential sources of revenue for further outrages, and prey on poor women because they can. She knows how drunks behave and how they excuse each other in euphemisms, as General Tracy excuses Uncle Woodford's drunken insults as 'merely the folly of a man in a condition which disarms resentment' (p. 149). In Smith's dark vision of a society poisoned by slavery, war, selfishness and greed, where people shun the returning soldier who has survived his country's savage wars, drunkenness aggravates the selfishness and brutality of males flaunting their privileges. The unjust laws are made even more irrational by benefiting and protecting the rapacity of drunken fools and beasts.

The use of animal imagery to describe male drunkards becomes ideological in Mary Wollstonecraft's *Vindication of the Rights of Women* (1792), where drunken husbands are irrational beasts, preventing their wives from achieving rational selves, and in her *Maria; or the Wrongs of Woman* (1798), where drunken predators reduce their female prey to equally subhuman beings. In such a world neither men nor women can cultivate their souls. Mary Wollstonecraft speaks out boldly against drunkenness specifically both in *Maria* and in *Vindication*. Her personal experience of raging drunks is a well-known spur to her rage at the dependency of women on such privileged animals, for, if they are animals, why are they privileged? Wollstonecraft's fury at drunken men in her theory and fiction burns from her girlhood experiences, which never leave her, for her father's alcoholism destroyed her mother.[47]

Wollstonecraft refuses to euphemize the nature of male profligacy. She lays bare its intimate foulness, noting the 'tainted breath' of the returning drunk crawling into bed.[48] The charm of the 'courtier', 'dandy', or 'gentleman', as glimpsed during courtship (even Elizabeth Bennet was almost swept away by Mr Wickham), his unpredictable disappearances and expenditures, suddenly become illuminated by the proximity of marriage. Now the new wife learns the truth of the dark side of sociability and popularity; now that her portion belongs to him to use as he wishes, there is no need to disguise it from her.[49]

The secret lives of wives emerge in Wollstonecraft: robbed, beaten, imprisoned, raped, starved, deprived of their children, willless, hopeless, isolated, and forced to behave publicly as if all were well, with a man who no longer washes. Wollstonecraft shows this degradation in the middle-class marriage of Maria Venable to George, and in the ruination of her jailor Jemima at the hands of drunken masters, drunken street people, and drunken 'johns'. As a maid Jemima endures the 'disgusting caresses' and 'blows and menaces' of her drunken master, so 'intoxicated' that he makes her the 'prey of his brutal appetite' in view of his wife, who turns her rage on Jemima instead of on him (pp. 56–7). Ejected from the

house, destitute, she becomes 'a slave, a bastard, a common property': 'Become familiar with vice ... I picked the pockets of the
drunkards who abused me; and proved by my conduct, that I
deserved the epithets, with which they loaded me at moments
when distrust ought to cease' (p. 59). Elevated suddenly to service
in the home of an invalided gentleman, Jemima sees this drunken
comportment at a higher level. Her master, 'a man of great talents,
and of brilliant wit' is 'a worn-out votary of voluptuousness'. He
dies suddenly, 'for he had recourse to the most exhilarating cor-
dials to keep up the convivial tone of his spirits', and his intellectual encouragement ceases, throwing her again 'into the desert of
human society' (pp. 60–2). The drunkenness of even the enlightened man fails Jemima, and she now finds herself guarding Maria
in the madhouse where Maria's husband has committed her.

Maria's middle-class life has been similarly blighted by drinking
brutes, and her story, with interpolated tales of other abused
women,[50] still shocks the twentieth-century reader attuned to
stories of such sorrows. After a quick summary of her childhood
with a tyrannical father and an indolent mother who loved only her
son, Maria tells how she married George Venable, without realizing
that under his genial mask he 'had acquired habits of libertinism'
(p. 80). Once married and in control of Maria's inheritance from her
uncle, George reveals his debts, his greed, his indifference and his
power, aggravated by drunkenness. Wollstonecraft minces no
words in describing the physical revulsion she feels for his person,
especially knowing that he returns to her befouled by 'wantons of
the lowest class, who could by their vulgar, indecent mirth, which
he called nature, rouse his sluggish spirits':

> He now seldom dined at home, and continually returned at a late
> hour, drunk, to bed. I retired to another apartment; I was glad, I
> own, to escape from his. ... His intimacy with profligate women,
> and his habits of thinking, gave him a contempt for female en-
> dowments; and he would repeat, when wine had loosed his
> tongue, most of the common-place sarcasms levelled at them, by
> men who do not allow them to have minds, because mind would
> be an impediment to gross enjoyment. (pp. 94–5)

Wollstonecraft wonders why women are 'reproved for neglecting
their persons', when men are not required to be clean. Maria is sickened by her husband's 'squallid appearance' at the breakfast table:
'The squeamishness of stomach alone, produced by the last night's

intemperance, which he took no pains to conceal, destroyed my appetite. I think I now see him lolling in an armchair, in a dirty pow-
dering gown, soiled linen, ungartered stockings, and tangled hair,
yawning and stretching himself', and pouring brandy into his tea
(p. 95). Wollstonecraft links drunkenness with sexual revulsion, insisting that women have no obligation to gratify a husband against
their own desires. Wollstonecraft's frankness about erotic degradation is revolutionary, for even twentieth-century studies have been
slow to recognize this revulsion.[51]

In addition to her emphasis on fleshly realities in the war
between Bacchus and Venus, Wollstonecraft stresses the double
standard and the injustices of the marriage laws. A husband would
be pitied if he had a wife 'rendered odious by habitual intoxication', but a wife must 'sentimentalize herself to stone, and pine her
life away, labouring to reform her embruted mate'. On top of this,
'he may even spend in dissipation, and intemperance, the very
intemperance which renders him so hateful, her property ... for
over their mutual fortune she has not power, it must all pass
through his hand' (p. 102). The husband spends not only her inherited and sometimes earned money but also money intended for
their children, while the wife has no legal right to direct her
money's use. 'The tender mother cannot *lawfully* snatch from the
gripe of the gambling spendthrift, or beastly drunkard, unmindful
of his offspring, the fortune which falls to her by chance; or (so
flagrant is the injustice) what she earns by her own exertions. No;
he can rob her with impunity, even to waste publicly on a
courtezan; and the laws of her country – if women have a country –
afford her no protection or redress from the oppressor ...' (p. 108).
Men's power and patriarchal laws 'bastille' women in *Maria*, a
novel about interlayered prisons, of body, mind, family, preconceptions or 'mind-forg'd manacles', and real prisons, while
Wollstonecraft's more famous *Vindication* addresses the folly, trivi-
ality, narrow-mindedness, indolence and dependency of women
whose lack of education has kept them from developing their
minds, establishing financial independence, and cultivating their
souls. If they are dependent on brutes, they will sink into brutishness themselves. Wollstonecraft urges the new wife to raise her
sights above 'the animal kingdom':

> Let her only determine, without being too anxious about present
> happiness, to acquire the qualities that ennoble a rational being,

and a rough inelegant husband may shock her taste without destroying her peace of mind. She will not model her soul to suit the frailties of her companion, but to bear with them; his character may be a trial, but not an impediment to virtue.

Without education or self-directed interests the wife is dependent; dependent, she must be submissive, 'smiling under the lash at which [she] dare[s] not snarl',[52] a 'mere propagator of fools', born but to rot.

Because the husband is protected by the euphemisms and codes of his male cronies, the isolated wife experiences all the more intensely the hostility between the sexes. The husband belongs to the larger world of men where he has been accepted, foibles and all, since public school days and where he can be bolstered in his clubs, sporting events, gambling salons, visits to houses of prostitution and theatres, while the wife waits alone for his riotous return reaffirmed in his maleness. In his male associations (which Wollstonecraft actually calls 'herding'[53]) he is bolstered not just in his importance but also in his drinking habits and in his early use of derogatory slang to describe women, whether they are whores, bossy mothers, or repressive frowning unhappy wives, comical topics to banter about along with pistols, horses, fights, politics and travel. Returning with this vocabulary ringing in his head, and his head swimming from drink, he is the more belligerent and derogatory.

Maria Edgeworth's *Belinda* (1801) mocks the crazy London society, corrupted by frivolous men, but extending to several women, Harriot Freke, 'mad with spirits' and Lady Delacour, a laudanum addict.[54] The novel is a remarkable anticipation of twentieth-century analyses of women's reactions to drunken husbands, for Lord Delacour is a confirmed drunkard whose intelligent Lady plays the manic coquette to disguise her loneliness and then resorts to larger and larger doses of laudanum to subdue the pain of an imagined and perhaps metaphorical breast cancer, lying most of the day in a darkened room and hatching suspicions and cruelties, even rejecting her own daughter, Helena.

Because she chose to marry a fool to provoke the man she loved, Lady Delacour becomes 'proficient in the dear art of tormenting' (p. 29); the fool in turn takes 'to hard drinking, which soon turned him, as you see, quite into a beast' (p. 33). Lord Delacour's intoxication provokes many of the dramatic scenes in the novel, such as his jealous invasion of his Lady's secret cabinet (pp. 112–19); Lady

Delacour blames his drunkenness on a 'buck parson' who taught him to drink (p. 289) and on the wittily named Lord Studley (p. 294) but not on her own coldness, manipulation, vanity, 'dissipations', a word used frequently in the novel to denote the waste of fashionable preoccupations to assuage ennui, and her own frankly described retreat into opium.

Lady Delacour is a complex and fascinating character, an early pattern for the study of wives of alcoholics. She laments that she has wasted her talents and lost herself: 'What am I? The outside rind is left – the sap is gone. The tree lasts from day to day by miracle – it cannot last long' (p. 261). Even as she nearly kills herself with calling for opium, she watches her own degradation and deplores her idle frolics (including a cross-dressing duel) and cruelties. She knows that her empty marriage (contrasted in the novel to the Percevals' companionate marriage at Oakley-Park) has led to interactively destructive addictions.[55] At the end of the novel, having told her story and clarified her own responsibility for her husband's condition, her daughter's exile, the death of a former lover, and other disasters that she has engineered to show her power, she is saved by her ward Belinda. Belinda gives her a sense of her own worth and a trust in the goodness of others that allows her to begin to appreciate her husband (who correspondingly stops drinking), slowly to abstain from laudanum, and even to embrace her daughter.

Lord Delacour and Lord Studley are not the only drunkards in *Belinda*; even the hero, Clarence Hervey, consorts with heavy drinkers and is one of the 'candidates for bacchanalian fame'. Winning a wine-tasting duel, Clarence 'laughed and sang with anacreontic spirit, and finished by declaring that he deserved to be crowned with vine-leaves' (p. 77). His adventures with Sir Philip Baddeley and Lord Rochfort find him drowning in the Serpentine while his cronies discuss their next drinking bout (pp. 76–84). Their frivolous indifference to his near death warns him against bacchanalian excesses. The sound of men's voices talking together is very different in these novels by Edgeworth and Smith from the brisk smug voices of Hannah More's domesticated male labourers. Here upper-class men curse, dare each other, goad each other on to further outrages, and laugh uproariously at past excesses. Maria Edgeworth consulted her brothers for details about the forbidden world of male festivities and recreated their sporty 'Damme's' in her brisk dialogues. Lady Delacour, Harriot Freke, and even the 'odious Luttridge' (an excellent shot) long to share in the excitment of this male world or to recreate a similar wildness in the routs of rivalrous women.

Late-eighteenth-century wives faced the isolation, secrecy, self-blame, and verbal, emotional and physical abuse that late-twentieth-century wives of alcoholics face, but they also had the law against them. Mary Poovey has delineated these laws which so sharply curtailed the freedoms of women and which were fixed just before the Romantic period in William Blackstone's 1758 formulations of wives as non-persons.[56] Worse yet, economic changes such as the enforcement of strict settlement of entail and the increase of wealthy and upwardly mobile merchant families made older sons of landed gentry more valuable, and the plentiful supply of daughters correspondingly less valuable; young landed gentlemen, puffed up with their scarcity on the marriage market, did not need to ingratiate themselves with women, or even behave as sensitive human beings; women desperate to marry land and money would put up with their vices.[57]

Where, theoretically at least, twentieth-century wives have legal recourse against their husband's drunken abuse (though women's shelters and meetings of Alanon reveal that these sympathetic laws often have little power), eighteenth- and nineteenth-century women lost their portions when they married, did not have rights to their children, and could be incarcerated as insane (as in the case of Mrs Lennard in Smith's *Old Manor House* and of Wollstonecraft's Maria who writes from the madhouse) or sold to cronies at their husbands' whims (as in the case of Maria whose husband takes money from Mr S. — in return for sex with her, the insult, 'selling me to prostitution' [pp. 110–11] that precipitates her flight, capture and incarceration). The laws about women's property have changed, but the loss of self-confidence that gradually results from belittlement, shame and fear of repeated violence continues to chain women to their alcoholic husbands.[58]

What is astonishing about these Romantic fictions by women is their daring mockery of male group habits and their forthrightness about the injustices in the law. With the exception of Edgeworth's Harriot Freke, women who themselves become drunkards are rare in Romantic literature, though anecdote shows them to exist, for example Dorothy Wordsworth's Queen of Patterdale, and Marianne Hunt, Leigh's lifelong burden. George Crabbe is one of the few Romantic writers, male or female, to imagine a prostitute's reasons for turning to drink.[59]

Although Anne Brontë's *The Tenant of Wildfell Hall* (1848) has been credited with being the first novel to depict alcoholism in the family, and the most accurate in being drawn from observation of her brother Branwell Brontë's alcoholism and laudanum addiction, the novel in fact follows by fifty years the first women's fictions about alcoholic husbands. It extends the frigid disapproval of the wife that Wollstonecraft explored. But it shows that the wife of an alcoholic is not always just a feeble victim; she suffers her own personality changes, for Helen Graham's disappointment freezes the sources of her spontaneity. She knows that 'instead of being humbled and purified by my afflictions, I feel that they are turning my nature into gall. This must be my fault as much as theirs who wrong me.'[60] In the central diary section of the novel Helen describes her gradual realization of her husband's sottishness, his long disappearances in London with his dissipated cronies, his public affair with Lady Loborough, his steady instruction of their six-year-old son in manly drinking, Helen's cold rage, desiring that her husband 'drink himself dead' (p. 330), and her escape from him to save the boy's innocence. Disapproval and disgust distort the once innocent wife: 'her countenance/ Could not unfrown itself', to return to Theodore Roethke's 'My Papa's Waltz', for in *The Tenant*, too, the father's drunken charm woos the boy from the mother: '"Mamma, why don't you laugh? Make her laugh, papa – she never will"' (p. 356).

The coldness that Helen Graham finally loses by learning to trust the hero of the frame narrative is refined to steely ferocity 66 years later by James Joyce, an expert in the hostility between drinking and domesticity, who was dumped many a night dead drunk at Nora Barnacle's hotel door. Joyce describes the steadfast war between Bacchus and Venus and the wife's triumph in several stories in *Dubliners* (1914). In 'The Boarding House', 'Counterparts', and 'Grace' the husband's drunkenness achieves short-term power, but then the abused wife takes her revenge by ostracizing (Mr Mooney, 'a shabby stooped little drunkard', a white rabbit, in 'The Boarding House'), by bullying (the technique of Mrs Farrington, when her husband is sober, in 'Counterparts'), and by babying (Mrs Kernan's power play when her husband tumbles down stairs in 'Grace'). Joyce's fictional wives use 'the dear art of tormenting' to emasculate their husbands, the obverse of the drunken impotence with which this chapter began. The rage of Wollstonecraft's wives has been transformed into power.

A few important changes in outlook occur in fiction and verse about alcoholics in the decade after the Regency. For one, women become drunkards themselves, and are blamed for destroying their homes. If they are not drinkers they are blamed for their unsupportive distance. For another, the drinking-song is turned on its ear as a temperance song, and drinking loses its classical, Renaissance and Romantic ambiguity under a new domestic regime.

By the 1840s women are deeply involved as drunkards and blame is heaped upon them for destroying their families, though these families were often fatherless to begin with. When the contagion of drink enters the wife's soul, she succumbs to alcoholism as a result of her husband's cruelty. George Eliot depicts this process in 'Janet's Repentance' (1857), where the drunken Janet stands 'stupidly unmoved in her great beauty, while the heavy arm is lifted to strike her' (p. 285) and Clara Lucas Balfour, one of the finest temperance writers, describes the blighted families of drunken mothers in *Glimpses of Real Life*.[61] Balfour warns against wives who bring their hard-working husbands down; she records the gossip in assorted dialects:

> 'but the wife, Sir, drinks! Ah, she jist does drink! Why she'd drink the Thames dry, if it was but gin. This very night she was brought home by a policeman, all the boys in the place a hooting of her; and as soon as she got in, she broke every thing she could lay hands on, and abused the sick man in his bed – the brute that she is!'

Mothers in Balfour's stories have 'breasts so withered and hardened, and seared by liquid fire, that the very stones in the streets were tender by comparison' (p. 77). Victorian female drunkards proliferate, humiliating and impoverishing their husbands, as does Stephen Blackpool's gin-soaked wife in Dickens's *Hard Times*. The female drunkard's personality changes are as corrosive as men's, breeding in her powerlessness a combination of terror, contempt and bitterness, as Jean Rhys has her drunken heroine Sasha beg for pity from men and then twist her plea into an insult – 'You Apes!' – in the epigraph to this chapter.

Drink is incompatible not just with sex but with domestic virtues such as supporting a family. As we saw, Hannah More's very early temperance narratives pit male drunkenness against the wife-dominated home, a tyrannical, busy domesticity that is suffocatingly snug. The fear of wildness forecasts mid-century temperance writings by both men and women. In the Revd E. Beardsall's *Temperance Hymns and Songs* (1844) the metre and images that delighted Moore and Coleridge join the temperance cause:

Oh, shun the bowl, when rich delight
Shines loveliest, mortal, in thy sight;
Oh, loathe the charms that tempt to sip,
And dash the goblet from thy lip.

For 'neath the nectar'd pleasures tide
The rankest dregs of woe abide;
And every drop that cheers thy heart,
Will madden more the poison's smart.[62]

Anapestic tetrameter couplets that were sung to rouse men's drinking groups are now sung by penitent drunkards in meeting-rooms in church basements. The temperance songs strike the inspiring note and then subvert it:

Thou sparkling bowl! Thou sparkling bowl!
Though lips of bards thy brim may press,
And eyes of beauty o'er thee roll,
And song and dance thy power confess,
I will not touch thee; for there clings
A scorpion to thy side, that stings!

Thou crystal glass! Like Eden's tree,
Thy melted ruby tempts the eye,
And, as from that, there comes from thee
The voice, 'Thou shalt not surely die.'
I dare not lift thy liquid gem:
A snake is twisted round thy stem.[63]

The sparkling bowl, associated with bards and lovers, is as delusory as Eve's tree, twined with a fatal serpent, who speaks in the familiar words from *Paradise Lost*. The tempting ruby beverage has turned to poison.

These ironic anti-drinking drinking-songs belie the usual gloomy associations of temperance writing. Where some poems are somber –

The Drunkard's house is desolate,
    His children cry for bread,
The woe-worn countenance of his wife
    Bespeaks the husband dead,[64]

or,

Self-punished here the drunkard is,
With woes on every hand,
Guilt, poverty, and dark despair
Dance round – a ghastly band![65]

and some take a ghoulish delight in the tortures of drunkards in
hell, many use the lure of the drinking-song to tempt men to enjoy
themselves and then to mock that enjoyment:

Fill to the Brim! but ah! we know
Full well a thousand daggers lie,
Where Pleasure's semblances may show
Their gilded fronts, concealing woe,
And piercing griefs, which ceaseless flow
A swelling tide of misery.[66]

Among other forms that harangue the drunkard into sobriety are
ballads, dialogues and narratives of downfall such as 'William
Bright: A Tale', modelled perhaps on Wordsworth's 'Michael',[67]
and a play by Beardsall named 'Trial of John Barleycorn, alias
Strong Drink'.[68]

Popular culture takes the drinking-song, never 'high culture'
even at its best, and uses the form against itself, heaping irony on
irony. Then high culture slips it back again, as the comic poet
Thomas Hood (1799–1845), friend of Lamb, Coleridge and Keats,
mocks the temperance song in his rowdy poem, 'A Drop of Gin!,'
published in *Punch* in 1843:

Gin! Gin! a Drop of Gin!
What magnified Monsters circle therein!
Ragged, and stained with filth and mud,
Some plague-spotted, and some with blood!

Hood mocks the 'magnified monsters', the 'Creatures scarce
human' that temperance writers create with their exaggerations; he,
too, enlists *Paradise Lost*, but to mock the demonizing of drunkards:

Gin! Gin! a Drop of Gin!
The dram of Satan! the liquor of Sin! –
    Distill'd from the fell
    Alembics of Hell,
By Guilt and Death, his own brother and twin!

That Man might fall
Still lower than all
The meanest creatures with scale and fin.

Instead of lashing 'with such rage/ The sins of the age', Hood calls
for mercy and pity; instead of snubbing 'the ragged pauper, misfortune's butt',

Hardly acknowledg'd by kith and kin –
    Because, poor rat!
    He has no cravat;
A seedy coat, and a hole in that! –

he calls for understanding of failure:

No light heart, tho' his breeches are thin, –
    While Time elopes
    With all golden hopes,
And even with those of pewter and tin, –
    The brightest dreams,
    And the best of schemes,
All knock'd down like a wicket by Mynn, –
    Each castle in air
    Seized by Giant Despair,
No prospect in life worth a minikin pin... [69]

Faced with lawsuits, debts and disappointments, who would not
wish to 'lose the rheumatic/ Chill of his attic / By plunging into the
Palace of Gin!'? Hood's own alcoholism makes him sympathize,[70]
but so, too, does his horror of censorship and single-minded right-
eousness, the new tone of moralizing that begins in philanthropic
evangelicalism and fuels the new temperance movement. What has
happened to an age where pleasure is forbidden and despair a
crime? Could scoldings by women be changing the way men enjoy
their freedom?

The change in tone in the 1840s reminds us retrospectively how
remarkable was the Romantic achievement in holding a fragile
balance in their representations of drinking, whether they explored
the fragmentation of self, the defeats of the will, the pressure of
hedonistic anxiety, the power of predictive language, or the vivacity of poetic fervour. Although they expressed their anger at the
social cost to groups and the human debasement for individuals,

they nevertheless also exulted in wildness and release. Their rich and complex investigation into both pleasure and pain has not been regained in later representations of drinking.

Notes

INTRODUCTION

1. Thomas B. Gilmore, 'James Boswell's Drinking', *Eighteenth-Century Studies* 24, 3 (Spring 1991), 337–57. Boswell's drinking, which follows the criteria of modern definitions of alcoholism, can be contrasted with Samuel Johnson's, for Johnson stopped at will.
2. Felicity A. Nussbaum, *The Autobiographical Subject: Gender and Ideology in Eighteenth-Century England* (Baltimore and London: Johns Hopkins University Press, 1989), pp. 103–17, wonderfully describes the Humean flux of Boswell's sense of identity, sometimes dramatized in two voices of the *retenu* and the *étourdi*, a dividedness found often in the alcoholic. The late-eighteenth-century arguments about personal identity are discussed in connection with Lamb in Chapter 3.
3. To extend into the present the phrase from Anne K. Mellor, 'Why Women Didn't Like Romanticism: The Views of Jane Austen and Mary Shelley', in *The Romantics and Us: Essays on Literature and Culture*, ed. Gene W. Ruoff (New Brunswick: Rutgers University Press, 1990), pp. 277–87.

1   DIONYSIAN MYTHS AND ALCOHOLIC REALITIES

1. Robin N. Crouch, 'Samuel Johnson on Drinking', *Dionysos: The Literature and Addiction Triquarterly* 5, 2 (Fall 1993), 19–27. Johnson's drinking and interest in other drinkers has received attention, especially by contrast with Boswell's drinking. When Johnson saw that too much wine was depleting his consciousness, he stopped drinking for twenty years and resumed in moderation for the last ten years of his life, often warning his drunken friends to do the same. On his wife Tetty's death from drink and laudanum, see the sensitive analysis in W. Jackson Bate, *Samuel Johnson* (New York and London: Harcourt Brace Jovanovich, 1975) pp. 236–9, and 261–76.
2. Joseph Gusfield, 'Passage to play: rituals of drinking time in American society', in *Constructive Drinking: Perspectives on Drink from Anthropology*, ed. Mary Douglas (New York and Port Chester: Cambridge University Press, 1987), pp. 73–90.
3. *The Wild Man Within: An Image in Western Thought from the Renaissance to Romanticism*, ed. Edward Dudley and Maximillian E. Novak (Pittsburgh: University of Pittsburgh Press, 1972), revives the figure of the inner animal.
4. E. R. Dodds, *The Greeks and the Irrational* (Berkeley and Los Angeles: University of California Press, 1968), p. 76.

5. Is Pentheus at fault for refusing to yield to the god and for trying to maintain order in his kingdom? Is he at fault for denying the irrational elements in himself and therefore, in his inflexibility, cracking?

6. Arthur Evans, *The God of Ecstasy: Sex-Roles and the Madness of Dionysos* (New York: St. Martin's, 1988) explores the complex notions of women's sexuality, transvestism and homosexuality in the play.

7. Lillian Feder, 'Dionysiac Frenzy and Other Ancient Prototypes of Madness', in *Madness in Literature* (Princeton, N.J.: Princeton University Press, 1982), pp. 35–76, believes that 'the story of Dionysiac power, fertility, pleasure, and madness conveys the efforts of human beings to regulate their own feelings and conduct', and that only those who deny the god's power suffer 'violence and anguish'. It is thus Pentheus who is out of control, rather than the god and his followers.

8. Richard Broxton Onions, *The Origins of European Thought* (Cambridge: Cambridge University Press, 1951; 1973), pp. 214–30.

9. Walter F. Otto, 'The Vine', *Dionysus: Myth and Cult*, trans. Robert B. Palmer (Bloomington and London: Indiana University Press, 1965), pp. 143–51.

10. Virgil, *The Pastoral Poems*, trans. E. V. Rieu (Harmondsworth, Middlesex: Penguin Books, 1949), p. 56.

11. Ovid, *Heroides and Amores*, trans. Grant Showerman (Cambridge, Mass: Harvard University Press, 1958), pp. 346–55.

12. Edgar Wind, 'The Flaying of Marsyas', *Pagan Mysteries in the Renaissance* (New York: Norton, 1958; 1968), pp. 172–85.

13. Paul Barolsky, *Infinite Jest: Wit and Humor in Italian Renaissance Art* (Columbia and London: University of Missouri Press, 1978), pp. 30–1; 46–9; 52–5; 97–100; 210–13.

14. Leonard Barkan, *The Gods Made Flesh: Metamorphosis & the Pursuit of Paganism* (New Haven and London: Yale University Press, 1986), pp. 39–41, notes nature, personal identity, and a state of 'half-prophetic, half-destructive madness' as Bacchus's distinctive areas of influence.

15. *Phaedrus*, 237 d, e, 238 a, b, *The Collected Dialogues of Plato*, ed. Edith Hamilton and Huntington Cains (Princeton: Princeton University Press, 1961), p. 485.

16. Alice Fiola Berry, 'Apollo versus Bacchus: The Dynamics of Inspiration (Rabelais's Prologues to *Gargantua* and to the *Tiers livre*)', *PMLA* 90, 1 (January 1975), 88–95.

17. André Winandy, 'Rabelais' Barrel', *Intoxication and Literature*, Yale French Studies 50 (1974), 8–25.

18. Michel de Montaigne, 'On drunkenness', *The Essays*, trans. M. A. Screech (London: Allen Lane, The Penguin Press, 1987), p. 386.

19. 'Carnival' is the term made central by Mikhail Bakhtin in *Rabelais and his World*, trans. Helene Iswolsky (Bloomington: Indiana University Press, 1984) to describe the upside down freedom of drunken festivals of self-loss and transformation. See C. L. Barber, *Shakespeare's Festive Comedy: A Study of Dramatic Form and its Relation to Social*

Custom (Princeton, N.J.: Princeton University Press, 1959; reprinted 1963), for an analysis of Bacchus in Nashe's *Summer's Last Will and Testament* and of Falstaff.

20. John Gay, 'Wine, A Poem' (1708), *Poetry and Prose*, ed. Vinton A. Dearling (Oxford: Clarendon Press, 1974), p. 21 ff. Gay's 'Ballad. On Ale' (pp. 442 ff.) associates ale with native English patriotism, liberty, health, mirth, harmony and inspiration. The ballad form itself reflects Englishness, as opposed to the foreign import epic and the imported wine it sings.

21. Joan Larsen Klein, 'The Demonic Bacchus in Spenser and Milton', *Milton Studies* 21 (1985), 93–118.

22. A. E. Housman, 'A Shropshire Lad', LXII, *Complete Poems*, ed. Basil Davenport (New York: Henry Holt & Co., 1959), p. 88.

23. Recent studies emphasizing the instability of Romantic beliefs include Susan J. Wolfson, *The Questioning Presence: Wordsworth, Keats, and the Interrogative Mode in Romantic Poetry* (Ithaca: Cornell University Press, 1986) and Andrew M. Cooper, *Doubt and Identity in Romantic Poetry* (New Haven: Yale University Press, 1988).

24. Mikhail Bakhtin, *Rabelais and his World*, trans. Helene Iswolsky (Bloomington: Indiana University Press, 1984), pp. 301–2.

25. Brian Harrison, *Drink and the Victorians: The Temperance Question in England 1815–1872* (Pittsburg: University of Pittsburg Press, 1971), p. 40.

26. Charles Dickens blames urban squalor for the degradation of drunkards in 'Gin Shops', *Sketches by Boz: Illustrative of Every-Day Life and Every-Day People* (London: Oxford University Press, 1957), p. 187.

27. M. Dorothy George, *London Life in the Eighteenth Century* (New York: Harper & Row, 1964), pp. 38 and 300, credits legislation in 1751 and the dearth of corn for a decline in drinking. John Frederick Logan, 'The Age of Intoxication', in Enid Rhodes Peschel (ed.), *Intoxication and Literature, Yale French Studies* 50 (1974), 81–94, uses only material provided by George to argue that 'the period between 1780–1820 witnessed some improvement in social conditions, as well as a general decline in gin drinking.' Gregory A. Austin, *Alcohol in Western Society from Antiquity to 1800: A Chronological History* (Santa Barbara, Ca.: ABC–Clio Information Services, 1985), pp. 350–8, states that drunkenness is moderating but in fact quotes many contemporary sources describing inebriation among the upper and lower classes. Austin writes, 'By the end of the century, many forces are at work which are beginning to reduce consumption levels. Although drunkenness is not advancing as some later temperance workers allege, it is still a major problem among all classes into the early 19th century' (p. 366). In this claim, he reveals the general uncertainty about levels of drinking in the population as a whole, among different classes, and for individuals. Jean-Charles Sournia, *A History of Alcoholism*, trans. Nick Hindley and Gareth Stanton (Oxford: Basil Blackwell, 1990), pp. 20–5, is also uncertain about the changing levels of English drinking.

28. Harrison paraphrases the uncertainty of a commentator in 1872: '"nothing was more puzzling than the statistics of drunkenness, for if

he was to judge by his own observation and by what others had told him of their experience, he would say that in the last fifty years there had been a marked improvement in this respect and in the general conduct of the people. But if, on the other hand, he were to look to statistics, the picture was by no means reassuring."' Hansard's Parliamentary Debates, Third Series, vol. 230, c. 722 (30 June 1876); vol. 211, c. 489 (8 May 1872), cited in Brian Harrison, 'Drink and Sobriety in England: 1815–1872: A Critical Bibliography', *International Review of Social History* 12 (1967), 204–76, p. 207–8.

29. M. M. Glatt, 'The English Drink Problem: Its Rise and Decline through the Ages,' *British Journal of Addiction* 55, 1 (July 1958), 51–67, p. 55.

30. Roy Porter, 'Introduction', Thomas Trotter, *An Essay, Medical Philosophical, and Chemical On Drunkenness and its Effects on the Human Body*, ed. Porter (London: Routledge, 1988), p. xi.

31. Henry Fielding, *An Enquiry into the Causes of the late Increase of Robbers, &c, with some Proposals for Remedying this Growing Evil* (London: Millar, 1751), p. 18. Hogarth's *Beer Street* and *Gin Lane* plates of 1751 make a similarly strong argument against the new, destructive popularity of spirits and in favour of soothing and inspiring British beer.

32. *Capitalism and Material Life 1400–1800*, trans. Miriam Kochan (New York: Harper and Row, 1973), pp. 158 and 170.

33. W. J. Rorabaugh, *The Alcoholic Republic: An American Tradition* (New York and Oxford: Oxford University Press, 1979), pp. 50–173.

34. Quoted in Rorabaugh, p. 44.

35. *CCL*, 1, 474.

36. Roy Porter, 'The Drinking Man's Disease: The "Pre-History" of Alcoholism in Georgian Britain', *British Journal of Addiction* 80 (1985), 385–96.

37. Porter, pp. 386, 388. T. G. Coffey, 'Beer Street: Gin Lane: Some Views of 18th-Century Drinking', *Quarterly Journal of Studies on Alcohol* 27 (1966), 669–92, contributes other drunkards to a list compiled by Roy Porter, pp. 681–2.

38. Hermione de Almeida, *Romantic Medicine and John Keats* (New York: Oxford University Press, 1991), pp. 3–12 and 22–65. Although de Almeida does not mention the study of drunkenness, perhaps because of its impressionistic and sociological methods, many doctors watched drunken patients (soldiers, sailors, labourers) develop cirrhosis, delirium tremens and dementia, as Sournia, *A History of Alcoholism*, pp. 23–4, has noted.

39. For this shift in outlook see Clifford Siskin, *The Historicity of Romantic Discourse* (New York: Oxford University Press, 1988), p. 189.

40. Carl Linnaeus of Sweden launched 'a private crusade against abuse of alcohol', and sponsored an anonymous dissertation on 'Inebriantia', as Henry Herbin Parker shows, *Linnaeus on Intoxicants: Pharmacology, Sobriety, and Latinity in 18th Century Sweden*, University of Illinois, Urbana-Champaign, Ph.D. dissertation, 1977.

41. Thomas Trotter, M. D., late physician to His Majesty's Fleet under the command of Admiral Earl Howe, *An Essay Medical, Philosophical,*

and Chemical On Drunkenness and its Effects on the Human Body
(London: Longman, Hurst, Rees, and Orme, 1804), 2nd edn, dedicated to Dr Jenner. It has recently been reprinted with a useful
biographical and scientific introduction by Roy Porter (London and
New York: Routledge, 1988).

42. Arnold M. Ludwig, *Understanding the Alcoholic's Mind: The Nature of
Craving and How to Control It* (New York: Oxford University Press,
1988), acknowledges the complexity of these overlapping forces.

43. John Dunlop, *Artificial and Compulsory Drinking Usage in Great Britain
and Ireland, containing the characteristic and exclusively national, convivial laws of British society, with the peculiar compulsory festal customs of
ninety-eight trades and occupations in the three kingdoms; comprehending
about three hundred different drinking usages* (London: Howston and
Stoneman, Paternoster Row, 1839).

44. 'The Drunkard's Death', *Sketches by Boz: Illustrative of Everyday
Life and Every-Day People* (London: Oxford University Press, 1957),
pp. 48–94; see also 'Gin-Shops', 182–7.

45. p. 4. I am grateful to Chris Rubenstein for finding this article by Dr
Lettsom.

46. Erasmus Darwin, 'Of Drunkenness', *Zoonomia*, 4 vols (London:
Joseph Johnson, 1801), I, 357–68.

47. Described by Basil Montagu, *Some Enquiries into the Effects of
Fermented Liquors, by a Water-Drinker* (London: Joseph Johnson, 1814),
pp. 20–3.

48. *Hygeia: or Essays Moral and Medical, on the Causes Affecting the Personal
State of our Middling and Affluent Classes*, 3 vols (Bristol, 1802), 1, 26–8.

49. *Hygeia*, 3, 25–30.

50. *Hygeia*, 3, 4–5.

51. *Hygeia*, 3, 38–9.

52. *Hygeia*, 3, 87–97.

53. Dr Anthony Carlisle, 'Of the moral influence of fermented liquors',
quoted in Basil Montagu, *Some Enquiries into the Effects of Fermented
Liquors, by a Water-Drinker*, pp. 178–9.

54. In *Pierce Penniless His Supplication to the Devil*, Thomas Nashe
classifies eight kinds of drunkards:

> The first is ape drunk, and he leaps, and sings, and holloes, and
> danceth for the heavens. The second is lion drunk, and he flings
> the pots about the house, calls his hostess whore, breaks the glass
> windows with his dagger, and is apt to quarrel with any man that
> speaks to him. The third is swine drunk, heavy, lumpish, and
> sleepy, and cries for a little more drink and a few more clothes.
> The fourth is sheep drunk, wise in his own conceit when he cannot
> bring forth a right word. The fifth is maudlin drunk when a fellow
> will weep for kindness in the midst of his ale, and kiss you, saying,
> 'By God, captain, I love thee; go thy ways, thou dost not think so
> often of me as I do of thee; I would (if it pleased God) I could not
> love thee so well as I do.' And then he puts his finger in his eye
> and cries. The sixth is martin drunk, when a man is drunk and

drinks himself sober ere he stir. The seventh is goat drunk, when, in his drunkenness, he hath no mind but on lechery. The eighth is fox drunk, when he is crafty drunk, as many of the Dutchmen be, that will never bargain but when they are drunk.

The Unfortunate Traveller and Other Works, ed. J. B. Steane (Harmondsworth: Penguin Books, 1972), pp. 107–8.

55. Francis Place, *Improvement of the Working People: Drunkenness – Education* (London: Charles Fox, 67 Paternoster Row, 1834), p. 8. This Pamphlet is in the North Library, British Library, as yet not reprinted.

56. Engels, *The Condition of the Working Class in England*, trans. W. O. Henderson and W. H. Chaloner (Palo Alto, Cal.: Stanford University Press, 1968), pp. 115–16, describes the industrial worker's degraded life: 'The worker is under every possible temptation to take to drink. Spirits are virtually his sole form of pleasure and they are very readily available.' Sensitively describing the worker's cheerless exhaustion, dreariness, uncertainty, filth, and hopelessness, Engels concludes:

> These and a hundred other influences are so powerful that no one could really blame the workers for their excessive addiction to spirits. In view of the general environment of the industrial workers, drunkenness ceases to be a vice for which the drunkard must accept responsibility. It becomes a phenomenon which must be accepted as the inevitable consequence of bringing certain influences to bear upon workers, who in this matter cannot be expected to have sufficient will-power to enable them to act otherwise. The responsibility lies with those who turned the factory hand into a soulless factor of production and have thus deprived him of his humanity.

Providing statistics and tables on the mass drunkenness of men, women, and children in Manchester, Engels emphasizes that the middle classes have dehumanized the lower classes: 'while burdening the workers with numerous hardships the middle classes have left them only the two pleasures of drink and sexual intercourse... If people are relegated to the position of animals, they are left with the alternatives of revolting or sinking into bestiality' (pp. 141–2).

57. In 1834 W. J. Fox praised Francis Place's three-penny pamphlet 'On Drunkenness' and Place himself as 'one who forms a valuable portion of the few links that yet hold together the different orders of this classified country in their unhappily progressive alienation.'

58. Place Papers, British Library, Additional Ms. 35, 151, ff. 220–1.

59. Information about Montagu's life can be found in *The Early Letters of William and Dorothy Wordsworth (1785–1805)*, ed. Ernest de Selincourt (2 vols, Oxford: Clarendon Press, 1935), 1, 138–41; 153; 164–5, 193–5. 'Vexed' references to his not repaying the Calvert legacy can be found on pp. 230, 234, 243, 316, 326–7, and 331. Coleridge writes Josiah Wedgwood about Montagu's irresponsibility 4 Feb. 1800 (*CCL*, 1, 567–8). Ralph M. Wardle, 'Basil and Anna Montagu:

Touchstones for the Romantics,' *Keats–Shelley Journal* 34 (1985), 131–71, describes wittily Montagu's many failed schemes and eventual life of luxury.

60. In *William Wordsworth: A Biography; The Early Years 1770–1803* (Oxford: Clarendon Press, 1957), Mary Moorman reveals that Montagu's unpublished manuscript memoirs in the Dove Cottage Library mention the years of dissipation after his first wife's death when he lived in London with the feckless Wordsworth, but that subsequent pages have been torn out. The excised pages would tell much about Wordsworth as well as Montagu.

61. For such lists of American literary alcoholics see Donald Newlove, *Those Drinking Days: Myself and other Writers* (New York: Horizon Press, 1981); Tom Dardis, *The Thirsty Muse: Alcohol and the American Writer* (New York: Ticknor and Fields, 1989), pp. 1–22; Donald W. Goodwin, *Alcohol and the Writer* (New York and Harmondsworth: Penguin Books, 1990), pp. 1–7 and 172–208; John W. Crowley, *The White Logic: Alcoholism and Gender in American Modernist Fiction* (Amherst: University of Mass. Press, 1994), pp. ix–xi. Thomas B. Gilmore has explored the surprising reluctance of critics of twentieth-century literature to come to terms with the drunkenness of major and minor authors in *Equivocal Spirits: Alcoholism and Drinking in Twentieth-Century Literature* (Chapel Hill and London: University of North Carolina Press, 1987), pp. 3–17.

62. W. J. Rorabaugh, *The Alcoholic Republic: An American Tradition* (New York: Oxford University Press, 1979).

63. Such as Dickens's Crook, Hardy's Mr Durbeyfield and the Mayor of Casterbridge, Zola's Gervaise, Dostoyevsky's Marmeladov, though in fact these have been noted rarely. See Mairi McCormick, 'First Representations of the Gamma Alcoholic in the English Novel', *Quarterly Journal of Studies on Alcohol* 30 (1969), 957–80.

64. See M. H. Abrams, *The Milk of Paradise* (New York: Harper & Row, 1934; 1962); Alethea Hayter, *Opium and the Romantic Imagination* (Berkeley and Los Angeles: University of California Press, 1970); Elisabeth Schneider, *Coleridge, Opium, and Kubla Khan* (Chicago: University of Chicago Press, 1953); Molly Lefebure, *Samuel Taylor Coleridge: A Bondage of Opium* (New York: Stein and Day, 1975).

65. Michael G. Cooke, 'De Quincey, Coleridge, and the Formal Uses of Intoxication', *Intoxication and Literature* 50 *Yale French Studies*, (1974), p. 30.

66. Thomas De Quincey, *Confessions of an English Opium-Eater*, (London: Oxford University Press, 1949), p. 201.

67. John Frederick Logan, 'The Age of Intoxication', *Yale French Studies* 50 (1974), 81–95, though Logan applies this phrase to the whole nineteenth century.

68. Johann Wolfgang von Goethe, *The Sorrows of Young Werther and Selected Writings*, trans. Catherine Hutter (New York: Signet, 1962), p. 58.

69. Hazlitt notes Crabbe's sociological versifying when he asks, 'If our author is a poet, why trouble himself with statistics? If he is a statistic

writer, why set his ill news to harsh and grating verse? ... A Malthus turned metrical romancer,' Crabbe 'professes historical fidelity' (*Spirit of the Age*), HCW, 11, 167.

70.   George Crabbe, 'Inebriety' (1775), section 1, ll. 108–17, section 2, pp. 49–74, section 3, l. 14, *The Complete Poetical Works*, ed. Norma Dalrymple-Champneys and Arthur Pollard (3 vols, Oxford: Clarendon Press, 1988), 1, 21–40, and note 613–14.

71.   Crabbe, *The Complete Poetical Works*, 1, 217–18.

72.   George Crabbe, 'Hester', *The Complete Poetical Works*, 1, 334–6.

73.   George Crabbe, 'The Borough' (1810), *The Complete Poetical Works*, 1, 461–5 and 506–9.

74.   'An Address to the People on the Death of the Princess Charlotte', *Shelley's Political Writings*, ed. Roland A. Duerksen (New York: Meredith, 1970), p. 85.

75.   Joseph Raben, 'Shelley the Dionysian', in *Shelley Revalued: Essays from the Gregynog Conference*, ed. Kelvin Everest (Totowa, N.J.: Barnes & Noble, 1983), pp. 21–36.

2   ROMANTIC HOMAGE TO THE DIONYSIAN BURNS: WORDSWORTH AND OTHERS

1.   For the immediate popularity of Burns's 1786 edition, see Donald A. Low, introduction, *Robert Burns: The Critical Heritage* (London and Boston: Routledge & Kegan Paul, 1974), pp. 15–20. Narrating the development of the reverence for Burns as a peasant poet, Nicholas Roe, 'Authenticating Robert Burns', *Essays in Criticism* 46, 3 (July 1996), 195–218, cites references to Burns's 'pleasure', 'weakness', and 'blemishes'.

2.   Low, *ibid.*, p. 21, explains that 'it was not until 1926, when Sir James Crichton-Brown published *Burns from a New Point of View*, that the poet's death was shown to have been caused by rheumatic fever and heart disease, not alcoholism.'

3.   George Thomson, an unsigned obituary notice, in Low, *The Critical Heritage*, pp. 99–100.

4.   Memoir, 1797, cited in *The Critical Heritage*, p. 125.

5.   James Currie, *The Works of Robert Burns; with an Account of his Life, and a Criticism of his Writings, to which are prefixed, some observations on the character and condition of the Scottish peasantry* (4 vols, Liverpool: J. M'Creery, 1800), pp. 156–7.

6.   John Dunlop, *The Philosophy of Artificial and Compulsory Drinking Usage in Great Britain and Ireland* ... (London: Houlston & Stoneman, 1839), pp. 94–5.

7.   Alan Bold, 'Robert Burns: Superscot', in *The Art of Robert Burns*, ed. R. D. S. Jack and Andrew Noble (London: Barnes and Noble, 1982), pp. 226–7.

8.   Pat Rogers, 'More Dirt, less Deity', review of James Mackay, *Burns, A Biography* (Edinburgh: Mainstream, 1992), in *TLS* (1 Jan. 1993), 3–4.

9. 'Tam o'Shanter', *The Poems and Songs of Robert Burns*, ed. James Kinsley (3 vols, Oxford: Clarendon Press, 1968), 2, 557–64, ll. 105–8.

10. David Daiches, *Robert Burns and his World* (New York: Viking, 1971), p. 101.

11. Low, *The Critical Heritage*, p. 106.

12. Letter from Dorothy to Jane Pollard, 16 Dec. 1787, cited in Low, *The Critical Heritage*, p. 92.

13. Lionel Trilling, 'The Fate of Pleasure', *Beyond Culture: Essays on Literature and Learning* (New York and London: Harcourt Brace Jovanovich, 1965), pp. 50–76, first proposes the study of Romantic pleasure. Richard Onorato, *The Character of the Poet: Wordsworth in The Prelude* (Princeton,N.J.: Princeton University Press, 1971), p. 161, suggests the infantile origins of Wordsworth's pleasures.

14. Wordsworth and Coleridge, *Lyrical Ballads*, ed. R. L. Brett and A. R. Jones, (London and New York: Routledge, 1963), p. 99, ll. 391–2. For 'sexual appetite, and all the passions connected with it', see *Preface*, p. 265.

15. 'Michael', *PWW*, 1, 457, l. 79.

16. 'Preface to the *Lyrical Ballads* 1802', in *Lyrical Ballads*, ed. Brett and Jones, p. 258.

17. 'Preface to the *Lyrical Ballads*' (1800), in *Lyrical Ballads*, ed. Brett and Jones, p. 248.

18. Wordsworth, 'The Two Part Prelude of 1799', *Prelude 1799, 1805, 1850*, ed. Jonathan Wordsworth (New York: Norton, 1977), part 2, p. 19, ll. 225–7 and 210–14.

19. Cited in Richard Perceval Graves, *A. E. Housman: The Scholar–Poet* (New York: Charles Scribner's Sons, 1979), p. 97.

20. Among those commentators are Geoffrey Hartman, Thomas Weiskel, and Richard Onorato. Laurence Lockridge, *Ethics of Romanticism* (Cambridge: Cambridge University Press, 1992), pp. 244–5 suggests that at the death of his brother John in 1805 his terror increases, and he withholds his feelings from others.

21. Willard Spiegelman, 'Wordsworth at Work and Play', *Majestic Indolence: English Romantic Poetry and the Work of Art* (New York: Oxford University Press, 1995), p. 44; p. 49 for Wordsworth's 'inherent puritanism'.

22. Mary Jacobus, '"Dithyrambic Fervour": The Lyric Voice of the *Prelude*', in *Romantic Writing and Sexual Difference: Essays on the Prelude* (Oxford: Clarendon Press, 1989), pp. 160–71.

23. CCN, 1, entry 1434. Coleridge seems to have stayed at the Inn, depressed by his own illness, lovelessness, and the squalor of Scotland. Just before arriving in Dumfries they stopped at an Inn that served 'no Beer! – What then? Whisky, Gin, & Rum – cries a pale squalid Girl at the Door, a true Offspring of Whiskey-Gin-&-Rum drinking Parents' (entry 1433). The evening of the 18th he notes his unhappiness with the company of William and Dorothy: 'I went to sleep, after dinner, Aug. 18th, & reflected how little there was in this World that could compensate for the loss or diminishment of the Love of such as truly love us/ and what bad Calculators

Vanity & Selfishness prove to be in the long Run' (entry 1436). Coleridge went off on his own two weeks later, desperately trying to hike his way out of his opium addiction and suffering violent withdrawal symptoms along the route. In taking his leave, he recognized a truth about himself: 'O Esteesee! that thou hadst from thy 22nd year indeed made *thy own* way & *alone!*' (entry 1471).

24. Stephen Parrish, *The Art of the Lyrical Ballads* (Cambridge, Mass.: Harvard University Press, 1973), p. 121. Mary Jacobus, *Tradition and Experiment in Wordsworth's Lyrical Ballads 1798* (Oxford: Clarendon Press, 1976), p. 90, declares 'If Cowper is the most important influence on the blank verse of the Conversation Poem and "Tintern Abbey," Burns must be the most important influence on Wordsworth's lyric writing. What he provided was not so much specific source-material as an approach to poetry.'

25. *Preface to the Lyrical Ballads* (1800), p. 245.

26. 'In Memory of William Butler Yeats', *The Collected Poetry of W. H. Auden* (New York: Random House, 1945), p. 51, ll. 62–3.

27. Mark L. Reed, *Wordsworth: The Chronology of the Middle Years 1800–1815* (Cambridge, Mass.: Harvard University Press, 1975), pp. 222–3.

28. A further personal connection is possible. Ernest C. Ross, *The Ordeal of Bridget Elia: A Chronicle of the Lambs* (Norman: University of Oklahoma Press, 1940), pp. 68–9, tells of 'an ugly rumor afloat about the death of the late John Wordsworth... that Captain Wordsworth had been drunk at the time of the wreck. ... There had not been a whisper from the owners of the ship that Captain Wordsworth had been drunk, but the underwriters, following their custom of holding captains responsible regardless of circumstances, had attributed the loss to drunkenness.'

29. Basil Montagu's alcoholism and shadowy role in the Wordsworths' lives is discussed on pp. 55–6, 109–10.

30. Frances Ferguson, *Language as Counter-Spirit* (New Haven: Yale University Press, 1977) shows this epitaph form and theme to be essential to Wordsworth's aim of inducing his reader to pause and watch.

31. 'Home at Grasmere', *PWW*, 1, 706, ll. 335–7, 'composed for the most part probably between about late June and early September 1806', that is, around the time of the lyrics to Burns; Dorothy Wordsworth, 'The Grasmere Journals', Dec. 1801, *Journals of Dorothy Wordsworth*, ed. Mary Moorman (Oxford: Oxford University Press, 1971), pp. 72–3.

32. Stephen Parrish, *The Art of the Lyrical Ballads*, (pp. 222–6) suggests that 'the delicate moral sympathy' of 'Death and Doctor Hornbook' is also a model here, though Wordsworth fails to achieve a similar delicacy. Mary Jacobus, *Tradition and Experiment*, pp. 252–5, suggests that 'Tam O'Shanter' also influences Wordsworth's 'The Idiot Boy'.

33. E. S. Shaffer, 'The Hermeneutic Community: Coleridge and Schleiermacher', in *The Coleridge Connection: Essays for Thomas McFarland*, ed. Richard Gravil and Molly Lefebure (London: Macmillan, 1990), pp. 217–21.

34. 'Benjamin the Waggoner, A Ryghte merrie and conceitede Tale in Verse. A Fragment' (1819), John Hamilton Reynolds, *Peter Bell, Benjamin the Waggoner, and The Fancy*, ed. Donald H. Reiman (New York & London: Garland Publishing, Inc., 1977), pp. 29–50, begins with the following stanza:

> Another tale in verse I'll sing,
> Another after that I'll drag on;
> Now tell me, Bess, I prithee tell,
> Shall it be of the Potter Bell,
> Or Benjamin who drives the Waggon?

35. William Wordsworth, *Benjamin the Waggoner*, ed. Paul F. Betz (Ithaca, N.Y.: Cornell University Press, 1981), p. 53, ll. 114–17. For a precise record of the stages of composition and various influences, see Betz, introduction, pp. 3–30.
36. Letter to Coleridge, Feb. 1799, from Nordhausen, *The Early Letters of William and Dorothy Wordsworth (1785–1805)*, ed. Ernest de Selincourt (Oxford: Clarendon Press, 1935), I, 222.
37. John Wilson, cited in Low, *The Critical Heritage*, p. 296. A rare mention of this Letter in recent criticism occurs in Annette Wheeler Cafarelli, *Prose in the Age of Poets: Romanticism and Biographical Narrative from Johnson to De Quincey* (Philadelphia: University of Pennsylvania Press, 1990), pp. 76–8.
38. Preface (1800) to *The Lyrical Ballads*, ed. Brett and Jones, p. 246. Lionel Trilling, in 'The Fate of Pleasure', shows (p. 50) how readers of Wordsworth almost always omit this qualifying phrase that completely changes the meaning of the sentence. Trilling's essay is the starting point for studies of pleasure in Wordsworth and Keats.
39. *Friend* 2, 74; Byron, letter to Miss Anne Isabella Milbanke, 12 Feb. 1814, *BLJ*, 4, 56.
40. Samuel Johnson, *The Life of Richard Savage*, ed. Clarence Tracy (Oxford: Clarendon Press, 1971), describes Savage's 'intemperate desire for pleasure', his tavern life, his drunkenness, and his refusal to pay his debts. Virginia Spencer Davidson, 'Johnson's Life of Savage: The Transformation of a Genre', in *Studies in Biography: Harvard Studies 8*, ed. Daniel Aaron (Cambridge, Mass.: Harvard University Press, 1978), pp. 57–72, shows the complex interplay of author and subject. She writes (p. 71): 'In the career of Savage, Johnson saw the ineluctable justification for his profound mistrust of self-indulgence and the demonstration of the necessity for human responsibility even if it must be in a context of essential inadequacy. But in the very midst of his disapprobation arises the turbulent, even romantic, imagination that Johnson, through rigid self-discipline, attempted to control.'
41. Moorman describes the beginnings of the confession in Montagu's memoirs, ripped off at this point before a full disclosure.
42. See Ralph M. Wardle, 'Basil and Anna Montagu: Touchstones for the Romantics', *Keats–Shelley Journal* 34 (1985), 131–71.
43. For Basil Montagu's role in the quarrel see *CCL*, 3, 296–7.

44. Thomas De Quincey, *Recollections of the Lakes and the Lake Poets*, ed. David Wright (Harmondsworth: Penguin, 1970), pp. 93–5, narrates the awkward problems of entertaining a wine-drinking poet in a tee-total house.
45. Cited by Stephen Gill, *Wordsworth: A Life* (Oxford: Clarendon Press, 1989), p. 288; see Gill, passim, for troubles with Montagu. Wardle describes the later mockery of his water-drinking.
46. Hazlitt, 'On Burns, and the Old English Ballads', *HCW*, 5, 130–2.
47. Cited in Rogers, 'More Dirt, Less Deity', p. 4.
48. As he calls him in letters from 1817 on, for example in *BLJ* 8, 66 and 68.
49. Aileen Ward, *John Keats: The Making of a Poet* (New York: Viking, 1963), pp. 198–201. John Glendening, 'Keats's Tour of Scotland: Burns and the Anxiety of Hero Worship', *Keats–Shelley Journal* 41 (1992), 76–99, examines these poems in terms of Keats's preference for a southern over a northern way of life.
50. Stuart Sperry, *Keats the Poet* (Princeton: Princeton University Press, 1973), pp. 132–4.

3 FRAGMENTED PERSONS: CHARLES LAMB, *JOHN WOODVIL AND* 'THE CONFESSIONS OF A DRUNKARD'

1. Thomas B. Gilmore, 'James Boswell's Drinking', *Eighteenth Century Studies* 24 (1991), 337–57. The distinction between Johnson and Boswell is also clearly noted in Robin N. Crouch, 'Samuel Johnson on Drinking', *Dionysos: The Literature and Addiction Triquarterly* 5, 2 (Fall 1993), 19–27.
2. Charles J. Rzepka, *The Self as Mind: Vision and Identity in Wordsworth, Coleridge, and Keats* (Cambridge, Mass.: Harvard University Press, 1986), pp. 23–6, describes the 'pluralism of identities', the subsequent 'feelings of emptiness and insubstantiality', and 'the correspondent derealization of the embodied self', that begin in this troubled period. Felicity Nussbaum, *The Autobiographical Subject: Gender and Ideology in Eighteenth-Century England* (Baltimore: Johns Hopkins University Press, 1989), pp. 103–26, reveals that Boswell applied Hume's doubts about personal identity directly to his own fluctuating self, a 'dissipated, inconstant fellow', and saw himself in a continual flux. His drunken self, like Lamb's and Coleridge's, surprised him with unpredictable acts and feelings.
3. For the shift toward a discourse of addiction, see Clifford Siskin, *The Historicity of Romantic Discourse* (New York and Oxford: Oxford University Press, 1988), pp. 164–94.
4. Roy Porter has shown that as early as 1740 some doctors were already lamenting their lack of control over their own drinking in 'The Drinking Man's Disease: The "Pre-History" of Alcoholism in Georgian Britain', *British Journal of Addiction* 80 (1985), 385–96.
5. Contemporary Anglo-American philosophers who address Hume's bundle theory of personality include A. M. Quinton, Bernard

Williams, Anthony Flew, F. M. Berenson, Peter Carruthers, Roderick M. Chisholm, Rom Harre, Peter J. McCormick, Robert Nozick, Derek Parfit, Sydney Shoemaker, Zeno Vendler, Godfrey Vesey.

6. David Hume, *A Treatise of Human Nature*, ed. Ernest C. Mossner (Harmondsworth: Penguin, 1969), pp. 299–300.
7. For a profound discussion of existential shipwreck in Romanticism generally and in Coleridge in particular, see Thomas McFarland, *Coleridge and the Pantheist Tradition* (Oxford: Clarendon Press, 1969), pp. 314–16.
8. *Treatise*, I, 6, 7, pp. 311–12.
9. *Treatise*, I, 6, 7, pp. 314–16, passim.
10. David Hartley, *Observations on Man, His Frame, His Duty and His Expectations* (1749), ed. Theodore L. Huguelet (2 vols, Gainsville, Fla.: Scholars' Facsimiles & Reprints, 1966), pp. 50–1 and 393–5. Jerome Christensen, *Coleridge's Blessed Machine of Language* (Ithaca: Cornell University Press, 1981), closely examines the power of Hartley's theories over Coleridge and his contemporaries.
11. Cited in *OED* from sermon LXXIX, *Works* (1872), VI, 445.
12. Immanuel Kant, *Anthropology from a Pragmatic Point of View*, trans. Mary J. Gregor (The Hague: Martinus Nijhoff, 1974), p. 9. See *The Critique of Pure Reason*, trans. F. Max Muller (Garden City, N.Y.: Doubleday, 1966), pp. 248–64, for his arguments for the person based on 'a transcendental unity of apperception'. See *Fundamental Principles of the Metaphysic of Morals*, trans. Thomas K. Abbott (Indianapolis: Bobbs Merrill, 1949), p. 46, for his definition of the ethical person. I have written about the influence on Coleridge of Kant's refutations of Hume in Anya Taylor, 'Coleridge on Persons in Dialogue', *MLQ* 50, 4 (Dec. 1989), 357–74; and in 'Coleridge on Persons and Things', *European Romantic Review* 1, 2 (Winter 1992), 163–80.
13. Kant, *Anthropology*, pp. 43–8, 74, and translator's introduction, p. xvii.
14. *LL*, 1, 36.
15. Gerald Monsman, *Confessions of a Prosaic Dreamer: Charles Lamb's Art of Autobiography* (Durham, N.C.: Duke University Press, 1984), p. 13.
16. Thomas McFarland, 'Charles Lamb: The Politics of Survival', *Romantic Cruxes: The English Essayists and the Spirit of the Age* (Oxford: Clarendon Press, 1987), p. 47.
17. The approach of madness, heard as 'a dull trampling sound', is described with horrified precision by Charles Lloyd, as recounted in Thomas De Quincey, 'Society of the Lakes II', *Recollections of the Lakes and the Lake Poets*, ed. David Wright (London: Penguin, 1970), pp. 323–30. De Quincey speaks with revulsion of the cruelties in the asylums for the insane.
18. Winifred F. Courtney, *Young Charles Lamb 1775–1802* (New York and London: New York University Press, 1982), pp. 347–8, n. 7.
19. *The Complete Works and Letters of Charles Lamb*, ed. Donald S. Klopfer (New York: Modern Library, 1935), p. 31. Page references to Lamb's essays, poems, and plays will be to this readily available volume, and will appear in the text as *LCW*.
20. Jane Aaron, *A Double Singleness: Gender and the Writings of Charles and Mary Lamb* (Oxford: Clarendon Press, 1991), explores the siblings'

'atypical merging of gender roles', and suggests that these constant companions reject aggressive, authoritarian styles and prefer a 'feminine' attentiveness to others. Their 'choice' of styles arises from their lack of access to social power (p. 147) and adoption of attitudes characteristic of 'social dispossession'.

21. *King Lear* IV, 1, 58–65.
22 . James White, *Original Letters, Etc., of Sir John Falstaff and his Friends* (1796), ed. Charles Edmund Merrill, Jr. (New York and London: Harper & Brothers, 1924), pp. 120–1, 'Sir John to Antient Pistol'.
23. 'Charles Lamb's Autobiography' (18 April 1827), *Complete Works*, p. 356.
24. Mark Taylor, 'Prospero's Books and Stephano's Bottle: Colonial Experience in *The Tempest*', *Clio* 22, 2 (1993), 101–13.
25. This tradition of drinking-songs will be discussed in Chapter 4.
26. Fred V. Randel, 'Eating and Drinking', *The World of Elia: Charles Lamb's Essayistic Romanticism* (Port Washington, N.Y., and London: Kennikat Press, 1975), pp. 113–37, gives many references to eating, as symptoms that Lamb was deprived of mothering, but hardly mentions drink.
27. Manning to Lamb, August 1800, quoted in Winifred F. Courtney, *Young Charles Lamb 1775–1802*, p. 258.
28. 'A Farewell to Tobacco', p. 526.
29. *The Diary of Benjamin Robert Haydon*, ed. Willard Bissell Pope (5 vols, Cambridge, Mass.: Harvard University Press, 1960–3), 2, 173–6.
30. E. V. Lucas, *The Life of Charles Lamb* (2 vols, continuous pagination, London: Methuen, 1921; reprinted 1968), p. 768. Subsequent references in the text are to EVL.
31. Lamb's biographers often ignore and usually excuse his drinking as 'understandable'. Ernest C. Ross, *The Ordeal of Bridget Elia: A Chronicle of the Lambs* (Norman: University of Oklahoma Press, 1940), is one biographer who refers often to Charles's drunkenness, particularly as it unsettles Mary.
32. 'Counterparts', *Dubliners* (New York: Viking, 1982), p. 90.
33. David Cecil, *A Portrait of Charles Lamb* (New York: Charles Scribners, 1983), pp. 122–3. Despite her important contribution to an understanding of Charles and Mary Lamb's madness, Jane Aaron in *A Double Singleness* persistently denies the reality of Charles's alcoholism, saying, for example, that his night in the stocks in 1809 showed only his marginal social position, and that the 'Confessions of a Drunkard' revealed that drink did not relieve depression. Such denial of alcoholism is common even for commentators on twentieth-century writers.
34. Again, the strange problem of biographers denying the alcoholism of their subjects arises. Thomas B. Gilmore, as we saw, noted this denial among the biographers of Boswell; Tom Dardis, *The Thirsty Muse: Alcohol and the American Writer* (New York: Ticknor and Fields, 1989), describes it at work among biographers of Hemingway, Fitzgerald and Faulkner.
35. Henry Crabb Robinson, *Diary, Reminiscences, and Correspondence*, ed. Thomas Sadler (2 vols, London and New York: Macmillan and Co,

1872; reprinted 1967), I, 165: 'Coleridge spent an afternoon with us on Sunday. He was delightful. Charles Lamb was unwell, and could not join us. His change of habit, though it on the whole improves his health, yet when he is low-spirited leaves him without a remedy or relief.'

36. *LCW*, pp. 368–70.

37. Katherine Anthony, *The Lambs: A Study in Pre-Victorian England* (1948; reprinted Westport, Ct.: Greenwood Press, 1973), pp. 101 and 224–5. Coleridge's joke about the origins of the word appears in Chapter 4.

38. Neither Alan Richardson, *A Mental Theatre: Poetic Drama and Consciousness in the Romantic Age* (University Park and London: Pennsylvania State University Press, 1988), nor Julie A. Carlson, *In the Theatre of Romanticism: Coleridge, Nationalism, Women* (Cambridge: Cambridge University Press, 1994), mention the play, though both credit Lamb's contributions as a theatre critic.

39. Jane Aaron, *A Double Singleness*, pp. 149–50, arguing that Lamb opposes masculinity and male aggression, writes, 'The "stains of manhood" also bring about a parent's death in *John Woodvil*.' These 'stains' presumably include Woodvil's desire to participate in the manly drunkenness of the age, but Aaron mentions his drinking only in the phrase, 'In the pride of his liquor'. George L. Barnett, *Charles Lamb* (Boston: Twayne Publishers, 1976), pp. 45–7, does say that the hero was drinking. The most sustained analysis of the play, in Wayne McKenna, *Charles Lamb and the Theatre* (New York: Barnes & Noble, 1978), pp. 55–63, clearly explains the weaknesses of plot and character, but does not mention drink.

40. *John Woodvil, A Tragedy, LCW*, 428.

41. The play's 'jumble' and 'hodgepodge', its inconsistencies and discontinuities, are described by McKenna, *Charles Lamb and the Theatre*, pp. 56–62.

42. 'The Drunkard's Death', *Sketches by Boz: Illustrative of Every-Day Life and Every-Day People* (London: Oxford University Press, 1957), pp. 484–5.

43. 'Elpenor: A Drunkard's Progress: AA and the sobering strength of myth', *Harper's Magazine* 273, 1637 (October 1986), 42–8.

44. The replacement of the original 'person', however divided and porous, with a phantom being is an important image in descriptions of the alcoholic Hartley Coleridge, to be examined in Chapter 5.

45. Gregory Bateson, 'The Cybernetics of "Self": A Theory of Alcoholism', *Psychiatry* 34 (Feb. 1971), 1–18. Loy D. Martin, *Browning's Dramatic Monologues and the Post-Romantic Subject* (Baltimore and London: Johns Hopkins University Press, 1985), pp. 257–63, uses Bateson to connect the dramatic monologue to the 'drunkalogue' of Alcoholics Anonymous and to ground both in the fragmented subjectivity and alienation of person from system initiated in Romanticism.

46. Brother Ralph's soliloquy in James Agee, *A Death in the Family* (New York: Avon, 1938), pp. 52–9, reproduces a similar maudlin self-involvement and self-loathing.

47. 'Elpenor', cited above, perceives that drinking is closely intertwined with story telling and story telling with 'spawning possible selves', pp. 45–7.

4 COLERIDGE AND ALCOHOL: SONGS AND CENTRIFUGES

1. Charles Lamb, 'The Old Familiar Faces', *HCW*, 518.
2. Tom Moore, *Irish Melodies, The Poetical Works* (London: H. Frowde, 1910), pp. 210, 213, 218. *The Poetical Works of Lord Byron* (London: Oxford University Press, 1945), p. 56. For the 'bladders of rhyme,' 'Fragment of an Epistle to Thomas Moore,' p. 76.
3. Frederick W. Hackwood, *Inns, Ales, and Drinking Customs of Old England* (reprinted London: Bracken Books, 1985), is a rich compendium of names and legends. For the inn or public house as a retreat during the 1820s from cold, darkness or anger at home, see Brian Harrison, *Drink and the Victorians: The Temperance Question in England 1815–1872* (Pittsburg: University of Pittsburg Press, 1971), pp. 37–63. For English inns in Shakespeare see Mark Taylor, 'Falstaff and the Origins of Private Life', *Shakespeare Yearbook* 3 (1992), 63–83.
4. William Blake, 'The Little Vagabond', *The Poetry and Prose of William Blake*, ed. David Erdman (Garden City, N.Y.: Doubleday & Co., 1965), p. 26.
5. I have discussed the connection between seventeenth-century drinking-songs and drinking-songs by Coleridge and Keats in 'Coleridge, Keats, Lamb, and seventeenth century drinking songs', in *Milton, the Metaphysicals, and Romanticism*, ed. Lisa Low and Anthony John Harding (Cambridge: Cambridge University Press, 1994), pp. 221–40.
6. J. C. C. Mays, 'Poetical Works', talk delivered in session 698, *The Collected Coleridge*, at the Modern Language Association Meeting in Chicago, 30 Dec. 1995. Mays avers that his forthcoming edition of the *Poetical Works* will corroborate the image of Coleridge that I am presenting in this chapter.
7. Max F. Schulz, *The Poetic Voices of Coleridge: A Study of his Desire for Spontaneity and Passion for Order* (Detroit: Wayne State University Press, 1964), p. 172, mentions 'Coleridge's drinking songs, *jeux d'esprit*, and adaptations of German lyrics' as missing 'the creative energy which pulsates through Burns's "The Jolly Beggars," for instance.' No further mention of the drinking-songs is made, either in the song chapter or the Farrago chapter.
8. *CCP*, 2, 978–9.
9. John Skelton, 'The Tunning of Elinour Rumming', in *The Renaissance in England: Non-dramatic Prose and Verse of the Sixteenth Century*, ed. Hyder E. Rollins and Herschel Baker (Boston: D. C. Heath and Co., 1954), pp. 77–81, ll. 101 and 555. John Gay, 'A Ballad. On Ale', *Poetry and Prose*, ed. Vinton A. Dearling (2 vols, Oxford: Clarendon Press, 1974), 2, 442–4.

10. *CCL*, 3, 321–2.
11. Three prints of music, song, and design from the mid-eighteenth century, in The Wellcome Institute Library, frames 19852 and 51428.
12. Previously unpublished. Copied by Sara Coleridge in back fly-leaf of vol. 2 of 1834 *Poetical Works of Samuel Taylor Coleridge* (London: William Pickering, 1834) in Coleridge's House in Nether Stowey. Described by Derrick Woolf, 'Sara Coleridge's Marginalia', *Coleridge Bulletin*, new series 2 (Autumn 1993), pp. 13–14.
13. *Marginalia*, ed. George Whalley (3 vols, Princeton: Princeton University Press, 1980), 1, 369.
14. Max F. Schulz, *The Poetic Voices of Coleridge* was the first to notice Coleridge's many ways of expressing various selves.
15. *CCL*, 1, 67–8, 71, 72n., 73, 80, 99, 107, 110, 126.
16. Richard Holmes, *Coleridge: Early Visions* (New York: Viking, 1989), p. 60.
17. *CCL*, 1, 148, 174, 192–3, 322, 333, 270.
18. Holmes, p. 85.
19. For Lamb's mentions of the pub see *LL*, 1: 32, 33, 65, 78, 93, 110, 113, 114, 124, 198; 3, 62.
20. *LL*, 1, 198.
21. *OED* cites Burns's poem 'O May, thy morn', ii, for an earlier use: 'Here's to them that, like ourself, Can push about the jorum', another Burns reference passing between these two Burns enthusiasts.
22. William Jerdan, *Autobiography* (1852–3), 4, 233; cited in David Perkins, *English Romantic Writers* (New York: Harcourt, 1967), p. 388.
23. 'Edinburgh Medical Journal', *Marginalia*, 2, 365.
24. *Coleridge the Talker: A Series of Contemporary Descriptions and Comments*, ed. Richard Willard Armour (Ithaca, N.Y.: Cornell University Press, 1940).
25. 'The Nightingale', *CCP*, p. 266, l. 86.
26. *Biographia Literaria*, ed. James Engell and W. Jackson Bate (2 vols, Princeton: Princeton University Press, 1983), 2, 66–7.
27. *Ibid.*, 49–51.
28. Letter to J. J. Morgan, 11 June 1814, *CCL*, 3, 506–7, a letter that tells the joke about the word 'erysipelas': 'the first man in England afflicted with it was called Harry – a great Toper. Every time the Doctor visited him, he said to Him – Harry! sip the less – which being constantly repeated by the man's friends became the name of the Disease, & by quick pronunciation got corrupted into Erysipelas.'
29 . As she does, for instance, about the central role of gin in the 1810 quarrel with Wordsworth, Molly Lefebure, *The Bondage of Love: A Life of Mrs. Samuel Taylor Coleridge* (New York: W. W. Norton and Co., 1986), pp. 198–200. She does not quote the specific charges of the letters but generalizes to 'bad habits,' which then are interpreted as drug habits.
30. *CCL*, 2: 884, 897, 1027; see also 2: 917, 919, 930, for similar avowals.
31. *CCL*, 2, 984 n.
32. Thomas De Quincey, *The Confessions of an English Opium-Eater* (London: Oxford University Press, 1949) p. 201– passim.

33. *CCL*, 3, 490; in a letter to Lord Byron, 10 April 1816, *CCL*, 4, 626–7, he describes his gradual realization of his danger and 'slow self-destruction'. However, Molly Lefebure, *The Bondage of Love*, believes that Coleridge and his wife hide the secret knowledge of his opium bondage as early as 1804.
34. *CCN*, 3, 4344.
35. *The Life and Correspondence of John Foster*, ed. J. E. Ryland (2 vols, London: Jackson and Walford, 1846), I, 445. I am grateful to David Miall for showing me this reference.
36. *CCN*, 2, 2557.
37. *WDW Letters*, pp. 192, 110, 128, 356.
38. Cited by Molly Lefebure, *The Bondage of Love*, p. 175.
39. See Chapter 2 above, pp. 55–6.
40. These charges are painfully noted by E. L. Griggs, *CCL*, 3, 296–7 and subsequent letters of 1810 and 1811.
41. Thomas De Quincey, *Recollections of the Lakes and the Lake Poets*, ed. David Wright (Harmondsworth: Penguin Books, 1970), pp. 93–5. But in his later essay on his own estrangement from Wordsworth (p. 380) he blames this quarrel on Wordsworth's desire to ridicule Montagu's vain scheme of improving Coleridge by telling Montagu that Coleridge was a 'poor opium-martyr' suffering from 'sensual effeminacy', one example of Wordsworth's many cold betrayals of friends.
42. John Frederick Logan, 'The Age of Intoxication', *Intoxication and Literature, Yale French Studies* 50 (1974), 81–95.
43. Samuel Taylor Coleridge, *Lectures 1795*, ed. Lewis Patton and Peter Mann (Princeton: Princeton University Press, 1971), pp. 74, 237, 236, 247.
44. *Lectures 1795*, pp. 246, 250.
45. *Lectures 1795*, p. 312 n.; *Essays on His Times*, ed. David V. Erdman (3 vols, Princeton: Princeton University Press, 1978), 1, 219–25, and 225 n. 13.
46. *Lectures 1795*, p. 355. The editors suggest that Coleridge may also be drawing on phrases from Dr John Arbuthnot.
47. *The Watchman*, ed. Lewis Patton (Princeton: Princeton University Press, 1970), pp. 346–50.
48. *CCL*, 6, 935.
49. *CCL*, 3, 312 (18 March 1811).
50. *The Friend*, ed. Barbara E. Rooke (2 vols, Princeton: Princeton University Press, 1969), 1, 103–6; 2, 70–1. Arden Reed, 'The Sot and the Prostitute', in *Romantic Weather: The Climates of Coleridge and Baudelaire* (Hanover: University Press of New England, 1983), pp. 109–11, summarizes this essay in the following way: 'If man is capable of bettering himself but fails to do so, the reason can only be that he is ignorant of the correct means. With instruction, which above all means proper rhetorical care, man will cease to be vicious, and hence miserable, because he will come to see that vice simply in not in his own interest.' Reed believes that 'certain misgivings creep into the Friend's argument as it proceeds' and undermine 'the optimism one has come to expect'. 'By the end it is no longer certain

whether education can continue to comprehend vice, or whether vice might not impose its own teachings.' But by reading Coleridge's essay as an optimistic praise of education, Reed does not acknowledge that Coleridge is discussing exactly that splitness between surface and depth that Reed's critical method claims to have discovered. I discuss what I believe to be his misrepresentation of Coleridge in 'Coleridge and Alcohol', *Texas Studies in Literature and Language* 33, 3 (Fall 1991), 364–5.

51. Samuel Taylor Coleridge, 'Temperance' (6 June 1788), *Shorter Works and Fragments*, ed. H. J. Jackson and J. R. de J. Jackson, *The Collected Coleridge* (20 vols, Princeton: Princeton and Routledge, 1995), II, 3–4. *CCN*, 1, 1706 note.
52. *CCL*, 6, 934, n. 1.
53. *CCL*, 3, 489–91. The divided being of the addict and drunkard is familiar from Lamb's 'Confessions', and is a characteristic noted in contemporary studies of alcoholism by Gregory Bateson and Norman Denzin.
54. Additional Mss., British Library, 47,533, ff. 32–3.
55. As noted in Chapter 3, Kant distinctly connects drunkenness with the loss of personal identity. I have discussed Coleridge's work in distinguishing between persons and things in two essays: 'Coleridge on Persons in Dialogue', *Modern Language Quarterly* 50, 4 (December 1989), 357–74; and 'Coleridge on Persons and Things', *European Romantic Review* 1, 2 (Winter 1991), 163–80.
56. Additional Mss., British Library, 47, 545, f. 38b, 14 Feb. 1831.
57. *CCL*, 1, 474. As distressed as he is about drinking in England, he observes it in 1806 in Italy as well: 'Noticed at Terni the dreadful prevalence of dram-drinking/ Wine did them all harm! – Coffee they did not care for/ but Acqua Vita! – Aye, that indeed! and on being supposed absent to my great amusement all coming to get a sup, one after the other/ – O fearful! – ', *CCN*, 2, 2842.
58. 'Jeremy Bentham', *The Spirit of the Age* (1824), *HCW*, 11, 12.
59. William Hazlitt, 'On Burns, and the Old English Ballads', *HCW*, 5, 126–5.
60. Stanley Jones, *Hazlitt: A Life: From Winterslow to Frith Street* (Oxford: Oxford University Press, 1991), pp. 178–81. Ralph M. Wardle, *Hazlitt* (Lincoln: University of Nebraska Press, 1971), p. 178, also mentions this courageous renunciation. Donald Reiman, 'Lamb and Hazlitt', *Intervals of Inspiration: The Skeptical Tradition and the Psychology of Romanticism* (Greenwood, Fla.: The Penkeville Publishing Co., 1988), p. 101, is one of the few critics to speak of Hazlitt's personal struggle with alcohol.
61. *CCL*, 6, 904.
62. *CCL*, 6, 933–5.
63. Samuel Taylor Coleridge, *Lectures 1808–1819*, ed. R. A. Foakes, (2 vols, Princeton: Princeton University Press, 1987), 1, 43–57. In a note (p. 43) Foakes states that no source has been found for these notes, and that the passage is much richer than Coleridge's 1812 lectures on the Greek drama, which were indeed largely borrowed from Schlegel.

64. Coleridge, *Marginalia*, 2, 582.
65. *Marginalia*, 2, 119.
66. John B. Beer, *Coleridge the Visionary* (New York: Collier, 1962), pp. 63, 68, 73, 103, 221, 274, 275, 282.
67. Letter to Thelwall, 19 Nov. 1796, *CCL*, 1, 260.
68. Plato, 'Phaedrus', *The Collected Dialogues*, ed. Edith Hamilton and Huntington Cairns (Princeton: Princeton University Press, 1961), pp. 491 and 511, 244 a and 265 a and b.
69. Giovanni Pico della Mirandola, *Oration on the Dignity of Man*, trans. Charles Glenn Wallis (Indianapolis: Bobbs-Merrill Company, 1940), pp. 13–14.
70. *Thomas Taylor the Platonist: Selected Writings*, ed. Kathleen Raine and George Mills Harper (Princeton: Princeton University Press, 1969), pp. 204–63; 361–426.
71. Taylor, pp. 499–501.
72. *CCN*, 1, entries 62 and 803 (7).
73. *CCN*, 1, 1646, November 1803. This idea appears in a self-lacerating note about projects that had not been completed, such as 'On Man, and the Probable Destiny of the Human Race', 'Hymns, Sun, Moon, Elements, Man & God', and 'Destruction of Jerusalem'.
74. Coleridge, 2 Sept. 1833, *Table Talk*, ed. Carl Woodring (2 vols, Princeton: Princeton University Press, 1989), 2, 443, and Woodring's note.
75. *CCN*, 2, 2842.
76. *CCN*, 3, 3263, and Coburn's 6-page note on it.
77. *OED* cites Paracelsus as the main source for the earthly, debased gnomes that accompany other spirits such as salamanders, sylphs, and nymphs and Alexander Pope in the preface to the *Rape of the Lock* as attributing gnome lore to the Rosicrucians.
78. In writing of Coleridge's images for partial being, Edward Kessler, *Coleridge's Metaphors of Being* (Princeton: Princeton University Press, 1979), pp. 39–82, depicts Phantoms as fragments of vain energy. Gnomes might belong in this grouping.
79. 'On Napoleon's deceit', *Essays on His Own Times*, 1, 91.
80. The debate is focused in the dialogue between Coleridge's 'Dejection: An Ode' and Wordsworth's 'Ode: On Intimations of Immortality from Recollections of Early Childhood'.

5   IN THE CAVE OF THE GNOME: HARTLEY COLERIDGE

1. Janet Geringer Woititz, *Adult Children of Alcoholics* (Pompano Beach, Florida: Health Publications, 1983), p. 4, lists qualities of adult children of alcoholics: they judge themselves without mercy, have difficulty with intimate relationships, overreact to changes over which they have no control, constantly seek approval and affirmation, usually feel that they are different from other people, are super responsible or super irresponsible, are extremely loyal, even in the

face of evidence that the loyalty is undeserved, tend to lock themselves into a course of action without giving serious consideration to
alternative behaviours or possible consequences; they lie and loathe
themselves. Hartley Coleridge has many of these characteristics.

2. Claude Steiner, *Games Alcoholics Play: The Analysis of Life Scripts* (New
    York: Grove Press, Inc., 1971), examines parental injunctions and
    scripts that alcoholics follow. Steiner's work on games builds on Eric
    Berne, 'The Alcoholic', *Games People Play* (New York: Grove Press,
    1964), pp. 73–81.

3. Coleridge's interest in Rousseau's theory of the free child of nature,
    as it appears in *Emile*, is discussed by A. S. Byatt, *Unruly Times:
    Wordsworth and Coleridge in their Time* (London: Hogarth Press, 1989),
    pp. 170–86. Coleridge's observations on marriage as humanizing can
    be found in *CCN*, 3, 2729 and in *Marginalia*, 1, 704. R. A. Foakes, ed.
    Lectures 1808–1818, 1, 105–9, summarizes his views on educational
    theories.

4. *Opus Maximum*, Victoria College Library, Toronto, mss (3 vols), 2,
    64–9. In his study Coleridge anticipates the work of twentieth-
    century psychologists such as Margaret Mahler and Erich Fromm.

5. Wordsworth mocks prodigies in *The Prelude* (1805), V, 290–357.
    Hopes that environments might create minds were dimmed by 1800,
    as suggested in a letter from Coleridge to Godwin disputing the idea
    that 'impressions and ideas constitute our Being'.

6. John Munder Ross, 'In Search of Fathering: A Review', in *Father and
    Child: Developmental and Clinical Perspectives*, ed. Stanley H. Cath,
    Alan R. Gurwitt and John Munder Ross (Boston: Little, Brown and
    Co., 1982) indicates that the father has appeared as 'an austere and
    remote overlord uninvolved in the care of his children' until very
    recent studies beginning in the 1970s. Despite Coleridge's anticipa-
    tion of this involvement, we should not apply our own expectations
    about good, consistent, ever-present fathers to a father working out
    these problems in 1796.

7. *LL*, 1, 200.

8. March 1801, *CCN*, 1, 923 and 918.

9. *LL*, 1, 105; Wordsworth's 'Ode: Intimations of Immortality...',
    stanzas 7 and 8, for the 'best philosopher'.

10. *CCL*, 1, 176 and 317.

11. *Poems of Hartley Coleridge*, ed. Derwent Coleridge, 2 vols (London:
    Moxon, 1851), 2, 127.

12. The word 'engrossment' is used in contemporary studies of fathers
    being enraptured by their newborns and feeling themselves and the
    baby to be larger than life and magnetic. See Martin Greenberg and
    Norman Morris, 'Engrossment: The Newborn's Impact upon the
    Father', in *Father and Child: Developmental and Clinical Perspectives*, ed.
    Stanley H. Cath, Alan R. Gurwitt, and John Munder Ross, pp. 87–99.

13. In a letter to Thomas Poole (*CCL*, 1, 236) he is emphatic about his dis-
    appointment, saying he was 'annihilated' by the news, overcome
    with 'stupefied Feelings', and that when he saw the baby he 'did not
    feel the thrill & overflowing affection which I expected – I looked on

it with a melancholy gaze – my mind was intensely contemplative and my heart only sad.' Perhaps this was partly because the baby's forehead was, as he says, 'villainously low'.

14. In a letter to Thelwall (*CCL*, 1, 246) he credits these notions to Fénelon, though more ancient sources for the pre-existence of the soul are also mentioned in other letters (*CCL*, 1, 260–2).

15. Derwent Coleridge, 'Memoir of Hartley Coleridge', *Poems of Hartley Coleridge*, 1, cix and cx.

16. James Engell, 'Introduction', *The Early Letters* (New York: Oxford University Press, 1995), has discovered evidence that two of the older Coleridge siblings committed suicide, that Samuel's older sister's death was traumatic for him, and that his role as the fragile survivor was crucial for his later insecurities. Engell writes (pp. 21–2), 'Mental or physical trauma that is unresolved, that is not integrated into everyday behaviour, often leads individuals to exhibit several classic, well-recognized traits. In modern standard medical literature these include waif-like behaviour, a sense of being distracted or dissociated from the present moment, feelings of guilt or remorse – especially if the individual survives while others have perished – and a very pronounced tendency to abuse either drugs or alcohol, or both.' Donald Reiman, 'Coleridge's Art of Equivocation', *Intervals of Inspiration*, pp. 107–52, explores the many forms that Coleridge's early rivalry with Francis and guilt over surviving him take in his later relations with his contemporaries.

17. Dorothy Wordsworth observes to Lady Beaumont during Coleridge's two and a half year absence in Malta and London: 'Dear little Creature! He said to me this morning on seeing Johnny cry after his Father who was going to take a walk "If he had the sense to know where *my* Father is he would not cry when his is going such a little way,"' 5 Jan. 1805, *Early Years*, p. 526.

18. *Table Talk*, ed. Carl Woodring, 1, 331. In his note to this entry of 4 Jan. 1833 Woodring applies the reference directly to Hartley's inheritance of Coleridge's addiction, Hartley's drunkenness, and the disaster of 1820. That nature *and* nurture contribute to alcoholism is a recent advance in studies of the problem. Gilbert S. Omenn, 'Heredity and Environmental Interactions' in *Genetics and Alcoholism: Procedings of the International Titisee Conference Held in Black Forest*, ed. H. Werner Goedde and Dharam P. Agarwall (New York: Alan R. Liss, Inc., 1987), p. 324, writes, 'a significant semantic advance in the debate about hereditary and environmental factors in alcoholism was the introduction of the phrase "Nature and Nurture..." The use of the conjunction "*and*" was intended to make clear that genetic factors and environmental factors interact. ...'

19. His friends were sharply aware of the dangers of the family atmosphere. At various times Wordsworth, Southey, and even loyal Lamb (who often applauded naughtiness) pleaded desperately to get Hartley away from the influence of his cross-addicted father, especially at the time of Hartley's first long vacation in 1815, when he was to stay with Coleridge and the Morgans at Calne. See *LL*, 3,

180–3 and note 5 for Southey's and Wordsworth's worries. For Hartley this summer vacation with his father was a time of flowering, when his life could have taken an upward course if he had followed it.

20. Derwent Coleridge, 'Memoir of Hartley Coleridge', 1, cxvi, for a glimpse of Hartley 'running along the fields with his arms outstretched, and talking to himself.'

21. *Poems of Hartley Coleridge*, note to dedicatory sonnet.

22. Derwent Coleridge, 'Memoir', 1, xx.

23. *CCL*, 5, 111–12.

24. *Marginalia*, 1, 41–2.

25. *CCL*, 1, 236, 247.

26. *Biographia Literaria*, 1, 116–23. He explains that in associationist theory 'the whole universe co-operates to produce the minutest stroke of every letter, save only that I myself, and I alone, have nothing to do with it, but merely the causeless and *effectless* beholding of it when it is done.' He seems to wonder how anyone with sense could have believed such a foolish theory, when every act and word speaks against it.

27. *LL*, 1, 75.

28. For an example of his dislike of his own name, *CCL*, 2, 1126.

29. 18 Dec. 1847, *New Poems*, ed. E. L. Griggs (London: Oxford University Press, 1942), p. 92.

30. *CCP*, 177.

31. *WDW Letters*, 90–1.

32. 'To my Unknown Sister-in-Law', *Poems*, 1, 114–16. Hartley does not know his sister-in-law because Derwent, the clergyman, must now guard his reputation and spurn his disreputable brother. Fran Carlock Stephens, *The Hartley Coleridge Letters: A Calendar and Index* (Austin, Texas: University of Texas Humanities Research Center, 1978), quotes Derwent, 'that circumstances of your reputation have made it impolitic for me to see you.'

33. *CCN*, 1, 1713 and note.

34. *CCN*, 2, 2418.

35. Claude Steiner, *Games Alcoholics Play: The Analysis of Life Scripts*, p. 30.

36. Derwent Coleridge, 'Memoir', 1, lix and lx.

37. *Letters of Hartley Coleridge*, ed. Grace Evelyn Griggs and Earl Leslie Griggs (London: Oxford University Press, 1936), p. 99.

38. *CCL*, 5, 113.

39. Coleridge, *Table Talk*, ed. Carl Woodring, 1, 377.

40. Judith Plotz, 'Childhood Lost, Childhood Regained: Hartley Coleridge's Fable of Defeat', *Children's Literature* 14 (April 1986), 138.

41. *Marginalia*, 2, 142.

42. Norman K. Denzin, *The Alcoholic Self* (Newbury Park: Sage Publications, 1987), p. 21.

43. *LL*, 1, 134.

44. *CCL*, 5, 251.

45. *Poems*, 2, 13, appended to end of volume from 1833.

46. Robert Southey, *Selections from the Letters*, ed. John Wood Warter (4 vols, London: Longmans, 1856), 1, 24.
47. *CCL*, 5, 112.
48. *CCL*, 6, 798.
49. Derwent Coleridge, "Memoir", 1, clxxxv.
50. From a letter to his mother, cited Derwent Coleridge, 'Memoir', 1, cix.
51. *New Poems*, p. 88.
52. 'Resolution and Independence', ll. 113–14, and Derwent Coleridge, 'Memoir', 1, lxx.
53. Noted in Sister Mary Joseph Pomeroy, *The Poetry of Hartley Coleridge: A Dissertation* (Washington: D.C.: Michie C., 1927), p. 62.
54. Derwent Coleridge, 'Memoir', 1, xci.
55. Steiner, *Games Alcoholics Play*, p. 26.
56. John Zinner and Roger Shapiro, 'Projective Identification as a Mode of Perception and Behaviour in Families of Adolescents', *International Journal of Psycho-Analysis* 53 (1972), 526. The authors are 'deeply impressed with the power that parental anxiety holds in tipping the balance'.
57. Judith S. Seixas and Geraldine Youcha, *Children of Alcoholism: A Survivor's Manual* (New York: Harper & Row, 1985), p. 60.
58. *CCL*, 5, 252.
59. E. L. Griggs, *Hartley Coleridge: His Life and Work* (London: University of London Press, 1929), p. 70. This book is the beginning of Griggs's long, sensitive and influential fascination with Hartley's struggles.
60. *CCL*, 3, 9–11.
61. Derwent Coleridge, 'Memoir', 1, cix–cx.
62. Judith Plotz, 'Childhood Lost, Childhood Regained: Hartley Coleridge's Fable of Defeat', p. 138, says that Hartley's notebooks are 'full of rebukes at the boy Hartley thirty or forty years earlier for his bad memory or his lack of pertinacity.'
63. Molly Lefebure, in *The Bondage of Love*, defends Sarah Fricker Coleridge against charges that she was an unsuitable wife for Coleridge because of her lack of sympathy with the poet's intellectual pursuits, and blames the breakdown of the marriage on Coleridge's addiction to opium, which she claims dominated his every thought from as early as 1795. Though Lefebure admires Sarah's humour and loyalty, Hartley's retrospective letters suggest that she was what Coleridge thought, selfish, worretting and concerned with appearances. Fran Carlock Stephens, *The Hartley Coleridge Letters: A Calendar and Index*, pp. 146–51, summarizes letters from Mrs Coleridge to her son that whine about her own health, and 'berate', 'chide', and 'lecture' him about his every lapse, going on for a half page on how to pack a trunk. His despair is explained in letter A26.
64. Letter 34, from London, 1831, *Letters of Hartley Coleridge*, p. 127.
65. Melanie Klein, 'On Identification (1955)' in *Our Adult World and Other Essays* (New York: Basic Books, 1963).
66. Julia Kristeva, 'The Pain of Sorrow in the Modern World: The Works

of Marguerite Duras', *PMLA* 102, 2 (March 1987), 147. Doubles, carbon copies, and replicas form a 'deathly symbiosis'; such mirroring produces unstable identities that invade each other (148–51). If this 'unfulfillable dissatisfaction' applies to mothers and daughters, it may also apply to fathers and sons.

67. Alice Miller, *Prisoners of Childhood: How narcissistic parents form and deform the emotional lives of their gifted children*, trans. Ruth Ward ((New York: Basic Books, 1981), pp. 64–115.

68. Daphne Du Maurier, *The Infernal World of Branwell Brontë* (Garden City: Doubleday, 1961), pp. 138–43, describes the visits of Branwell, aged 22, to the 43-year-old Hartley, and compares the fates of the two alcoholics, both of whom had been obsessed with imaginary kingdoms: 'The urge that had driven Hartley Coleridge to drinking, and to what must have seemed to his friends an aimless existence in the hills amongst simple people, was surely the same flight from reality that drove Branwell deeper, year by year, into the infernal world. Here he was master, here he controlled his puppets, and here the inordinate ambition which, both in himself and in Hartley Coleridge, fought to overcome a sense of inferiority could best be satisfied, where it could meet no challenge.'

69. William Hazlitt, 'Essay XI: On the Conduct of Life; or, Advice to a School-Boy', *HCW*, 17, 86–100.

70. E. L. Griggs, 'Foreword to the Letters of 1820 concerning Hartley Coleridge's Loss of his Fellowship at Oriel College, Oxford', *CCL*, 5, 57–78. Letters 1241–57 about the crisis extend to p. 132. E. L. Griggs's early biography of Hartley also discusses this disaster at length. Molly Lefebure, *Bondage of Love*, explains that the truth was kept from his mother, who continued to believe that her boy had been victimized unfairly.

71. Derwent Coleridge, 'Memoir', 1, lxxvi.

72. *CCL*, 5, 79.

73. *CCL*, 5, 111–12.

74. *CCL*, 5, 233.

75. *CCL*, 5, 110–11.

76. *CCL*, 5, 114.

77. 'Memoir', 1, lxxv.

78. *CCL*, 5, 254.

79. *CCL*, 5, 232.

80. 'Memoir', 1, xciii.

81. Ibid., xciv and xcv.

82. *CCP*, pp. 425–6, ll. 8–10, 14, 22–3.

83. 'Sonnet iv', *Poems*, 2, 6.

84. *New Poems*, pp. 98–101.

85. *Poems*, 1, 111.

86. *Poems*, 1, 168: 'And if thou hast, where could'st thou write it better / Than on the feeder of all lives that live?'

87. Hartley Coleridge, *Essays and Marginalia*, ed. Derwent Coleridge (2 vols, London: Moxon, 1851), 1, 33–4.

88. *CCL*, 5, 98.

89. Hartley Coleridge, 'On the Character of Hamlet', *Essays and Marginalia*, 1, 171.
90. *CCL*, 6, 648.
91. *CCL*, 6, 797–8.
92. *CCL*, 5, 249–51.
93. Coleridge, 'Christabel', 1.303.
94. Coleridge, *Marginalia*, 2, 49–85.
95. Hartley Coleridge, 'Dedicatory Sonnet to S. T. Coleridge', in *New Poems*, p. 3.
96. As in *CCL*, 6, 551 and 645.
97. *Opus Maximum* manuscript, 2, 90.
98. In *Opus Maximum*, 2, 179–81, Coleridge writes that 'individual persons are the result of finite Wills... A will that does not contain the power of opposing itself to another Will is no Will at all.'
99. Raymond Carver, 'Chef's House', *Cathedral* (New York: Vintage, 1989), pp. 31–2.

6   'JOY'S GRAPE': KEATS, *COMUS*, AND *PARADISE LOST* IX

1. Hermione de Almeida, *Romantic Medicine and John Keats* (New York: Oxford University Press, 1991).
2. John Milton, *Paradise Lost*, ed. Alastair Fowler (Harlow: Longman Group, 1971), pp. 485 and 496. I am grateful to Professor Anne Barbeau Gardiner for pointing out to me many years ago that in *Paradise Lost* intoxication accompanies the Fall. See Merritt Hughes, 'Acrasia and the Circe of Renaissance', *Journal of the History of Ideas* 4 (1943), 381–99.
3. Writers on Milton who might be expected to mention this passage because of their close readings, such as Arnold Stein and Christopher Ricks, do not. Even Howard Schultz, *Milton and Forbidden Knowledge* (New York: MLA, 1955), whose book has a chapter called 'Traditions of Sobriety', does not mention it. Only B. Rajan discusses it. B. Rajan, *Paradise Lost and the Seventeenth Century Reader* (London: Chatto & Windus, 1962), p. 155, n. 8, writes:

> Also unusual is Milton's description of the fruit as an intoxicant (XI, 793; IX, 837–38; IX 1008 ff.; IX, 1046 ff.). The *De Doctrina Christiana* does not imply this. In fact, chapter ten suggests that the fruit had no powers of any kind. Of the fourteen other commentators I have consulted, the majority agree with the 'De Doctrina', and none provide any encouragement for the version in *Paradise Lost*. So, if we were to take this version at its face value, it would run counter to tradition and also to what we know of Milton's beliefs. Hence I feel that it is simply a figure of speech, introduced in order to stress still more the gross physical aftermath of Sin and that Milton does not believe in the conceit or intend his audience to believe it.

Dennis H. Burden, *The Logical Epic: A Study of the Argument of Paradise Lost* (Cambridge, Mass.: Harvard University Press, 1967), p. 145, mentions Eve's 'heightening' as a pun on drunkenness in IX, 793.

4. 'Ode on a Grecian Urn', *KCP*, p. 373, ll.29–30.

5. He omits the many recommendations of drink, for example, 2 Sam. 16: 1–2; Gen. 27: 25; Jer. 16: 7; Eccles. 2:3; Eccles. 2: 24, as compiled by John Maxwell O'Brien and Sheldon C. Seller, 'Attributes of Alcohol in the Old Testament', *The Drinking and Drug Practices Surveyor*, Alcohol Research Group, 18 (Aug. 1982), pp. 18–24.

6. John Milton, chapter IX, 'Of the First Class of Special Virtues Connected with the Duty of Man towards Himself', *The Christian Doctrine, The Works of John Milton* (New York: Columbia University Press, 1934), 17, 213–17. See William Riley Parker, *Milton: a Biography* (Oxford: Clarendon Press, 1968), pp. 194, 198–9, 446–7, for Milton's personal advocacy of temperance.

7. *The Romantics on Milton: Formal Essays and Critical Asides*, ed. Joseph Anthony Wittreich, Jr. (Cleveland: Case Western Reserve Press, 1970), and Beth Lau, 'Keats's marginalia in *Paradise Lost*', in *Milton, the Metaphysicals, and Romanticism*, ed. Lisa Low and Anthony John Harding (Cambridge: Cambridge University Press, 1994), pp. 151–71, record Keats's reactions in the margins of his texts.

8. *The Romantics on Milton*, ed. Wittreich, p. 553.

9. Blake's phrase is from plate 5, 'The Marriage of Heaven and Hell', *The Poetry and Prose of William Blake*, ed. David V. Erdman (Garden City, N.Y.: Doubleday, 1965), p. 35. Several recent studies have examined Milton's sympathy for, and knowledge of, ecstatic traditions: Richard Halpern, 'Puritanism and Maenadism in *A Mask*', in *Rewriting the Renaissance: The Discourses of Sexual Differences in Early Modern Europe*, ed. Margaret W. Ferguson, Maureen Quilligan, and Nancy J. Vickers (Chicago and London: Chicago University Press, 1986), pp. 88–105; Christopher Kendrick, 'Milton and Sexuality: a symptomatic reading of *Comus*', in *Re-membering Milton: Essays on the texts and traditions*, ed. Mary Nyquist and Margaret W. Ferguson (New York and London: Methuen, 1987), pp. 43–73; and Jacqueline DiSalvo, 'Fear of Flying: Milton on the Boundaries Between Witchcraft and Inspiration', *English Literary Renaissance* 18 (Winter 1988), 114–37.

10. To use the wonderful word, paired with taste, of Christopher Ricks, *Keats and Embarrassment* (Oxford: Clarendon Press, 1974).

11. 'Ode on Indolence', l. 15, *KCP*, p. 375.

12. Christopher Ricks introduces this important term for Keats's physicality, but may find intoxication itself too embarrassing to mention.

13. Even Jeffrey Baker, *John Keats and Symbolism* (Sussex: Harvester Press and New York: St. Martin's Press, 1986), rushes past this stanza 3.

14. Stuart Sperry, *Keats the Poet* (Princeton: Princeton University Press, 1973), p. 285.

15. Helen Vendler, *The Odes of John Keats* (Cambridge, Mass.: Harvard University Press, 1983), p. 161.

16. He writes his brothers 5 Jan. 1818 (*KL*, 1, 197), 'I have had a great deal of pleasant time with Rice lately, and am getting initiated into a little Cant – they call dr[i]nking deep dying scarlet, and when you breathe in your wartering they bid you cry hem and play it off – they call good Wine a pretty tipple, and call getting a Child knocking out an apple, stopping at a Tave[r]n they call hanging out.'

17. Annette Wheeler Cafarelli, 'How theories of romanticism exclude women: Radcliffe, Milton, and the legitimation of the gothic novel', in *Milton, the metaphysicals, and romanticism*, pp. 84–113, shows (pp. 95–6) that Ann Radcliffe 'posited *Comus* as the ancestor of the gothic novel's distressed female held captive', all the more influential because 'the new Eve of *Comus* ... is triumphant in her fortitude.'

18. Shakespearean allusions in this stanza have been examined by Jonathan Bate, *Shakespeare and the English Romantic Imagination* (Oxford: Clarendon Press, 1989), pp. 191–7, and by Mark Taylor, 'Keats' "Ode to a Nightingale"', *Explicator* 36, 3 (Spring 1978), 24–6.

19. Werner William Beyer, *Keats and the Daemon King* (New York: Oxford University Press, 1947),p. 359, dismisses the importance of Bacchus for Keats: 'The legendary Bacchus, with the various minor features gleaned from Diodorus and Rabelais and Ovid, is actually an irrelevant adornment. In itself it had no intrinsic relation to the pattern or theme of Endymion, the gradations of happiness and quest for immortality.'

20. Willard Spiegelman, 'Keats's Figures of Indolence', *Majestic Indolence: English Romantic Poetry and the Work of Art* (New York: Oxford University Press, 1995), pp. 83–107. For the influence of Spenser and Milton on Keats's suspending, hanging, waiting, and 'ripening', see Patricia Parker, *Inescapable Romance: Studies in the Poetics of a Mode* (Princeton: Princeton University Press, 1979), pp. 159–218.

21. J. Lemprière, D. D., *Classical Dictionary, containing a copious account....* (London: T. Cadell and W. Davies in the Strand, 1804).

22. Robert Gittings, *John Keats* (Boston: Little, Brown and Company, 1968) p. 158.

23. For example, Charles I. Patterson, Jr., *The Daemonic in the Poetry of Keats* (Urbana: University of Illinois Press, 1970), pp. 66–77, reads the song as a song of sorrow, embracing the actual, learning to view sorrow as 'an inseparable part of human existence', even 'a desirable part'. 'Sorrow', he writes (p. 74), 'is an avenue to wide, deep, and varied knowledge of our world and of its possibilities.' Susan J. Wolfson, *The Questioning Presence: Wordsworth, Keats, and the Interrogative Mode in Romantic Poetry* (Ithaca and London: Cornell University Press, 1986), p. 246, mentions it only as the 'Sorrow Song'.

24. For the omnipresence of annihilation in Keats's thinking, see Donald Reiman, 'Keats and the Abyss', *Intervals of Inspiration: The Skeptical Tradition and the Psychology of Romanticism*, pp. 263–306.

25. *The Diary of Benjamin Robert Haydon*, II, 317–18 and 463.

26. Robert Gittings, *John Keats*, pp. 27, 30.

27. *The Keats Circle: Letters and Papers*, ed. H. E. Rollins, (2 vols, Cambridge, Mass.: Harvard University Press, 2nd edn, 1969), 2, 319–21, but see lxxii–lxxiv for Clarke's absence during Keats's time of manly drinking.
28. Talk delivered at the John Keats Bicentennial Conference, Harvard University, 7 Sept. 1995.
29. Entry 140, *The Keats Circle*, 1, 302–9.
30. Walter Jackson Bate, *John Keats* (Cambridge, Mass.: Belknap Press of Harvard University Press, 1963), pp. 274–5.
31. Gittings, pp. 178–80.
32. Bate, pp. 463–4.
33. Aileen Ward, *John Keats: The Making of a Poet* (New York: Viking Press, 1963), p. 255.
34. See Sperry, *Keats the Poet*, pp. 36–71, for Keats's use of chemical terms such as volatility, fermenting, spiritualizing, etherealizing, essences, and distillation, to describe the work of imagination and language.
35. Anya Taylor, *Coleridge's Defense of the Human* (Columbus, Ohio: Ohio State University Press, 1986), pp. 119–43, discusses this intertwining of science and spirituality in the scientists Coleridge read and in his interpretations of them.
36. William Hazlitt, *Lectures on the English Poets* (1824), HCW, 5, 372.
37. As noted in Brown's list of Keats's books, *The Keats Circle*, 1, 253–60.
38. Sperry mentions distilling and fermented liquors in note 30, p. 45.
39. Christopher Ricks, *Keats and Embarrassment*.
40. Farewell letter to Charles Brown from Naples, 1 Nov. 1820, *KL*, 2, 351.
41. Mr Abbey seems to have been afraid of her sexual power, but his reminiscences have been suspect, if only selectively so, as Gittings suggests, pp. 13, 18, 25.
42. Susan Wolfson, 'Keats and the Manhood of the Poet', *European Romantic Review* 6, 1 (Summer 1995), 1–37, discusses the gendering of criticism of Keats.
43. *Keats and Embarrassment*, p. 133.
44. Gittings, pp. 451–3.
45. 'On Effeminacy of Character', cited in David Bromwich, *Hazlitt: The Mind of a Critic* (New York: Oxford University Press, 1983), pp. 368–9.
46. *Lectures on the English Poets*, HCW, 5, 127. For the influence of Hazlitt on many aspects of Keats's feelings and language see Bromwich, *Hazlitt: The Mind of a Critic*, pp. 362–401.
47. *The Diary of Benjamin Robert Haydon*, 2, 317–18.
48. In a letter on 5 Jan. 1818 (*KL*, 1, 198), Keats tells George and Tom about Lamb's behaviour at a dinner at Haydon's: 'Lamb got tipsy and blew up Kingston – proceeding so far as to take the Candle across the Room hold it to his face and show us wh-a-at-sor(t)-fello-he waas I astonished Kingston at supper with a pertinacity in favour of drinking – keeping my two glasses at work in a knowing way.' He reproduces Lamb's stutter and drunken hostility and is proud of his own capacity to drink.
49. Is he drinking 'sparkling red burgundy'? A spirited correspondence in *The Times* of London (1977) includes suggestions that he diluted

his wine with gaseous waters, preferred odious concoctions, poured his wine too quickly, or drank pink gin (reprinted for the John Keats Bicentennial Conference, The Palimpsest Press, Sept. 1995).

50. Bromwich, *Hazlitt: The Mind of the Critic*, p. 380, writes, 'Keats's second stanza opens with a private joke against himself, "O, for a draught of vintage." Claret had appeared in his letters among the accessories proper to the full life of sensations. Now it is lovingly described, but with an awareness that its effect is to dull sensation and to obscure identity.'

51. Tilottama Rajan, 'On the Threshold of Tragedy: Keats's Late Romances', *Dark Interpreter: The Discourse of Romanticism* (Ithaca and London: Cornell University Press, 1980), pp. 115- 25. Rajan's brilliant adaptation (pp. 143–203) of Nietzsche's Dionysianism to represent a core of destructive will ironically present as an undertow to Apollonian representation illuminates the double perspective of generation and dissolution in Keats's Hyperion poems, but does not include the free and wild Bacchus whom Keats celebrates. Keats uses the name 'Bacchus'; Rajan's 'Dionysius' is an anachronistic though apt application of Nietzschean awareness onto Keats.

52. See Robert M. Ryan, *Keats: The Religious Sense* (Princeton: Princeton University Press, 1976), pp. 212–17, for his unconsoled death.

53. Donald Reiman, 'Keats and the Abyss', *Intervals of Inspiration: The Skeptical Tradition and the Psychology of Romanticism*, pp. 263–306.

7 BACCHUS CONTRA VENUS: ALCOHOLIC HUSBANDS AND THEIR WIVES

1. See John W. Crowley, *The White Logic: Alcoholism and Gender in American Modernist Fiction* (Amherst: University of Massachusetts Press, 1994), for the beginnings of a study of the difference between male and female drinking as depicted in literature. George Crabbe in *Hester*, as we saw in Chapter 1, was an early observer of drunkenness among women.

2. *The Rochester–Savile Letters, 1671–1680*, ed. John Harold Wilson (Columbus: Ohio State University Press, 1941), letter III, p. 33, cited in Felicity A. Nussbaum, *The Brink of All We Hate: English Satires on Women 1660–1750* (Lexington: University of Kentucky Press, 1984), p. 58. See also Carole Fabricant, 'Rochester's World of Imperfect Enjoyment', *JEGP* 73 (1974), 348, for Rochester's anxiety about impotence. In 1932 the psychiatrist Karen Horney asked, 'Is it not really remarkable (we ask ourselves in amazement), when one considers the overwhelming mass of this transparent material, that so little recognition and attention are paid to the fact of men's secret dread of women?' ('The Dread of Woman', in *Feminine Psychology*, ed. Harold Kelman [New York: W. W. Norton, 1967], p. 136).

3. Samuel Johnson, *Life of Savage*, ed. Clarence Tracy (Oxford: Clarendon Press, 1971), p. 140. Virginia Spencer Davidson, 'Johnson's *Life of*

Savage: The Transformation of a Genre', in *Studies in Biography: Harvard Studies 8*, ed. Daniel Aaron (Cambridge, Mass.: Harvard University Press, 1978), pp. 57–72, noted in Chapter 2, examines Johnson's interest in Savage's self destruction as a tragic circularity, where this tragic hero experiences no recognition of his own responsibility.

4. *BLJ*, 9, 15.

5. The word 'bowdlerized' came into existence in 1818, when Dr Thomas Bowdler published his sanitized Shakespeare; Moore's letters from Byron show the effect of this prudery in being starred with asterisks where he cleaned out racy passages.

6. Thomas Moore, *Memoirs of the Life of the Rt. Hon. Richard Brinsley Sheridan* (2 vols, 1858; reprinted New York: Greenwood Press, 1968), 2, 328.

7. Canto 2, stanza CLXXIX, *Don Juan*, ed. Leslie Marchand (Cambridge, Mass.: Riverside Press, 1958), p. 99.

8. Ellen Moers, *The Dandy: Brummell to Beerbohm* (New York: Viking, 1960), p. 169. In this chapter on Maginn, the editor of *Frazer's Magazine*, crony of Thackeray, and opponent of 'Puff', Moers cites Maginn's epitaph: 'A randy, bandy, brandy, no Dandy, / Rollicking jig of an Irishman!'

9. Coleridge, *CCL*, 5, 192–7, 15 Jan. 1822. Some of this advice is hypocritical, as when he contrasts Derwent's 'dissipations' with his own (revised in retrospect) collegiate diligence. Hazlitt's essays dismiss Moore's 'vapid, varnished sentiments, lip-deep'. 'Moore converts the wild harp of Erin into a musical snuff-box!' (on Moore in *The Spirit of the Age*, *HCW*, 11, 174). Contrasting Moore's 'fastidious' verse with Byron's ferocity, he chooses words like 'fine, soft, exquisite ... indolent, luxurious', to capture the femininity of Moore's work: 'Poetry, in his hands, becomes a kind of *cosmetic* art – it is the poetry of the toilette' (in 'Moore and Byron', *HCW*, 16, 412 -15).

10. 'Brummelliana' (*The London Weekly Review*), *HCW*, 20, 152–3.

11. Moers, *The Dandy*, pp. 36–7.

12. Eve Kosofsky Sedgwick, '*The Country Wife*: Anatomies of Male Homosocial Desire', in *Between Men: English Literature and Male Homosocial Desire* (New York: Columbia University Press, 1985), pp. 49–66, argues (p. 50) 'that the men's heterosexual relationships in the play have as their raison d'etre an ultimate bonding between men; and that this bonding, if successfully achieved, is not detrimental to "masculinity" but definitive of it.'

13. 'Circe' is her name in the homosocial community of Hemingway's *The Sun Also Rises*, where the manly drinking group, headed by the castrato, Jake, who may or may not be more manly than the non-drinker, Robert Cohn, is happiest without women. The happiness of men in groups is noted poignantly at the end of the fishing trip when Harris says 'I've not had much fun since the war' (New York: Charles Scribner's Sons, 1954), p. 129. Two opposing associations – of 'manliness' with healthy temperance and of 'manliness' with bellying up to the bar – conflict in twentieth-century American literature, as John W. Crowley demonstrates, with special reference

to *The Sun Also Rises*, in *The White Logic: Alcoholism and Gender in American Modernist Fiction* (Amherst: University of Massachusetts Press, 1994), pp. 32–5. Crowley discusses the ironies of homosocial bonding and drink, pp. 57–62. See also Mark Spilka, *Hemingway's Quarrel with Androgyny* (Lincoln: University of Nebraska Press, 1990).

14. Sedgwick's work on homosocial groups is far more refined and subtle than early theories that alcoholism results from latent homosexuality. A. A. Brill, *Lectures on Psychoanalytic Psychiatry* (New York: Vintage Books, 1956), p. 266, states this now outdated theory plainly:

> Under the influence of alcohol, one, as it were, 'forgets his troubles' or can realize one's wildest wish-phantasies. In studying such cases we find that the patients invariably wish to run away from heterosexuality. Every chronic alcoholic studied by me either never attained genitality and object-finding or there was some noticeable weakness in his development which sooner or later led to a regression to the oral autoerotic phase. Some gave histories of bad experiences with women, unhappy marriages or love affairs for which they invariably blamed the women. Their excuse for excessive drinking is that they are lonesome and seek companionship in bar rooms or clubs. And, as is known, the homosexual element is glaringly displayed in such gatherings whether they are of the upper or lower strata of society.

Otto Fenichel, *The Psychoanalytic Theory of Neurosis* (New York: W. W. Norton & Co., 1945), p. 379, is even more reductive: 'The unconscious impulses in alcoholics typically are not only oral but also homosexual in nature. It is only necessary to call to mind the numerous drinking customs to find confirmation of this fact.'

15. To John Cam Hobhouse, 19 May 1818, *BLJ*, 6, 40.
16. Caroline Franklin, *Byron's Heroines* (Oxford: Clarendon Press, 1992).
17. 18 September 1819, *BLJ*, 6, 69.
18. Moers, *The Dandy*, pp. 42–3.
19. *The Journals of Thomas Moore 1818–1841*, ed. Peter Quennell (London: B.T. Batsford Ltd., 1964), pp. 181–5.
20. 'Wreath the Bowl', *The Poetical Works of Thomas Moore*, ed. A. D. Godley (London: Oxford University Press, 1910), p. 213.
21. Thomas Moore, *Poetical Works*, p. 218.
22. Thomas Moore, *Poetical Works*, p. 210.
23. *The Early Poems of John Clare 1804–1822*, ed. Eric Robinson and David Powell (2 vols, Oxford: Clarendon Press, 1989), 2, 401–2.
24. *The Early Poems of John Clare*, 2, 710–11.
25. J. W. & Anne Tibble, *John Clare: A Life* (Totowa, N.J.: Rowman & Littlefield, 1972), pp. 48–51, 54–6, 66–70. For the accusations against him, see *The Prose of John Clare*, ed. J. W. and Anne Tibble (New York: Barnes & Noble, 1970), pp. 65–7, where he writes, 'I have often been accusd of being a drunkard & of being ungrateful towards friends & patrons by a set of meddling trumpery to whom I owe none.'

26. 'The Toper's Rant', from the manuscript of 'The Midsummer Cushion', printed by Arthur Symons in 1908, quoted in J. W. & Anne Tibble, *John Clare: A Life*, p. 323.

27. Some of these theories are set forth by Karl A. Menninger, 'Alcohol Addiction', *Man Against Himself* (New York: Harcourt, Brace and Co., 1938), pp. 160–84.

28. Letter to John Scott, 11 June 1816, *The Letters of William Wordsworth*, ed. John Scott (Oxford: Oxford University Press, 1984), pp. 190–1, on Burns; to Basil Montagu, 29 July 1829, p. 239.

29. 'The Recluse, part first, book first, Home at Grasmere' (1800–1806), *PWW*, p. 706, ll. 335–52.

30. *Journals of Dorothy Wordsworth*, ed. Mary Moorman (Oxford and New York: Oxford University Press, 1971), pp. 72–3, 22 December 1801.

31. *Letters of Dorothy Wordsworth*, ed. Alan G. Hill (Oxford: Clarendon Press, 1985), p. 101, 15 June 1809.

32. For a full study of Finch's place as a shadowy figure in eighteenth-century brightness, see Ruth Salvaggio, *Enlightened Absence: Neoclassical Configurations of the Feminine* (Urbana and Chicago: University of Illinois Press, 1988), pp. 105–26.

33. *Selected Poems of Anne Finch, Countess of Winchilsea*, ed. Katharine M. Rogers (New York: Ungar, 1987), p. 44.

34. 'The Bargain: A Song in dialogue between Bacchus and Cupid', *Selected Poems of Anne Finch*, p. 45.

35. 'The Prevalence of Custom', *Selected Poems of Anne Finch*, pp. 112–13.

36. Does this early eighteenth-century playfulness suggest a changed relation between the sexes? Were women less victimized, less legally dependent, and thus more carefree, and were men less dangerously drunken, than at the end of the century?

37. Dale Spender, *Mothers of the Novel: 100 Good Women Writers Before Jane Austen* (London and New York: Pandora, 1986), shares her outrage at the fates of many women novelists forced to scribble against time to support families abandoned by irresponsible men.

38. See Chapter 1 for the pressures of these changes in work patterns in relation to drink.

39. 'Patient Joe; Or the Newcastle Collier', in *Women Romantic Poets 1885–1832: An Anthology*, ed. Jennifer Breen (London: Dent & Sons, Ltd., 1992), pp. 20–2. Breen's anthology bears on its cover a reproduction of 'Bacchante', 'copy after Elisabeth Louise Vigée-Lebrun (1755–1842)', curiously promising a bacchanalian feminism, a promise undercut by this poem, More's other temperance poem, and a number of other poems in the volume.

40. M. G. Jones, *Hannah More* (New York: Greenwood Press, 1968), pp. 86–8, and 272–3, for a list of 'Cheap Repository Tracts attributed to Hannah More'.

41. George Cruikshank, *The Bottle* (1847), a series of eight plates influenced by Hogarth's *Rake* series, presents the melodramatic disintegration of a family. Martin Meisel, *Realizations: Narrative, Pictorial, and Theatrical Arts in Nineteenth-Century England* (Princeton: Princeton University Press, 1983), pp. 124–41, shows how these

narrative plates became tableaux for theatre. Cruikshank, himself a drunkard, after a long struggle with the bottle became a teetotaler.

42.   Charlotte Smith, *The Old Manor House*, ed. Anne Henry Ehrenpreis, introd. Judith Phillips Stanton (Oxford: Oxford University Press, 1989), p. 148.

43.   Felicia Dorothea Hemans, 'The Sceptic', *The Domestic Affections, The Restoration of the Works of Art to Italy* ... ed. Donald H. Reiman (New York: Garland Publishing, 1978), pp. 6–7.

44.   Mellor's thesis is expanded from different directions in 'On Romanticism and Feminism', in *Romanticism and Feminism*, ed. Anne K. Mellor (Bloomington: University of Indiana Press, 1988), pp. 3–9; 'Why Women Didn't Like Romanticism: The Views of Jane Austen and Mary Shelley', in *The Romantics and Us: Essays on Literature and Culture*, ed. Gene W. Ruoff (New Brunswick: Rutgers University Press, 1990), pp. 277–87; and 'A Criticism of Their Own: Romantic Women Literary Critics', in *Questioning Romanticism*, ed. John Beer (Baltimore: Johns Hopkins University Press, 1994), pp. 29–48, where Carol Gilligan's idea of women's distinctive 'ethic of care' characterizes the woman's community of writing.

45.   *The Poems of Charlotte Smith*, ed. Stuart Curran (New York: Oxford University Press, 1993), pp. 79–80 and 132–66.

46.   As noted in biographical synopses by Dale Spender, Jennifer Breen and Stuart Curran.

47.   Ralph M. Wardle, *Mary Wollstonecraft: A Critical Biography* (1951; reprinted Lincoln: University of Nebraska Press, 1967), pp. 5–7, writes of Mary's father, Edward:

> As his family grew larger, his expenses increased, and his inheritance dwindled. Gradually his temper grew morose, and he solaced himself by drinking heavily and tyrannizing over his docile wife. ... When drunk, Wollstonecraft could shift abruptly from extravagant fondness to brutality, and his wife and children learned to be prepared for either extreme. Sometimes Mary was obliged to rush between her parents to protect her mother from injury. And nights when she feared an outburst from her father, she used to sleep on the landing outside her mother's bedroom so that she could protect her from harm if Wollstonecraft flew into a rage. ... [H]owever much anguish it may have cost her, her experience with her father did much to shape the strongest qualities of her character in later life. By suffering his tyranny and combating it, she learned an abiding hatred for tyranny of all sorts and a fearlessness in fighting it.

48.   *Maria; or The Wrongs of Woman* (1798), introduced by Moira Ferguson (New York: Norton, 1975), p. 102. Dale Spender, *Mothers of the Novel*, pp. 257–62, points rightly to Wollstonecraft's revolutionary depiction of physical degradation in marriages to 'brutalising men': 'to be sure, Charlotte Lennox, Frances Sheridan and Charlotte Smith had hinted at the frustration and the bitterness below the surface in the lives of

many wives, but they *had* maintained the surface: Mary Wollstonecraft swept it all away.'

49. Ramona M. Asher, *Women with Alcoholic Husbands: Ambivalence and the Trap of Codependency* (Chapel Hill and London: University of North Carolina Press, 1992), observes in many case studies the wives' gradual realization that their husbands had turned into hostile, impotent strangers, leading them to doubt their own worth as persons.

50. Tilottama Rajan, 'Autonarration and Genotext in Mary Hays' *Memoirs of Emma Courtney', SIR* 32 (Summer 1993), 149–76, describes the complex of narrative layers in *Maria* (160–71).

51. Jacqueline P. Wiseman, 'The Malevolent Pendulum: Drunken and Sober Behavior of an Alcoholic as Perceived by his Wife', *The Other Half: Wives of Alcoholics and their Social-Psychological Situation* (New York: Aldine de Gruyter, 1991), pp. 93–161; 170–2, cites interviews with wives about sex, anxiety, economic fears, and the contagion of drinking. *Alcoholism Problems in Women and Children*, ed. Milton Greenblatt and Marc A. Schuckit (New York: Grune and Stratton, 1976), pp. 19–20, mentions the anger of wives of alcoholics briefly.

52. Mary Wollstonecraft, *Vindication of the Rights of Woman*, ed. Miriam Brody (Harmondsworth: Penguin Books, 1985), pp. 116–17.

53. *Vindication of the Rights of Woman*, p. 94, note 1.

54. Maria Edgeworth, *Belinda*, introduced by Eva Figes (London and New York: Pandora, 1986), p. 37.

55. The pattern of the husband's drunken hostility and the wife's opium-addicted retreat is again similar to Eugene O'Neill's parental duel in *Long Day's Journey into Night*.

56. In *Commentaries on the English Constitution* (1758) Blackstone writes, 'by marriage ... the husband and wife are one person in law; that is, the very being or legal existence of the woman is suspended during the marriage or at least is incorporated and consolidated into that of the husband; under whose wing, protection and cover, she performs everything', cited by Miriam Brody, introduction to Mary Wollstonecraft, *Vindication*, p. 34.

57. Mary Poovey, *The Proper Lady and the Woman Writer: Ideology as Style in the Works of Mary Wollstonecraft, Mary Shelley, and Jane Austen* (Chicago: University of Chicago Press, 1984), pp. 30–9.

58. George Eliot, 'Janet's Repentance', in *Scenes of Clerical Life* (1858), ed. David Lodge (Harmondsworth: Penguin, 1985), p. 350, describes the 'crushed' weakness of the wife brutalized by an alcoholic husband: 'there was a darker shadow over her life than the dread of her husband – it was the shadow of self-despair.'

59. In 'Inebriety III' (1775), *The Complete Poetical Works*, ed. Dalrymple-Champneys and Pollard, 1, 35–9.

60. Anne Brontë, *The Tenant of Wildfell Hall* (New York: Penguin, 1979), p. 323.

61. Clara Lucas Balfour, 'The Female Drunkard', *Glimpses of Real Life* (Glasgow: Scottish Temperance League and London: Houston & Wright & W. Tweedie, 1859), pp. 5–85. See Sheila Shaw, 'The Female

Alcoholic in Victorian Fiction: George Eliot's Unpoetic Heroine', in *Nineteenth-Century Women Writers of the English-Speaking World,* ed. Rhoda B. Nathan (New York: Greenwood Press, 1984), pp. 171–9, for additional female alcoholics suffering from detailed delirium tremens and withdrawal symptoms.

62. *Temperance Hymns and Songs for Public and Temperance Meetings,* compiled by Revd E. Beardsall (Manchester: J. Brook & Co., 1844), p. 137.
63. Beardsall, p. 121, song 146.
64. Beardsall, p. 113.
65. Beardsall, p. 114.
66. D. G. Paine, *Temperance Lays and Poems* (London: Paternoster Row, 1841), pp. 26–7.
67. Paine, pp. 87–111. This narrative also bears similarities to the death of Adam Bede's father, falling dead drunk in the snow.
68. (Manchester: Abel Heywood, 1840).
69. *Selected Poems of Thomas Hood,* ed. John Clubbe (Cambridge: Mass.: Harvard University Press, 1970), pp. 301–3. Notes record that Alfred Mynn (1807–61) was a 'famous cricketer, then at the height of his career'.
70. John Clubbe, *Victorian Forerunner: The Later Career of Thomas Hood* (Durham, N.C.: Duke University Press, 1963), pp. 48–9, 53–4.

Index